THE
ROAD TO
SPARTA

ALSO BY
DEAN KARNAZES

Ultramarathon Man:
Confessions of an All-Night Runner

50/50:
Secrets I Learned Running 50 Marathons in 50 Days—and How You Too Can Achieve Super Endurance!

Run!
26.2 Stories of Blisters and Bliss

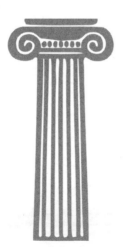
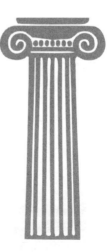

THE
ROAD TO
SPARTA

RELIVING THE ANCIENT BATTLE AND EPIC RUN THAT
INSPIRED THE WORLD'S GREATEST FOOTRACE

DEAN KARNAZES

RODALE.

RODALE *wellness*

Live happy. Be healthy. Get inspired.

Sign up today to get exclusive access to our authors, exclusive bonuses, and the most authoritative, useful, and cutting-edge information on health, wellness, fitness, and living your life to the fullest.

Visit us online at RodaleWellness.com
Join us at RodaleWellness.com/Join

Mention of specific companies, organizations, or authorities in this book does not imply endorsement by the author or publisher, nor does mention of specific companies, organizations, or authorities imply that they endorse this book, its author, or the publisher.

Internet addresses and telephone numbers given in this book were accurate at the time it went to press.

Rodale books may be purchased for business or promotional use or for special sales. For information, please write to:
Special Markets Department, Rodale Inc., 733 Third Avenue, New York, NY 10017.

Printed in the United States of America

Rodale Inc. makes every effort to use acid-free ♾, recycled paper ♻.

Book design by Joanna Williams

Photographs by Vladimir Rys, Elias Lefas, and Babis Giritziotis

Library of Congress Cataloging-in-Publication Data is on file with the publisher.

ISBN-13: 978-1-60961-474-4 hardcover

Distributed to the trade by Macmillan

2 4 6 8 10 9 7 5 3 1 hardcover

RODALE.

We inspire health, happiness, and love in the world. Starting with you.

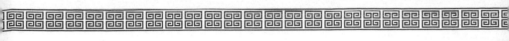

To Pheidippides and the ancient Greeks,
who lived and died for what they believed

CONTENTS

"The secret of happiness is freedom, and the secret of freedom is courage."
—THUCYDIDES

"It is not Greeks that fight like heroes, but heroes that fight like Greeks."
—WINSTON CHURCHILL

"Bid me run, and I will strive with things impossible."
—WILLIAM SHAKESPEARE

PREFACE

Though not much time has passed, much has changed in the world since the writing of this book, especially in Greece, the Middle East, and Europe. During the telling of my story, I wrote of a troubling immigration problem emerging in Greece, a country ill prepared to deal with such an issue. Since that time the Syrian refugee exodus has exploded into a global crisis, one that frequently dominates front-page news. In a single year that trickle of refugees washing upon the shorelines of Greece has grown into a tidal wave of displaced individuals seeking asylum and a safe haven from the brutal Assad regime.

The other unfortunate occurrence that has unfolded over the past year is the full-fledged collapse of the Greek economy. Things were bad while I was writing this book, but they have deteriorated further since then. The country required emergency bailout funding from its EU creditors, and to receive it accepted harsh austerity measures and crushing societal reforms. No age group has been spared. The younger Greek generation is grappling with 25 percent unemployment, and the aging population is coping with dramatically slashed pensions. Many blame the government and the rich for this, calling for higher taxes on the one percent to fix the problem.

But this is nothing new. I could sense these issues flaring

to a flash point during my visits to Greece. The telltale signs
were everywhere, if one bothered to look. Yet, to claim that I
was among the first to notice would be disingenuous. Plato
writes of the biggest threat facing the Republic as that of
income inequality. And the Battle of Marathon was about the
Greeks trying to preserve their nascent democracy from the
crushing tyranny of Persian totalitarianism. These events
preceded my observations by roughly 2,500 years.

Perhaps the more startling revelation is that in all this
time, not much has truly changed. Income inequality and disparities in wealth distribution are still hot topics, and cruel
tyrants continue attempting to repress their people to this
very day. Given that 2,500 years haven't fixed this situation,
maybe the government isn't the problem and higher taxes
aren't the answer. Perhaps instead these issues have more to
do with human nature than anything else.

That is one of the key insights I have gleaned from pen-
ning this work. No governmental policy will solve the problems we face. Unless we change our fundamental nature,
these same issues will persist for another 2,500 years, the
Greek theater continuing on for millennia.

Plato foretold of these troubles, but unlike so many of
today's leaders, he also developed a solution that addressed
the underlying human condition at its core. In place of
stitching together an ineffectual patchwork of laws and leg-
islation, he called for replacing the politicians, policy
wonks, and warmongers with thinkers, a measure meant to
bring about the enlightenment of humankind rather than
imposing more rules to regulate the way we live.

"There will be no end to the troubles of states, or
indeed of humanity itself, until philosophers become kings
in this world," he wrote.

It's an interesting proposition. A world guided by philosophers rather than by politicians—interesting, indeed.

I'll leave it at that.

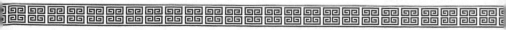

PROLOGUE

The story you are about to read has waited patiently for 2,500 years to be told. Doggedly persisting within the annals of history for centuries and millennia, the legendary tale of the first marathon has remained resolute in enduring the test of time, untiringly awaiting the splendor of its full revelation.

Anecdotal bits and shards have surfaced throughout the years—most famously the tale of the fabled run by Pheidippides (fye-DIP-ə-deez) from the battlefield at Marathon to Athens—but a deeper, more investigative assessment of what truly transpired during this very first marathon has yet to be told in a single, unifying narrative.

Until now.

The saga awaiting you tells the remarkable journey of a single, inspired athletic endeavor that forever preserved the course of humanity, the means by which this tremendous accomplishment was achieved being something that all humans, despite our many differences and disparities, have shared in common since the dawn of antiquity: our ability to put one foot in front of the other, and run.

Gus Gibbs, 1927

1

IMMIGRANT SONG

A hulking figure of a man, both in stature and in character, Gus Gibbs possessed the broad-shouldered physique of a Spartan warrior along with an equally domineering personality to match. Now in his autumn years, Gus was gregarious and spirited, but his life hadn't always been so carefree. Fifty years earlier, at the fresh age of 14, he'd arrived on American shores with 20 bucks in his pocket and not a word of English in his vocabulary. Since adolescence he'd been forced to fend for himself, alone and in a foreign land.

Enterprising and hardworking, Gus followed his instincts across the country, venturing wherever opportunity could be found and eventually settling on the West Coast, in Los Angeles. There, he met a beautiful young lady, Vasiliki, and they fell madly in love. He couldn't stand being without her. One night he appeared outside her bedroom window. "Billy, Billy," he tapped on the pane, "it's me, Gus. Open up."

She heard the rapping and slid the window open. "Gus, what are you doing here?"

"I've come to take your hand in marriage."

"But I can't."

He was puzzled. "Why? Do you not love me?"

"Yes, I love you deeply."

"Then why will you not marry me?"

"Because my oldest sister has yet to marry."

"Oh." Gus scratched his head as she slid the window shut.

He thought about the situation for a second and then moved over to the adjacent window. He tapped on it, and Eugenia's face appeared. Gus waved his hand back and forth several times, "Sorry, sorry." Eugenia was the middle sister.

He moved over one more time and knocked on a third window. Panayota looked out at him.

"Pack your bags," he told her. "We're going to get married."

She did as he asked and then crawled out the window. They eloped to Mexico that night.

Ironically, Panayota's family (or Patricia, as she was known) had emigrated from a region not far from Gus's origins. The two of them got along well together. Eventually, they raised a family of three children.

As the years passed, Gus invested his earnings from the restaurant business into acquiring rental properties, eventually building a portfolio sufficient to provide for his family and live a comfortable life in the flourishing metropolis of LA. A proud man who had come from nothing, it was quite gratifying to him to have created such a stable foundation for himself and his loved ones—the American dream come true.

Yet, despite all that he'd accomplished and everything he'd achieved, Gus remained perpetually restless. An incessant fire burned within the man. To him, it always seemed there was more that could be done; there were greater challenges still to be conquered. He would not permit himself to stop or to slow down, perpetually resisting any temptation to rest. His philosophy was: Show me a man who is content, and I will show you an underachiever. Gus was never quite satisfied with his place in the world. He was constantly striving to do more and to be more, though he wasn't always quite sure how to go about it.

Some of this pent-up ferocity was released through participation in sports and athletics. An avid wrestler, Gus dabbled
in the professional arena back in an era when wrestling was a
more noble pursuit. Athleticism was important in his ancient
culture, and those virtues stuck with him even in America.
His opponents used to say that getting in the ring with Gus
was like wrestling Hercules. He earned a reputation for being
a mighty fighter, fearless, even when taking on opponents
twice his size. His colossal chest and huge arms were imposing enough, but his legs, especially his calves, were so shock-
ingly overdeveloped that Gus often had to have the legs of his
trousers widened to fit over his calves.

Because he remained physically active throughout his
life, the years had been mostly kind to him. Bronze-skinned
and chisel-cheeked, with a full head of wavy, silver hair, Gus
looked the part of a Hollywood movie star. But like many
immigrants, his diet had progressively shifted from one of lean
meats and freshly harvested vegetables to one of heavily fatted,
fried, and overly salted foods. It was the American way. And
besides, it tasted better.

Returning home one bright and sunny afternoon, he
burst through the front door and lightheartedly called out,
"Patricia! Where is my lovely bride?"

It was a jovial, good-natured call he routinely sang out
upon returning home, even though they'd been married for
32 years. Despite decades together, Gus still maintained a
playful side. After all, wasn't that what life was about? No
amount of hard work could dampen this spirit, every glorious day was cause for celebration. This is what he'd been
taught as a boy. It was the way of the land he had come from
before arriving in America.

Suddenly, something peculiar occurred. The muscles in
his left arm started pulsing rather strangely. Gus cocked his
head—what was this? The sensation quickly spread to his

neck, and then farther up to his jaw. He stood silently, attempting to appraise the situation. Rather abruptly, his arm went entirely numb. He shook it several times, but the feeling did not return. What *was* this?

In that instant a crushing tightness squeezed his chest, as though an opponent in the wrestling ring had him in a body lock. The iron grip became so constrictive he could barely breathe. Staggering to reach the kitchen, he dropped to one knee. Gus was not a man to be seen on his knees. He thrust his arm upward in an attempt to grab the counter for stability, but his mighty arm did not cooperate, and he crumpled downward.

Now he was furious. "Arm, work!" he roared. "Do not forsake me arm; work!"

Blood coursed through his body in anger, but still there was no response from his arm. He would have none of this. He would not have his wife find him lying in an undignified heap on the kitchen floor as though pinned and defeated by a rival. This had never happened to him in the ring, and he would not permit it to happen to him now.

"If you do not lift me, arm, I will cut you off," he shouted. "Now, WORK!"

But his arm would not respond. He could not pry himself off the ground.

The door to the kitchen swung open. Patricia had heard the commotion and dashed in to see what was going on. She found him lying on the ground.

"Gus! What is happening?" She knew right away that something was terribly amiss.

"Patricia," he snarled, nostrils flaring, "bring me a knife!"

She looked down at him, quizzically. His request confused her. Patricia was a slight woman, of fair olive skin and light hazel eyes. Their union had begun as a convoluted one—after all, he had originally fallen in love with her youngest sister—though she had always found him quite handsome,

albeit a bit gruff and unrefined. No matter, she had sensed
that their relationship would endure despite their unexpected
union, and her intuition had been true. They'd been happily
married since the day she crawled out her bedroom window.

Gus broke the silence. "Bring me a knife, I tell you. I
must cut off my arm!"

Now she was concerned. She slowly stepped back. "I . . .
am . . . "

Walking backward, still staring down at him in grave
concern, she said, "I am calling for help."

"There's no need for that!" he yelled, eyebrows furrowed
in rage. "Just do as I ask. Bring me a knife and I will cut off
this uncooperative arm, and we can go about our day."

She started to tremble. Distraught, she didn't know what
to do, which wasn't like her. She always knew what to do,
how to handle things. But this was different. Her husband's
neck was growing increasingly purple, and the discoloration
was spreading upward toward his face. Something was horribly wrong.

"Come to me, darling," he requested, in a tone that was
now softer and more tender. What? She'd never heard such
passive words coming from her husband's lips. "Come, hold
me," he pleaded.

Never had she seen her husband scared before. Never
had he allowed himself to display any overt sign of weakness.
His ancestral pride would not permit such. She knelt down
next to him, and he noticed that she was whimpering.

"Just hold me," he said. After 32 years of marriage, those
were the final words exchanged between them before his
body went limp.

So ended the life of Gus Gibbs. Just like that, 64 years of
highs and lows, good times and bad, dreams realized and
dashed, all came to an abrupt conclusion. The death certificate following the autopsy listed occlusive coronary artery
disease as the cause, a heart attack. It was an all-too-common

affliction cast upon those who'd adopted the new American diet, with its greasy fast food and other unhealthy offerings. Fatty deposits of plaque had literally blocked his arteries.

The only peculiarity on the death certificate was that it didn't list his name as Gus Gibbs, but instead as Constantine Nicholas Karnazes. Like many foreigners concerned about potentially suffering the stigma that attaches to recent immigrants, he'd chosen an alias in an effort to assimilate more smoothly. Why do I know all of this? I know it because Gus Gibbs was my namesake, my grandfather.

Grandfather Constantine carrying me outside Saint Sophia Greek Orthodox Church, Los Angeles, 1964

2

WHO AM I?

My name is Constantine Nicholas Karnazes, son of Nicholas Constantine Karnazes, grandson of Constantine Nicholas Karnazes (aka Gus Gibbs), and so forth and so on throughout the ages. My grandfather's family raised goats in a little village called Silimna, located high in the hills above Tripoli on the Peloponnese peninsula of southern Greece. It was a tough existence, which in turn bred tough and resilient people. These are the origins of my paternal bloodline.

The other half of my DNA traces its lineage to the sun-drenched Greek island of Ikaria, situated in the Aegean Sea far from the mainland, a world unto itself. My maternal roots are here, in this unhurried place where food is harvested fresh from the land and neighbors are like family. In Ikaria simple pleasures still bring much joy, stress is unheard of, deadlines are wobbly, and the inhabitants live long, healthy lives. One of the famed Blue Zones, Ikaria has the highest concentration of centenarians on earth. It is an island, it's been said, where people forget to die.

My mother's lineage was never lost on her, even though we lived in LA. From the day I was born, we would spend sunup till sundown wandering around outside, seeing the sights, smelling the smells, walking through the park, talking to people along the way, and beholding the cycles of the seasons, just as her forebears had done on the misty blue islands of the Aegean in ancient times. Sometimes she would carry pruning shears and collect fruit and greens for dinner. I couldn't have known these things at the time, given that I was an infant being pushed around in a stroller, but perhaps these early childhood experiences seeped into my bloodstream, for starting at a young age I began to manifest a rather strong yearning for adventure and a strange penchant for endurance and self-discipline.

Some of my earliest childhood recollections, in fact, are of sitting quietly in the oversize cathedral of Saint Sophia Greek Orthodox Church in Los Angeles listening to an exhaustive Divine Liturgy, largely delivered in Greek, punctuated with endless refrains of "*Kyrie eleison*" (Lord, have mercy), always thrice repeated with the final verse delivered slower, more deliberately and drawn out, "Kee-ree-ay e-le-ee-sawn . . . " as if to be saying, "Okay, Lord, we *really* mean it this time; have some mercy, will ya please?!" Get a Greek Orthodox bishop going, and you could spend all day and much of the night in church. Endurance events in their own right, these sermons were not known for their brevity.

Yet I would sit there attentively for hours, even as I watched others slouching over and falling asleep in the pews. Many people used to tell my parents that I, the oldest of three children, was going to be a priest one day. But the truth was, I had little interest in the sermon itself (what 5-year-old boy could even understand this stuff?). What intrigued me was exercising my ability to hold steady and keep myself still and attentive while sitting assiduously through something I barely understood, hour after droning hour. I had a deep desire to master my body and mind, and sitting idly within the church's sacred nave while engaged in protracted liturgical worship was the acid test of willpower and self-command.

Above all, having complete discipline of mind and body mattered most to this 5-year-old.

One of my other early memories was that of our Easter Picnic festivities. Greek Orthodox Easter was, from what I could tell, just an excuse to throw one enormous party. Never had I witnessed so much wine, raucousness, and love all taking place in a single location. The quantities of food and celebration were beyond imagination, but what really struck me were the older Greek gentlemen dancing endlessly without rest or tiring. Most of them were recent arrivals from the old country, Greek immigrants whose children and grandchildren had migrated to America and then imported them over to the United States at a later date. These men were distinctive in the way they looked, dressed, and behaved. They seemed less interested in food and social carousing and more interested in moving with incredible form and exquisite mastery to the rhythmic sounds of the Hellenic Tunes, a local Greek band that strummed eight-string bouzoukis and tapped rousing chromatic riffs on the ancient santuri. These instruments didn't just play music; they infused passion directly into your soul.

Most of the men from the old country were in remarkable shape, lean and fit, with beautifully preserved olive skin and heads full of peppery gray hair. Their faces were chiseled and taut, and they danced with whomever would dance with them, even by themselves when everybody else tired. These were hardy men, resilient and self-reliant, wise in the ways of the world, men who had endured hardship and struggle in the old country far beyond anything their American-bred offspring would ever encounter. Their movements were expressive and stirring. They would dance the *zeïbekiko,* the *hasapiko,* and the *pentozali,* pure emotion bleeding onto the dance floor.

In between sets of music, when the band would take a break, I would watch as they exchanged shots of a clear liquid from little glasses, sometimes hoisting these oversize

thimbles into the air and cheering *"Opa!"* before consuming. I
later learned that these glasses were filled with an aperitif
known as ouzo, or the stronger distillate called tsipouro,
unless they were Cretans, in which case they'd drink raki.
When the band gathered the energy to resume playing, these
men were always the first to head back out onto the dance
floor, never stopping, never tiring.

Our family would often leave near midnight, and the
only remaining groups of people at the festival were these
old Greek men, still dancing as though the party had just
begun. The band had long since stopped, and now it was
just a scratchy prerecorded sound track playing over the
speakers, but the men didn't slow down. Their endurance
was extraordinary.

Why I would remember these particular things as a
child, I do not know. But those indefatigable dancing Greek
men would stick with me forever.

Another lasting childhood memory was that of a footrace
during my kindergarten year. It was an all-school affair that
pitted the children in my grade against the older kids in the
first and second grades. Judging from my experience during
free play at recess, I knew that I wasn't the swiftest kid
around, as other boys and girls could routinely outsprint me.
But this was a contest of four laps around the schoolyard, not
a quick dash.

The starting gun sounded and off we went. Most kids
darted out at a full sprint pace, racing as though they were
running a 100-yard dash, not four laps. By the end of the first
lap, I was somewhere in the middle of the pack.

By the end of the second lap, many of the initial sprinters
were complaining that the race was too long. But the teachers
kept telling them it was four laps and to keep going. Most of
them quit or started walking.

By the end of the third lap, nearly all of the kids were
walking from exhaustion or sitting on the sidelines. But I just

kept chugging along, not really paying attention to my position because there were still so many kids in front of me. I was one of the youngest out there, and I remember weaving in and out among the much taller kids as though running through a forest of trees.

Come the fourth lap, something remarkable occurred. Daylight emerged between the trees as I passed the final competitor. Amazingly, I found myself in front of everyone and leading the race. This struck me as odd; it was hardly the outcome I'd expected. Even more startling, I still had lots of energy left. I just kept running along, not feeling tired at all.

I came across the finish line a full half lap ahead of the nearest rival. Not once had I slowed or walked. I just kept going at a steady clip throughout the full duration of the race, and I felt like I could have kept going even after crossing the finish line.

The teachers didn't seem to make much of my victory, at least initially. They simply congratulated me and then went about corralling all of the other kids back into their classrooms. Later that day, however, I started to notice some teachers having side conversations and then glancing my way. I could tell they were talking about me, but I didn't know what they were saying. This kept happening throughout the afternoon, and I started to think that perhaps they were saying something good, something positive. I sensed they might have actually been stirred by what they'd witnessed that day on the playground. That was my first inclination that running held the power to move people in unexpected ways. Even though there wasn't much to it, running inspired.

Not that it really mattered to me. Sure, I'd won the race, but running laps around the playground didn't particularly interest me. What I really loved was running home *after* school. This was where true freedom could be found. The heck with running around in circles within the confines of some fenced-off, man-made institution; real adventure took place outside the school walls. Running through the park, chasing the ducks around the lake, breathing the fresh air blowing in off the Pacific, marveling at the great expanses before me, this was the stuff of life. A man's education shouldn't be limited to a classroom, not even at 6 years old—especially not at 6 years old.

Why is it that these thoughts and experiences were some of my earliest childhood recollections? Nature or nurture, it remains anybody's guess. Perhaps we really were born to run, as some have suggested, and certain people feel the pull of this primordial instinct more strongly than others. Whatever the case may be, an adventurous wanderlust seemed hardwired into my genetic constitution, a by-product of my ancestry, perhaps. And so I grew up exploring freely and, in doing so, discovered that my own two feet could carry me wherever I wanted to go.

"Perhaps you'll run a marathon, like Pheidippides," my dad once said to me.

"Who?"

"Pheidippides, the ancient Greek messenger who ran from the battlefield of Marathon to announce victory."

"Wow, that seems like a long way."

"He ran over 25 miles, and then he died."

"But he still delivered his message, right?"

"Yes," my father chuckled, "he still delivered his message."

It was a profound revelation. A man, a sacred Greek messenger, a runner just like me, had collapsed to the ground dead from exhaustion, but only after having fulfilled his life's duty. In my young heart's zeal, I could think of no more honorable way to go. From that moment on I knew my life's purpose. I wanted to be as Pheidippides. I wanted to run a marathon.

3

FIELDS OF FENNEL

M*arathon*. It is a word with universal recognition, though no universal meaning. Few people know the origin of the word, while even fewer know the secret truths behind the reality of Pheidippides's heroic undertaking. When asked the definition of *marathon*, most people would probably tell you it means anything of excruciatingly long duration requiring great endurance of its participants. For instance, we have marathon sessions of Congress, dance-a-thons, marathon episodes of *The Simpsons*, marathon lines around the block when Apple releases a new iPhone, and marathon traffic delays during rush-hour commutes. None of these answers would be correct, however. Those in the know would tell you that the definition of the word is a 26.2-mile footrace. But even they would be wrong.

The literal translation of the word *marathon* is: "a place full of fennel" (yes, that same aromatic herb you enjoy sautéed with vegetables, tossed in salads, or roasted alongside leg of lamb). Why fennel? Because when the invading Persian military forces landed on the shorelines of Greece in 490 BCE, they encountered a massive field of fennel. It is here that the Battle of Marathon took place. And that is the true etymology of the word—field of fennel. So I guess

all those bumper stickers on athletes' vehicles displaying
26.2 should actually be changed to read *Fennel*.

While the genesis of the word is rather entertaining, the
occasion itself is a bit more poignant. In fact, historians have
called the Battle of Marathon one of the most significant
events in the course of human history, for the very shape
and form of our modern world depended upon its outcome.
Had the invading Persian forces defeated the Greeks at Marathon, the evolution of Western society would have been
inexorably altered. The impact of this confrontation cannot
be overstated given that it occurred during a most fragile
juncture in the blossoming of contemporary human civilization. Our very existence hung in the balance.

As military historian Edward S. Creasy wrote in his
book, *The Fifteen Decisive Battles of the World*:

> The day of Marathon is the critical epoch in the his-
> tory of the two nations. It broke forever the spell of
> Persian invincibility, which had paralysed men's
> minds. . . . It secured for mankind the intellectual
> treasures of Athens, the growth of free institutions, the
> liberal enlightenment of the Western world, and the
> gradual ascendancy for many ages of the great prin-
> ciples of European civilisation.

If the Battle of Marathon holds such weight, then it may
not be overreaching to consider the feat of a single runner
the greatest athletic achievement of all time. Indeed, had
Pheidippides failed in his conquest, the Battle of Marathon
would have almost certainly concluded differently and the
history books been eternally rewritten. Few people realize
that the footsteps of an ancient Athenian *hemerodromos*[1] (day-
long runner) essentially preserved the fate of modern culture

---

[1]   Pronounced HEE-mer-O-drome-mos. The plural is hemerodromoi.

and forever influenced the values and way of life we know today. All of this because of a single runner; and all of this because of a single long-distance run.

The Battle of Marathon is one of history's earliest recorded military clashes, and the valiant drama of a single lone runner stands enduringly as one of the greatest physical accomplishments ever. The story of Pheidippides is one of the first known references to athleticism beyond sport, his long-distance run being notable not only in duration and expediency, but in heroism.

And, most remarkably, it all took place 2,500 years ago, long before the rise of energy gels, sports drinks, and medial posts on highly cushioned footwear. The vision of a lone runner making his way from the battlefield of Marathon to Athens to deliver news of the Greek victory, chest heaving mightily, armor shimmering brightly in the radiant Mediterranean sun, powerful legs thrusting forward, running with the hope of saving all of Greece and forever preserving democratic principles, was just the sort of oversize romantic fodder my young heart needed to ignite a passion. I was Greek, and running was something that brought with it great pride. I saw no higher calling.

Following that enlightened conversation with my father about Pheidippides's untimely but glorious death, I continued running right up to my freshman year of high school when I joined the San Clemente Tritons cross-country team. We runners were a grungy lot, free-spirited and aloof. People thought we were either really cool or really weird, and I guess we were a bit of both.

Although the race distances we competed in were fairly short in duration—typically 2.3 to 2.7 miles—we sometimes ran 70 or 80 miles a week in training. Not because we had to, but because we loved to.

My history teacher, Benner Cummings, was our cross-country coach. Benner was an interesting character, more of a mentor sage than a hard-nosed drill instructor. He referred to some of us stouter, sturdier runners on the team as "hillmen," because we specialized in conquering the hills. Calling me a hillman was Benner's subtle way of explaining to me that I was too slow to keep pace with the lankier sprinters, but that when the going got tough, when the incline steepened and the rocks and roots chewed men alive, I would excel.

Humble and unassuming, Benner was much the Socratic figure. One of the greatest thinkers of all time, Socrates once denounced, "I know nothing except the fact that I know nothing." Not formally trained as a coach, Benner claimed to know nothing, but he taught us everything.

"Run with your hearts and the body will follow," Benner used to tell us. Some of the parents were growing concerned about the high mileage we were racking up each week. Listen to your heart, Benner counseled. If the heart grows weary and uninspired, stop. If the heart remains impassioned and burning with desire, go. It was a simple philosophy, one that made sense to me. My heart was ablaze, so I went with it.

Being inherently drawn to extremes, I did something many thought was truly crazy during that first year of high school. Looking back on it, perhaps they were right.

Our school's annual fundraiser that year was an organized run around the high school track. The idea was for us students to solicit pledges for each lap we completed. A typical donor pledged a dollar per lap. If you were able to garner 10 donors, then you would be raising $10 per lap. Run five laps, and you'd be raising a total of $50 in donations. Not bad. But complete 10 laps, and you'd raise $100, which was even better (of course, running 10 laps wasn't easy). The donations raised went toward funding the school's library. This was a cause near and dear to my heart because my mom was a schoolteacher and always stressed the importance of reading and open access to books and literature. The library was an important place of learning to me, and I didn't just want it to survive, I wanted it to thrive.

Each lap around the track was a standard quarter-mile.

Some students were able to complete those 10 laps and raise an amazing $100 for the school library. A couple students managed to go even farther and run 20 laps, raising a hefty $200. One student was able to cover a remarkable 40 laps—10 full miles—raising $400 for the library!

I ran 105 laps. Yes, I raised the most money of anyone and made my mother proud, which was all well and good, but in the process of doing so I accomplished something even grander: I fulfilled my life's promise. You see, the total mileage covered during that intrepid gallivant around the high school track was the equivalent of a marathon. At 14 years of age my mission had been realized. I had become one with Pheidippides.

It took its toll on me. Completing that marathon wasn't easy. In fact, it was the toughest thing I'd ever done. Running 70 to 80 miles over the course of a week was one thing, but running 26.25 sustained miles in a single go was an altogether different proposition. There was pain. Avalanches of it, coming in sporadic waves and unpredictable pulses. Sometimes the pounding was acute and specific, as though a wooden mallet was repeatedly striking my kneecaps. Other times it was diffused and ephemeral, as if all of my cells were screaming out in concurrent agony, from the balls of my feet to the very tip of my nose. The pain also brought with it bouts of gut-wrenching nausea. Stop, my body kept telling me. Give up. This is too much. The mental battle was every bit as daunting as the physical one, a raw confrontation with self.

Friends and outsiders who had taken an interest in my endeavor surrounded me, so I did my best to put up a cheerful facade. But my struggles to persist must have been obvious to them; the internal strife was palpable and impossible to conceal. Feelings of self-doubt and doom were often followed by great waves of elation, as though I could run forever, only to shortly thereafter be overtaken by further rounds of darker, more disconcerting emotions. There were several points during the later stages of the run when my

mind seemed to disassociate entirely from my body, and a
peculiar numbness spread over me like a dense, halcyon
haze. These moments were not entirely disagreeable. In fact,
I felt almost nothing at such points. All sense of time and
place became distorted as though I'd crossed into a new
dimension, some sort of foggy parallel universe where
things didn't present as crisply and well defined as they do
here on earth. Then someone would hoot or yell my name,
and I'd be abruptly transmuted back to reality, bringing
with it more pain and an unsettling queasiness deep within
my bowels.

No wonder Pheidippides died, I thought to myself. Those
final few steps toward the finish of the 105th lap brought with
them a torrent of emotions. There were euphoria and jubila-
tion as people cheered, clapped, and slapped me on the back
in congratulatory attaboys as I wobbled by, but there were
also intermittent pulses of pain and mind-bending tenderness
in my muscles and joints so severe that they threatened to
topple me like a domino at any instant. And finally, there
was a profound sense of satisfaction in having accomplished
what I'd set out to do.

These deep feelings of accomplishment represented one
side of the emotional equation; the other side was an almost
infinite sense of relief. As my friend's mother dropped me off in
front of my house and I said goodbye and shut the car door, the
main thought I had at that moment was, "Thank God it's over."

I couldn't imagine taking another step beyond a marathon. But I would never have to. My conquest was complete
and I could now rejoice and relax. I'd done it; I'd completed a
marathon. There was nothing left to prove. All was good.

But the contentment in having fulfilled my destiny was
surprisingly short-lived. Things move quickly in high school,
and soon the exultation of having run a marathon was
replaced by an overwhelming sense of *What's next?* By the

conclusion of cross-country season, the fire in my belly had all but extinguished. Benner retired as our coach, and the motivation to keep running just wasn't there. Growing up near the beach in Southern California provided plenty of alternative activities. Surfing and volleyball became some of my pursuits, as did lifeguarding. I had nothing left to prove in running, so I hung up my running shoes—quite literally, by flinging them high into a tree branch—and moved on. Just as Pheidippides had died a noble death on the steps of the Acropolis, my life as a runner lofted away heavenward on the limbs of that tree.

Once a runner I may have been. But that was then. Now was a time to move on.

Off to the land down under

4

UNITED BY CALVES

Though running had exited my life, I still remained restless with an insatiable wanderlust and never-ending thirst for adventure. During my junior year of high school, I relocated to Sydney, Australia, as an American Field Service exchange student. Sure, I wanted to be a global ambassador and spread goodwill across borders, but mostly I wanted to pursue my new life's passion, surfing.

Australia is well known for some of the best breakers on earth, and it was the vision of riding the perfect wave that truly fueled my fire. I made it a point to attend school and be a good citizen when the surf wasn't up. But when it was, school became optional. I had my priorities squarely aligned.

The laid-back Aussie lifestyle suited me perfectly. My schoolmates were a hoot. The teenage Australian vernacular suffixed everyone's given identity with an *o*. For instance, Johnny Phillips was Johnno, David Smith was Davo, and Daniel Wojciechowski was Waddo. I was Karno (no one could ever properly pronounce my surname anyway, so it was just as well they called me Karno).

Endless days were spent laughing, surfing, and hanging out at the pub, an Australian institution where young men were taught the finer things in life, like choosing the best ales, picking a balanced pool cue, and throwing a straight dart. I hadn't a care in the world. Life was pretty much perfect. Until one day I got a strange phone call.

The voice on the other end was shaky and trembling. "Is this . . . Constantine Karnazes?"

Nobody called me Constantine in those days. My Greekness had long since departed. I was Dean. Or better, Karno.

"Yeah, this is Constantine Karnazes. Who might this be?"

There was a moment of silence in which I thought I heard muffled weeping and muted sobs, then the caller regained her composure, "We would like to meet."

Okay, who is this weirdo? I thought. And how did they get my number?

We hung up. The next day officials from the American Field Service headquarters contacted me. They explained that if such a meeting were to occur, representatives from AFS would accompany me. I agreed to the meeting, even though I wasn't sure whom it was I'd be meeting. It was like being a character in a surreal Kafka novel in which an important meeting is arranged but the party's identity remains a mystery. What happened next blew my mind.

Australia has some remarkable eateries, and at the time one of them happened to be a 360-degree revolving restaurant atop the Sydney Tower. It offered (and still offers) stunning views in every direction as you dine. As I walked past the buffet table, the smorgasbord of food was astonishing and the aromas were intoxicating. I couldn't wait to rip into some of those fancy meat dishes and gourmet cheeses. It was hard not to salivate in anticipation as we strode by. My hope was that this meeting would end quickly so we could roll up our sleeves and get down to eating.

As we approached our designated table, I could see three women awaiting our arrival. One of them was older, most likely in her seventies, with frosted, wavy hair and deep brown eyes. The other two bore a striking resemblance to each other. All of them were nicely clad and neatly groomed. I wore my standard attire: T-shirt, grungy surf trunks, and flip-flops.

When we reached the tableside, the older lady's eyes grew wide, and it appeared she was trembling. I tried not to take notice, but there was uneasiness in the way she stared at me and carefully watched my every movement, assessing, evaluating, and analyzing, as if looking for clues. Who were these people, and what did they want with me?

We sat down together, and a dizzying exchange of introductions and formalities ensued. Eventually the handshakes, name verifications, and ID checks concluded, and the officials who'd escorted me to the meeting politely excused themselves.

Now I was sitting alone with these three women, partitioned from the world in an awkward cell of silence. The older woman continued inspecting me with her eyes, as if searching for some meaning in a piece of art. Finally, the tension was interrupted. One of the two younger women spoke. Her voice was genial; her words were warm and articulate, soothing and disarming. She explained to me that we were related, somehow, some way. Things got progressively hazy from there. It wasn't that her explanation lacked clarity, but that *my* mind was awhirl with thoughts. She spoke in a rambling stream of consciousness about relationships, connections, coincidences, and family ties that all somehow related back to me, but her words streamed past me in a three-dimensional ticker tape of undecipherable code. The restaurant was spinning around in circles, and so was my head. Categorization is what I needed, hierarchy, some anchor of understanding to serve as a foundation for this tangled web of interrelationships that she was revealing. Her lips moved, but what came out was a mystifying cascade of names, pedigree, links, and associations like biblical gibberish. It was clear she held the advantage of time and perspective to piece this intricate chain of events together. But I had no such prior knowledge.

And so I sat there in a clueless fog.

"May I ask about your grandfather?"

Suddenly I was jolted from my daze. "My grandfather?"

They seemed surprised at how this question jostled me back to the present. "Yes, your father's father."

I thought about this for a while. As I did, I noticed the older lady sitting upright, attentively leaning forward seemingly readying to lurch ahead. She was clutching a handkerchief and kept rubbing it through her fingers. The other two glanced at her with that subtle look you give someone as a helpful reminder to remain composed and show restraint. Still, she hung on my every word.

"I didn't know him very well," I said. "He died when I was a young boy."

My words were a dagger to her heart. A flood of emotions exploded upon her aging face, and tears poured forth in watery, sobering moans of sorrow and pain. She clasped her hands to her chest and looked skyward, columns of moisture streaming down each tanned cheek. Her two companions moved closer, and the three of them hugged and wept, trying to console one another and somehow conceal this outward display of grief.

What had I done? What had I said?

I felt at once both a great desire to escape from this place and return to my familiar daily routine as if none of this had happened, and also a strange sense of providence as though being here was somehow part of my destiny. Of course, I also felt their pain; it was impossible not to. We were connected in some way, apparently, flesh and blood, and I couldn't simply bear witness to their anguish without feeling some shared sense of sadness myself. If I were somehow the conduit to this serendipitous reunion, then I bore a certain responsibility to surrender myself to faith and put aside my reluctance to engage in this public display of raw emotion. So I slid around the table and embraced them, becoming one with their heartache.

This is how I came to know my great aunt Helen, my grandfather's sister, and her daughters, Mary and Sophia, my cousins.

We met on many occasions during the course of my 1-year stay in the land down under, and every meeting was similar to the first. Helen would break down in tears, making the sign of the cross on her chest over and over, and we would all try to console her. She would often hold me, just hold on to my arm, the entire time I was with her. She would touch my face, rubbing her fingers along my cheeks and down my chin in a show of affection and a desire to gain a deeper familiarity with my constitution than words could convey. At first I found this practice weird—hell, it *was* weird, but not in her time and place. People outwardly expressed their feelings and emotions where she came from. There was none of this staunchly puritanical reserve and stiff-upper-lip mentality of modern Anglo society. People had no such hangups in her world; if you felt strongly about someone, you let it show. You didn't repress your feelings and emotions in the old country, and her emotional range was quite broad. She could just as easily shift from wallowing in tears of sorrow to thunderous outbursts of laughter to deep, reflective contemplation. She was, as the Greeks say, *polytropos* (a person of many twists and turns, moods and emotions). Over time I came to better understand these odd behaviors, if not fully appreciate them. They provided a richer insight into who my grandfather was and, by association, who I was.

The story of how this all came to be was quite remarkable. Helen was just 5 years old when her brother, Constantine Nicholas Karnazes, left Greece, though she remembered him quite fondly. My grandfather (aka Gus) was the oldest child in the family, and the only male. Helen was the

youngest of four girls. Constantine used to chase them
around the village, playing hide-and-seek with them for hours
on end. They had pet goats, and she remembered him showing her how to milk one. Their mother used to make cheese
out of this milk, feta cheese.

After young Gus departed for America in hopes of seeking a more prosperous life in which he could better help support his family back in the homeland, his letters arrived only
sporadically, if at all. Mail service to the little village in the
hills of Greece where my family came from was intermittent
and unreliable. They knew that he'd arrived safely in New
York City, clearing customs at Ellis Island in 1913, but his
whereabouts grew progressively vague as time passed. He
moved about the country, sending money when he could, but
oftentimes his letters never arrived. Eventually they lost contact completely. Helen vowed to someday reconnect with her
long-lost brother. That was her dream.

Eventually she relocated across the Mediterranean to
Egypt, married, and raised two beautiful daughters. She and
her husband built quite a prosperous empire before being
forced to flee the country in exile after the Six Day War,
when the Nasser regime took control of the country. They
lost everything and sought refuge in Australia, as did many
Greeks, I came to learn.

Helen thought about her brother often over the years, but
these were the days before Facebook and the Internet. Elec-
tronic mail didn't exist. As dreams of meeting went unful-
filled, his status became progressively less and less certain.
Until someone recognized my calves.

Yes, my calves. Word circulated in the Greek-Aussie community that someone spotted a boy with Karnazes-like calves.
Mary traced the lead to the *Sydney Morning Herald,* where a
story had been published about my coming to Australia as
part of the American Field Service high school ambassador
program. And that is how my Greek family found me. This

enchanting series of events was both magical, in that we were reunited with long-lost relatives whose whereabouts had been unknown for years, and tragic, in that I brought with me news of my grandfather's passing. It was also quite outrageous, in that all of this came to be because of an outsize set of calf muscles.

Although they were not athletes, Sophia and Mary had these same distinctive calves, as did Aunt Helen. On my side of the family, my father and both his brother and his sister—my uncle and aunt—possessed these same pronounced calf muscles. My dad claims it's a result of our ancestors chasing goats around the hills of Greece. Whatever the case may be, there's no mistaking these hulking anatomical protrusions.

The more I tuned in to this genetic linkage, however, the more I realized it wasn't just these oddly enlarged, bifurcated calf muscles that were unique, but also the entire musculature of our leg up to the glutes. Even in relatives who were inactive and slightly overweight, their girth showed only in their upper bodies, while their legs remained powerful and statuesque no matter how much extra heft their torsos carried. These improbably brawny specimens of legs, with their vascular networks of gnarled, rootlike arteries and capillaries interwoven throughout, appeared a freakish hybrid between a thoroughbred racehorse and an alpha male Brahma bull. Such robust lower extremities seemed custom built for locomotion over steep and rocky terrain.

Whether I liked it or not, I was bequeathed these same comically proportioned legs. Once again, my Greek heritage reared its Hellenic mug. The Greeks were an endearing people to be sure, but I had always maintained a detached degree of separation. Their culture was not the same as mine. They were from another place, another time. I was different from them. Or so I thought.

As I would come to learn, I could run from my ancestry, but I couldn't hide (unless, that is, I covered my legs).

5

ALL IN

And conceal my legs is precisely what I did for the next decade. The fairy-tale story would have been that I returned from my travels in Australia, dusted off my running shoes, and performed brilliantly in my remaining high school year, thus receiving a full-ride scholarship to run track at the University of Oregon, whereupon numerous collegiate records were shattered and titles won. Reality, however, was a bit less glamorous.

Instead of chasing running goals, the goals I chased were monetary and status oriented. I wasn't born to run; I was born in the USA. And the business of America is business. I pretty much followed the societal prescription for happiness. I attended an academically rigorous university (Cal Poly), graduated with distinction (class valedictorian), landed a good job with a Fortune Global 500 company (GlaxoSmith-Kline), gained some experience before attending business school (MBA University of San Francisco McLaren School of Management), made a ton of cash, acquired a bunch of shit, and lived happily ever after.

By the time I reached my late twenties, I was a millionaire (which was a good chunk of change back then, in an era before the Internet boom where "instantaires" can now amass great fortunes virtually overnight). I drove fancy cars, went to posh nightclubs, vacationed on yachts in Tahiti and in chalets in Aspen, bought lots of expensive things, and generally indulged in gluttonous materialistic lavishes. This was the recipe for success, I thought, and I was sure that eternal happiness would follow.

Only it didn't. Eternal happiness never came as a result; eternal emptiness did. And all the *things* in this world weren't able to fill the void. I'd been living within a cloud of delusions.

The seeds of discontent had been planted early on, when I suffered the tragic loss of my closest friend (who just so happened to be my kid sister). She was such a free-spirited and wise person, one of the few truly happy people I've ever known. Pary was forever encouraging me to follow my heart and do what I loved, not what society prescribed. I always chuckled at her, thinking that if I did what I loved, I'd be homeless. Corporate America was where happiness was found, I'd say. Fat paychecks and lots of perks dangled before your nose. Those are the things that fuel passion.

Pary died in a car accident on her 18th birthday, and I channeled my anger over her untimely death into a mindless drive to "succeed," never questioning whether my definition of success was misaligned with my personal values. Just do good and make lots of money, I thought. Those pesky little details like purpose, fulfillment, and contentment would work themselves out once the coffers were sufficiently overstuffed.

Unfortunately, the threads of disillusionment holding this finely woven veil together started unraveling as my 30th birthday approached. Thucydides had written, "The secret of happiness is freedom, and the secret of freedom is courage." These words sounded amazingly like those of Pary, yet they were written some 2,400 years ago. Once again, the connection to ancient Hellenic mores resurfaced in my life.

For the first time ever I started to second-guess my own

judgment and began questioning things. The inscription on the Oracle of Delphi reads, "*Gnōthi sauton*" (Know thyself). Did I really know myself? Was I in touch with the real me? Were these corporate paychecks giving me freedom, or were they shackling me in dependency? Did I have the courage to follow my unique calling in life and be true to mine own self? Nothing that I felt certain of before retained its original grasp on me; that placating carpet of conformity was yanked out from underfoot, and I was left scrambling for some toehold to buttress the slide. But no sturdy brace could be found, and I began spiraling downhill in an uncontrollable freefall.

This unbearable internal strife came to a head on the night of my 30th birthday, when I walked out of a bar in San Francisco, three sheets to the wind, stripped down to my fancy silk underpants, and started running south in a pair of old tennis shoes I used primarily for lawn mowing and gardening around the yard. I hadn't run since hanging up my shoes back in high school, but off I went. I didn't stop until the next morning when I hit the 30-mile mark in Half Moon Bay, completing a celebratory mile for each one of my unfathomable years of existence on this 4.6-billion-year-old rock we call planet Earth, this tiny speck of sand in a cosmic sea orbiting a single sun in the 200-trillion star Virgo Supercluster, which drifts like flotsam in an endless haze of mysterious dark matter. I lofted in those heavens that night of my 30th birthday running in the starlight, and in the morning things had changed. Everything that was important to me the day prior became less so the day after. That night forever altered the course of my life.

It wasn't that I didn't have a good job, because I did, and it wasn't that the company treated me poorly, because they certainly didn't. It's just that it wasn't the right place for me. While many of my colleagues thrived in such conditions, I withered like a grape desiccating on the vine.

I put up a convincing front, but on the inside there was

misery. It was clear I didn't belong there. But where, then, did I belong? Where was my place in this universe? That much was a little less certain.

One thing I did know for sure was that I'd run a hell of a long way that night of my 30th birthday. Not only had I locked strides with Pheidippides, I'd outpaced him, not stopping at the marathon distance but continuing onward to the 30-mile mark. Never had I heard of anyone running beyond a marathon, and I theorized that perhaps this was the farthest anyone had *ever* gone.

Until I met two men who were planning on going farther.

6

BEYOND

The Latin prefix *ultra* means "beyond." For instance, the term ultraviolet means light rays *beyond* violet. Ultrasonic means sound frequencies *beyond* sonic. It follows, then, that the term ultramarathon means a distance *beyond* a marathon.

This term hadn't existed in my lexicon prior to a chance encounter with two extraordinary individuals I ran into, quite literally, on a run. I should clarify—two individuals who *passed* me on a run. I wasn't used to being passed, but thankfully the duo stopped ahead of me (to do a round of pushups, no less).

They weren't a talkative pair, but eventually I was able to get some information out of them. Basic information. They were training for a race. A running race. A long-distance running race. A 50-mile long-distance running race.

Wait, 50 miles? Did I hear that right? I must have heard something wrong.

"How many days does the race last?" I asked.

No response.

"Is it, like, camping, where you hike during the day and sleep at night?"

Still no response.

"Are there hotels along the way, and supermarkets?"

Finally, a response: "Look, man, you just run."

"Yeah, but I mean how far each day? How many miles do you cover each day?"

He looked at me as though I were joking.

"What, does it take more than a few days?" I questioned.

"Buddy, the gun goes off and you start running. You stop running when you cross the finish line."

With that they both jumped to their feet and bolted off down the pathway, leaving me in a cloud of dust.

My cerebral circuitry was instantaneously overloaded. Breakers tripped, sparks flew, live wires dangled precariously. My mind had been blown. There existed a race longer than a marathon, apparently. I simply couldn't wrap my head around the idea of running 50 continuous miles—nearly two marathons back-to-back—but that is precisely what they said they'd be doing. I didn't like *driving* 50 miles; how was it possible for a human to cover such a distance on foot? I stood there transfixed, rubbing my temples and trying to make some sense of it all.

But another side of me was intrigued and, dare I say, enthralled. I wanted to try.

And so I did. And I lived. The aftermath wasn't pretty, but I managed to accomplish something I'd previously thought impossible.

It got more interesting from there. Training and life became inseparable, one and the same, intimately intertwined. My running shoes traveled with me wherever I went. Sometimes I would run a marathon before breakfast, and then run 10 or 12 miles that afternoon. On the weekends I could run for 8 or 10 hours a day. Training became life, and life became training.

After the 50-mile race I learned of a 100-mile run, nearly four marathons in a row! And the course wasn't held along some level stretch of pathway but on a grueling single-track trail cutting a swath across the rugged Sierra Nevada moun-

tain range.[1] The idea of covering 100 miles on foot was so
expansive to me that it absolutely obliterated all preconceived
notions of what was, and wasn't, possible. The limits of
human capability were completely redefined, and nothing
seemed out of reach any longer, in running or in life.

And so I went for it. After completing the 100-mile footrace I tackled a 135-mile race across Death Valley, in the middle of summer.[2] Upon finishing that beast it was on to
something bigger, longer. But what? I couldn't find a footrace
beyond 135 miles. So I signed up for a 199-mile, 12-person
relay race, solo.[3] The race director must have found it odd
that all 12 people on my team were named Dean Karnazes.

Running these long distances was liberating. Others
might have found it daunting and intimidating, and it was on
some level, but it was also a means by which to set the body
free and unbind the spirit. Vanished are the pittances and
mundane trivialities of everyday living when one is engaged
in an all-engrossing test of physical and mental fortitude.
Nothing else matters much when you are in the grips of great
pain, struggling to somehow persist and continue forging
onward against staggering odds. These endeavors would temporarily ruin my body but cleanse my soul. My spirit would
be awakened, and I would be left in a state of higher being,
the dismantled fragments of my essence eventually reconsti-
tuting into a better version of myself.

I began tackling ultramarathons across the country. The
hills of Vermont, the Rockies of Colorado, the deserts of
Sonora—soon there was a race in my calendar nearly every
month of the year.

Yet I wasn't naïve. The lights still needed to go on, and
food still needed to get on the table. Such were the realities of

---

[1] The Western States 100-Mile Endurance Run
[2] The Badwater Ultramarathon
[3] The Golden Gate Relay, Northern California

20th-century living. I had a family now, and being a responsible provider was important to me, *most* important to me.

People speak of finding balance. To me, that's a misplaced ambition. If you have balance, you do everything *okay*. But to excel at your craft, you need obsessive, unbridled fanaticism. Not only does excellence require such commitment, it demands it. A life worth living is frenetic, disjointed, breakneck, and quite fantastic. Balance doesn't lead to happiness—impassioned dedication to one's life purpose does.

Some might say that this is the price one must pay for high achievement. But with all the high achievers I've ever met, none of them speak of such a toll. Instead, they talk of boundless energy and infinite vigor that crosses into every element of their lives. The only time I hear people speak of dreary, exhaustive drudgery is when their daily work is misaligned with their life's calling.

I know this because that's precisely where my life was stuck. I loved running, but I still had a corporate job. Perhaps serendipitously, that was right when some representatives from the outdoor clothing manufacturer The North Face approached me. The setting seemed odd, though strangely appropriate. It was one o'clock in the morning, and I'd just finished running a 100-mile footrace through the mountains.

"We'd like to design a line of footwear for trail running," they said, "and we're wondering if you'd be interested in getting involved."

It was an intriguing proposition, but it meant I'd need to moonlight from my existing career, the one that paid the bills. I thanked them for their offer and told them I needed to think about it for a while. I took five steps toward the showers, then turned back.

"Okay," I said. "I'm in."

Despite being exhausted from running an ultramarathon, I didn't sleep much that night. Although it was just a small opportunity and wouldn't pay much, it represented

something much bigger. The notion that change takes time
is fanciful. Change happens in a flash. The underlying
magma may have been heating for a while, but when a well-
timed counterforce disrupts the system, change erupts
instantaneously, like a volcano, and suddenly nothing is
ever the same.

Here was an opportunity for me to potentially transition
out of my corporate job into something I loved. Sure, it would
take a lot of work and creativity to make ends meet. But if
not now, when? It was time to act, and it was time to act
decisively.

The North Face wasn't known as a running shoe company. Nike, Adidas, and Asics made running shoes. But when
I thought about it further, it made sense. What an ultramarathoner does is nothing like running around in circles on a
flat, oval 400-meter track. We ran over mountains and
through valleys, forging rivers and rocks on rugged, backcountry terrain. It was perfectly logical for a company like
The North Face to design footwear for such a setting. After
all, making the very best performance gear for the great outdoors was the heritage upon which the company was built. I
was hooked. Somehow I believed this opportunity with The
North Face could provide a stepping-stone to a more fulfilling
life. It was just the beginning, and I'd have to figure out other
ways to supplement earnings, but I knew that if I didn't pursue this opportunity, I'd spend the rest of my life regretting
my decision. This was my lucky break, my shot at forever.

I'll never forget walking into our kitchen one morning
and announcing to my wife that I was resigning from my job,
which was a terrifying proposition. I'd be walking away from
a dependable paycheck, a 401(k) matching program, stock
options, health-care coverage for our family, and a company
car. How would she take such information?

She looked at me and said, "I wondered what took you
so long."

I never looked back. We can either follow rules or follow dreams, and I went with the latter. Hundred-mile footraces became commonplace. Extreme races in extreme places, like the Sahara, Namibia, Antarctica, Patagonia, and the Atacama Desert, were tackled. No challenge seemed impossible, and I spent the better part of a decade pursuing every imaginable physical conquest on earth with never-say-die intensity.

Yet few of these races, despite their allure, adventure, and prestige, offered any cash purse. Even those champions I admired most in the sport had a hard time sustaining a career as an ultramarathoner. Ultramarathoning was something few people knew even existed, as previously I hadn't myself.

My intention in making this life-altering choice to join the ranks of ultramarathoners was not to shirk my responsibilities as a provider for my family, so I knew there would have to be more than just running if I were to make a legitimate go of it. Just because I could run great distances didn't mean the landlord was going to pardon the rent. My mission was to never yield, to be *polytlas* (long-enduring), somehow figuring out a way to make a stable ongoing living while pursuing this lifestyle along the fringes. To do that, I would need to be *polymetis* (resourceful) and look for every available option to support this unconventional vocation. Pheidippides may have been able to rely solely on his legs, but that was 2,500 years ago. Besides, I thought, he only ran a measly marathon, a mere pittance of the mileage I was accruing these days.

Boy, did I get that one wrong.

7

SPARE THE HORSES

Many runners are familiar with the story surrounding the origins of the modern marathon. As the well-worn legend goes, after the badly outnumbered Greeks somehow managed to drive back the Persians who had invaded the coastal plains of Marathon, an Athenian messenger named Pheidippides was dispatched from the battlefield to Athens to deliver news of Greek victory. After running 26.2 miles to the Acropolis, he burst into the chambers and gallantly hailed his countrymen with, *"Nike! Nike! Nenikekamen!"* (Victory! Victory! Rejoice, we conquer!). It was a glorious moment of celebration for all of humanity, and then he promptly collapsed from exhaustion and died.

It is an endearing story of perseverance and human triumph that serves to make every runner proud. Turns out, however, the story is bigger than that. Much bigger.

When I began to uncover the reality of what actually transpired, the truth didn't so much set me free as drive me nuts. Had we runners had the proverbial loincloth pulled over our eyes for all these years? We'd been brainwashed into believing that the marathon stood for the ultimate test of endurance, but there seemed more to it than that. So I resolved to learn what really took place with Pheidippides out there in the hillsides of ancient Greece.

To help sort matters out, I turned to one of the world's foremost authorities on the subject, Cambridge University Professor of Greek Culture Dr. Paul Cartledge. Never had I met a man who possessed such encyclopedic knowledge. Author of innumerable books and research papers on the topic, Professor Cartledge was a wealth of information and knowledge beyond anything contained in the history books because he gave the story a richness of context and setting that no sterile historical record could possibly provide.

Being British, a witty sense of humor accompanied his intellectual vastness. For starters, Dr. Cartledge preferred to reference Pheidippides by the aristocratic Athenian name of Philippides, the literal interpretation being "spare the horses" (seemingly because a trained hemerodromos could outrun a horse and thus preserve the poor creature's legs for less arduous tasks). However, frequently his tongue-in-check references cunningly revealed deeper insight, in this particular instance helping to explain why the Greeks dispatched messengers on foot rather than on horseback. Turns out that in the mountainous terrain of Greece, a trained hemerodromos could quite literally outrun a horse.

As we paced through the annals of history, the account of Marathon that began to emerge was something far more complex and mysterious than a simple 26.2-mile amble from the battlefield to Athens. And to tell the whole story we must step back in time, a long way back, to ancient Greek mythology.

Starting with the *Dialogi Deorum* (Dialogues of the Gods), ancient Hellenic storyteller Lucian tells of the heavenly messenger Hermes protesting to his mother, Maia, that in his role as hemerodromos he must carry his father Zeus's messages high and low, and when he returns, he hasn't even time to wash the dust off and tidy up before going out again. Having just gotten back from seeing Cadmus's daughter at Sidon, he hardly catches his breath before dashing off to Argos to check on Danae, and from there he must run directly to

Boeotia to see Antiope, though he is tired out already. So many women, so many miles, so little pleasure!

While this type of droll banter between the Gods is commonplace in Greek mythology, what is telling in this particular instance is that there is the mythical reference to the job of a hemerodromos in an era predating time. Hermes's gripe conveys the fact that hemerodromoi undertook demanding work that required inexhaustible endurance and great sacrifice. Hermes was something of a charmer, yet in his capacity as a hemerodromos he had sparse time to pretty himself between runs, nor was he afforded the luxury of being able to enjoy the women he visited during his tour of duty. Such tireless and unrewarded work this being a hemerodromos was!

While this reference to the hemerodromoi—day-long runners—existed in ancient Greek mythology, it is somewhat paradoxical that the modern Olympic Marathon, the one sports enthusiasts identify with ancient Greece, is one that had no place in the ancient Greek Games at all. Indeed, the modern marathon race, which attracts millions of runners worldwide every year, wouldn't even come into existence for another several thousand years. It is part of Greek lore, but not part of the original Olympic Games. In Greece, things aren't always as they seem, and perception isn't always reality.

To understand why such a paradox exists, we must visit ancient Olympia and examine the way Greek society was evolving. Throughout much of recorded history, the Greeks placed great value on physical fitness and sport, and in 776 BCE the inaugural Olympic Games were organized. Initially referred to as the Crown Games—owing to the fact that the prize for participation was a simple crown of laurel or olive leaves—athletes competed in them for the pure glory and love of sport. All male citizens were encouraged to take part; what mattered most was that one got in the game. O ΤΟΛΜΩΝ ΝΙΚΑ, the Greeks say (Who dares wins).

Although universal participation was the goal, overall performance still mattered. All contestants were essentially amateur athletes and competed on equal footing. But being one's best was important. The Greeks had a word for this, *aristeia* ("bestness" or personal excellence). So the citizen-athletes always gave their maximum effort.

As is the case with much lore, the romanticized view of the athletes of ancient Greece voluntarily competing naked to preserve the purity of sport is charming, though the genesis of this practice is a bit less altruistic. The reality stems from the 720 BCE Games in Olympia in which the sprinter Orhippos lost his loincloth during the championship footrace and didn't want to slow down to pull it back up. So he proceeded short-less and won the race. After this remarkable victory, others adopted the practice, thinking that running in the buff offered a strategic advantage because the legs were left unencumbered and thus able to fully stride without meeting resistance.

Eventually the Greek leaders began to notice that when men competed naked, all were equal, regardless of social status or background. They deemed this a good thing, and the practice of competing unclothed was widely promoted. Soon, athletes in every discipline were competing in the nude. Sports were the great neutralizer that rose above petty differences and trite disparities, thus elevating athletes to a higher plane, one that was beyond blithe trivialities and class differentiation. The symbolic act of removing one's clothing denuded a man of his pretentions and ego and stripped away prejudices and stereotypes, effectively eliminating social stratification. Athletes entered the arena as equals. Sports played a central role in the democratization of society, as there is no socioeconomic leveler like public nakedness. Imagine that: The pillars of democracy were founded by a guy who lost his shorts during a run.

Because of this willingness to appear naked before others, a trend of cultivating and exhibiting the perfect physique emerged. Physical excellence was highly prized, and the constructs of the idealized athlete started to materialize. The Greeks believed that physical strength was the soul manifested through the body. Thus, having a strong body foretold of a pure soul. Men spent long hours engaged in strenuous exercise, sculpting their bodies and perfecting their craft even though they weren't professional athletes, maintaining outside trades and professions all the while. Ironically, the only truly professional athletes were that class of citizens known as the day-long runners, hemerodromoi. But there was not an Olympic competition for this group of athletes, as no ultramarathons existed in ancient sport. What the hemerodromoi did was considered beyond competition, more akin to something sacred or an act of religion. Much is written about the training and preparation of Olympic athletes, and quite detailed accounts of the early Greek Games exist. Comparatively little is recorded of the mysterious hemerodromoi other than that they covered incredible distances on foot, over rocky and mountainous terrain, forgoing sleep if need be in carrying out their heroic duties as messengers of the people.

The original Olympic footrace distances were not ultramarathons, or even marathons for that matter, but relatively short sprints. The first of these running races was called a stade, and it consisted of a roughly 200-meter dash around the perimeter of the arena. Spectators who came to watch these athletic competitions sat in *stadiums* (from which the modern word is derived). The stade was the most prestigious of all Olympic sporting disciplines and was traditionally held as the concluding event of the Games.

As the games progressed over the years, a second footrace distance was introduced, the *diaulos*, or double stade. The *diaulos* consisted of two laps around the perimeter of the stadium. Eventually more and more athletic disciplines were added to the roster, such as boxing, discus throwing, a pentathlon, and various forms of wrestling. But all sporting events were held within the confines of the stadium, and footrace distances never approached anything close to a present-day marathon or ultramarathon. These prodigious distances remained the domain of the hemerodromoi.

In 560 BCE there was a minor movement to hold a foot-race of 800 meters, known as the *hippios* (meaning: there and back and there and back, or quadruple stade). *Hippios* was athletic jargon for *horsey*, meaning it was a longer than middle-distance race and thus probably best suited for horses. One of the first known US trail races is a particularly grueling endeavor held in Northern California called the Dipsea Trail Run. Later, an offshoot of this event emerged and was aptly named the Double Dipsea. Finally, for those who just don't know when to stop, a Quad Dipsea was founded (i.e., there and back and there and back, essentially a *hippios*). Having run this Quad Dipsea, I can attest firsthand that it is a race better suited for horses!

As the ancient Olympic Games gained momentum, a contest called the *hoplitodromos* was eventually introduced. This event consisted of a *diaulos* (double stade) but was run in helmet, breastplate, and greaves while carrying a heavy battle shield. This was the armor of the *hoplites,* the foot soldiers of ancient Greece, and sprinting a double stade in weighty battle gear, of approximately 60 or 70 pounds, was incredibly taxing and physically grueling. Due to its armored nature, the athletes this contest attracted were typically bulkier and built more sturdily than their svelte, stade-running counterparts. Speed was the most valued asset of a great stade runner, while strength and endurance counted most in the *hoplitodromos* competition.

The Greeks began to realize that having their infantry possess great power and stamina could be a strategic battle advantage. Over time the *hoplitodromos* competition became more of an Olympic sideshow than a dedicated event itself. These *hoplitodromos* events were held after the conclusion of the Games and allowed a broader range of competitors the opportunity to compete in an athletic contest (not unlike participants in the modern-day Warrior Dash or Spartan Race, which, legitimate as they may be, are still considered somewhat of a fringe event rather than a mainstream athletic contest). Great numbers of citizen-soldiers were drawn to these types of contests, and progressively they seceded from the Olympics altogether and evolved into something of a parallel venue, becoming more of a general training ground for the mass citizenry hoplite brigade on an ongoing basis rather than being held only once every 4 years.

Simultaneously, Athens began emerging as the cultural center of Greece and much of Eurasia. Large training complexes were established for men to develop their physical skills, stamina, and strength. Inside each of these towering arenas was typically an expansive courtyard filled with sporting equipment to accommodate athletes of all sizes and varieties, the bulk of those being everyday civilians. Hoplites, as they became known—common citizens trained in military ways—worked with a variety of exercise equipment and weaponry, most of which was designed and functioned very similarly, such as the piercing javelin or the sharp-edged discus. Seasoned hoplites and newcomers trained together, by design. The Athenians saw that having everyday people train alongside military elite created a citizenry that was supremely capable of defending itself, if need be, in the advent of war. Conditioning for war in times of peace is one function these training centers fulfilled.

Beyond being expansive sports and warfare training centers, these complexes evolved into places of learning, as well. It was in these centers that young male residents were educated and indoctrinated into the Athenian way. The Greek ideal was that sport should be preparation for life. Athenians viewed intellectual education and physical education as inseparable equals, both necessary preparation for a citizen to develop into a contributing member of the growing *demokrateia* (democracy, or self-rule by the people). In early Greek society there was no separation between the government and the people, because the people *were* the government. Over time, these facilities advanced into a combination of liberal arts colleges and sports training centers, known as *gymnasia*, from which the modern word gymnasium is derived (think 24 Hour Fitness, only staffed by Harvard professors). Preeminent among these centers was the *Academia*, where we get our modern word, academy. Students spent their time practicing running, jumping, throwing, and wrestling, while philosophy and mathematics professors sauntered about in the nearby alcoves—which were adorned with great statues and awe-inspiring works of art—always ready to engage in an enlightened conversation during periods of rest, or while working out together. Later, Aristotle would move outside the walls of the gymnasium and conduct his classes while walking around. His pupils became known as the Peripatetics (wanderers).[1]

Intellectual curiosity was encouraged, as was vigorous physical exercise and movement. The development of both mind and body was central to the Greek way of life. The Athenians came to believe that only when mind, body, and spirit were aligned in perfect harmony could true human potential be realized and *arête* (excellence and virtue) be achieved. These sanctified epicenters of sport and learning (i.e., gyms) were a place where the advancement of such principles could burgeon and thrive.

It was this quest for knowledge, not conflict, this insatiable passion for deeper understanding and cerebral expansion that pervaded Athens during the 5th century BCE. *Philosophia krateito photon—Phi Kappa Phi—*as the early Greeks advocated, "May love of wisdom rule humanity." A cultural renaissance was emerging in Athens, and the arts, sciences, and humanities were beginning to blossom.

Meanwhile, in the Greek city-state of Sparta, society was progressing in a radically different direction. Spartan boys were plucked from their families at the age of 7 and inducted

---

[1] Millennia later Nietzsche would expound, "Only those thoughts that come by walking have any value."

into the *agōgē*, where they were raised in crude barracks. Their training started early in life and was often harsh and unrelenting, the weak being thrust into a brutal fight for survival from the very onset of existence. Black broth and diluted wine were the dietary staples, and the occasional bath was cold. Spartan boys were taught two indispensable life lessons: Never retreat and never surrender. For a Spartan in battle the only two options were victory or death, nothing else.

Sparta was a hard land, rocky and unforgiving. This was a good thing. Soft lands, they reasoned, bred soft people, and by contrast, so too did the opposite hold true. The Spartans believed the rugged nature of their homeland helped harden them into tough and conquering people. For it wasn't the advancement of the arts and humanities that drove the Spartans; it was the development of the most dominant military regime in all the land, one capable of defending the city and annihilating trespassers. At this they were quite adept. Spartans were fearless in battle and showed no trepidation or mercy when engaged with an enemy. It was part of their ethos. As Spartan mothers used to tell their sons before sending them into battle, "Return with your shield or on your shield."

Spartan lavishes were few, and their meals were notoriously sparse and unrefined. A wealthy Athenian landowner had once visited Sparta and was asked to stay for dinner. He courteously obliged and politely ate his meal. Afterward, the Spartans asked him what he thought. "Now I know why a Spartan is not afraid to die," he answered. Apparently death wasn't a bad alternative compared with having to eat food like that again.

As brutish and unsophisticated as Spartan life could be, the principles of democracy were no less advanced in Sparta than they were in Athens. In fact, some might argue just the opposite was true. Spartans made all citizens *homoioi* (equals). In this landlocked Greek city-state, displays of public boastfulness were disdained, and flaunting one's athleticism was considered vulgar. Individual expressions of creativity or intellectual ascendancy—indeed anything that might convey a sense of superiority over another—were looked down upon. Duty and honor mattered most.

Even more progressive, Sparta was a place of great equality between the sexes, and women were every bit as valued, respected, and empowered as men. And this wasn't just lip service, either. Women served in important civic roles, helped develop public policy, and played a central part in shaping Spartan culture and societal mores. As well, Spartan women worked out and exercised with men, unlike in Athens where sports were confined entirely to the male citizenry. Spartan women were of tough body and tough mind. For all its loutish militaristic machismo, ancient Sparta was a place that would make Gloria Steinem proud. Sheryl Sandberg would be equally pleased. Spartan women didn't just "lean in," they came thundering in with both intellect and brawn. Later, Socrates himself made no distinction between men and women, saying, "We must pick suitable women to share the life and duties of guardians with men, since they are capable of it and the natures of both are alike."

Still, as progressive as it was in some ways, the mighty Greek city-state of Sparta remained dichotomously fusty and outmoded in other ways. For instance, it wasn't until the age of 30 that a Spartan male was allowed to venture from the barracks and marry. Even then, he wasn't permitted to leave the army and settle into a house of his own until the age of 60. A life of devoted service was what defined a Spartan—strength and honor—and during this period of history no other society had a more developed and sophisticated infrastructure for cultivating military supremacy than the Spartans did. They feared nothing and no one. When told of an approaching enemy, the Spartans did not ask how many are they, but where are they.

Such was the state of the Hellenic union in 494 BCE, the year Persian warships set out for the shorelines of Greece.

8

LET'S ROCK

Mick Jagger's throaty voice belted out another refrain as I worked my way into the tightly packed corral, The Rolling Stones blaring over the loudspeakers as the mass of anxious, excited, and scantily clad individuals stood restlessly awaiting the starting gun to go off at the 2007 San Diego Rock 'n' Roll Marathon. Twenty-six point two heart-pounding, music-pulsing, sweat-drenching miles later, I arrived at the finish line. It took 3:16 to complete the race.

Decent, considering I'd run 700 miles to get there.

One of the other runners spotted me jogging inward toward the starting line. He'd taken a shuttle from his downtown hotel, as had most race participants.

"How did you get here?" he asked, seeing me striding in.

"I ran."

"From the hotel?"

"From San Francisco."

That was the end of our conversation. I think he thought there was a hotel in downtown San Diego called The San Francisco or something.

The places I'd run through on my jaunt to join the day's starting line were a bit more remote and serene than the place where I was now standing. Rock 'n' Roll San Diego was the

final marathon in a long ultramarathon that had begun
12 days earlier in the bucolic little village of Sonoma, located
near my home in San Francisco. Nestled in what's known as
the Valley of the Moon, Mission San Francisco Solano is the
northernmost of the California Missions. From this starting
point in Sonoma, a string of 21 missions stretches southward
along the backbone of California, forming an interwoven network of sanctity en route to San Diego.

My career as an ultramarathoner had progressively
morphed, fractionating off from a sport that was already on
the margins. While I enjoyed competing in traditional ultramarathon races and had enjoyed some success in such, what I
loved most was embarking upon these less-structured running expeditions that ventured far outside the confines of a
set racecourse boundary. An extreme introvert by nature, I
found these types of excursions more consistent with my
inner persona. There was nothing I enjoyed more than stuff-
ing a few dollars in my backpack and heading out the door,
destination unknown. Sometimes I'd be gone for 2 hours,
sometimes 2 days.

At first I found this practice a bit unnerving, as did my
family. Why did this peculiar wanderlust keep manifesting in
me since boyhood? I started to think there was perhaps some
deeper mental dissonance at the root of these eccentric yearn-
ings. What was I running from, or to? We've all heard the
adage about the loneliness of the long-distance runner, but I
wasn't lonely at all. In fact, it was when I was out running
that I felt most complete. Only when I was running could I
feel truly liberated from the excruciating heaviness of existence. Oftentimes running would hurt, though nowhere close
to the insufferable pain of not running. Not running was
death—slow, insipid death. A day or two of not running was
tolerable, but a permanent state of not running was some
lesser form of existence.

Some might have discounted my behavior as flaky, a

coping mechanism for escaping the realities and pressures of everyday living. But I thought there might be more to it than this, a deeper meaning. Doing the things I did was my way of being true to myself. I wasn't the brightest of men. Along with the introversion, I was dyslexic. I didn't have great people skills, nor was I necessarily a good team player. But running great distances was something I could do, and something I loved to do.

So I did.

My inner Greekness had once again surfaced, and like a peripatetic disciple of Aristotle, I wandered. After starting my trek at Mission San Francisco Solano in Sonoma, I'd worked my way southward down the California coastline using this succession of missions as outposts and places of refuge along the route to San Diego, much in the same fashion the early settlers had done during their extended migrations, or, for that matter, the ancient hemerodromoi had done during their lengthy foot travels throughout the countryside of Greece.

Since the beginning of time, mankind has sought to communicate with one another to protect, to grow, and to develop as a race. Those societies and cultures that were able to disseminate and gather information most effectively tended to thrive and proliferate, while those that did a poor job of communicating got gobbled up or faded away. As humanity progressed and advanced, certain milestones in the development of communications literally altered the course of history.

Today we take for granted that in a single keystroke we can dispatch an e-mail across the globe, but it hasn't always been this way. Dialing back the clock to our humble beginnings, people used cave paintings and the beat of a drum to communicate and exchange ideas and relay critical information. Moving up the historical time line, the advent of telecommunications, fiber optics, and digital technology has had a major impact on the outcome of world wars and has influenced global events ever since their development in the 1970s.

But somewhere in between the use of smoke signals and instant messaging is a long and important period of our evolution where people relied primarily on, well, their own two feet to transfer and receive information. The Greeks realized that if they could build a more efficient infrastructure for communicating between city-states, they would be able to develop and thrive in comparison to other societies where less proficient means of information transfer were in place. Thus, the role of the hemerodromoi was a critical one. These esteemed foot heralds were the Greek equivalent of a faster Internet, and the distances they covered went far beyond those of modern-day marathons.

Given the importance of their duties, hemerodromoi were chosen carefully based not only on their physical abilities, but also their lineage and upbringing. Not only did hemerodromoi need to be extraordinary athletes, they also needed to be highly trustworthy and reliable. The reputation of one's family was critically important, as many times the messages being delivered or the intelligence being gathered was top-secret proprietary government information of great importance. In ancient Greece a family's standing in the community symbolized a tremendous amount. Traitors were not uncommon, and oftentimes such perpetrators came from lesser-known families of ill repute. Pheidippides, it bears mentioning, hailed from an established and highly regarded Athenian family.

The incredibly strenuous and exhausting work hemerodromoi performed tended to extract and expose the core of a man's essence. During such physical duress it is impossible to hide behind the façade of goodness if a darker side lurks within. Hemerodromoi were men of upstanding character, incorruptible and dedicated to the service of their fellow countrymen.

Watching the sunset and the moonrise night after night on my mission-to-mission ultra, I thought about what life must have been like as an ancient Greek foot herald. Running down the California coast covering 60 miles a day wasn't easy, but the hemerodromoi would have had a much rougher go of it. For one, most of the terrain I covered was along paved roadways. Sure, there were some steep ascents and descents, especially near the Santa Lucia mountain range east of Big Sur and along the steep passes crossing into and out of the Central Coast region, but it was all on tarmac. I didn't have to contend with rocky and rooted dirt trails like the hemerodromoi did. My foot always landed on a relatively smooth and even surface.

Further, the cushioned footwear I wore was engineered and constructed to cradle my foot in comfort and support while providing significant impact resistance. I learned these things through my work at The North Face developing running footwear. My socks were also designed with form and function in mind. They utilized moisture-wicking fabrics that effectively drew dampness away from my skin, thereby reducing friction and ultimately helping to prevent blisters.

My clothing, too, was manufactured for optimal performance and fit, composed of advanced synthetic materials that were highly breathable, provided UV protection against the harsh rays of the sun, and had few internal seams, which minimized chafing.

By contrast, hemerodromoi would have run in leather sandals, or in no footwear at all. In fact, many viewed shoes as an impediment rather than an advantage. An ancient scholium on Aristophanes noted:

> Dispensing with the shoes provides the feet with plenty of ease and lightness in movement, if they have been trained. Accordingly, one does not see hemerodromoi wearing shoes when on the road, and of the athletes the runners would not be capable of maintaining speed, if they were to run wearing shoes.

Many of the older Greek runners of our modern day
agree. The late George Psychoundakis, who as a young shep-
herd ran messages for the Resistance in German-occupied
Crete during World War II, concurred that Pheidippides and
the other hemerodromoi would likely have run barefoot.
Author of *The Cretan Runner,* Mr. Psychoundakis did not own
a pair of shoes until he was 15. Even then he rarely wore
them, and he ran great distances over rocky terrain. He tells
another story of a postwar sheep rustler living in the White
Mountains of Crete who eluded certain capture by removing
his boots to outrun authorities.

Perhaps the closest living equivalent to the ancient hemerodromoi are the native *Rarámuri* (commonly referred to as
the *Tarahumaras*) of the Copper Canyon in the Sierra Madre
Occidental of northwestern Mexico, those immortalized by
author Christopher McDougall in his bestseller, *Born to Run.*
In their native tongue, *rarámuri* means "runners on foot" or
"those who run fast." I visited these remarkable people, and
what I saw astounded me. Their ability to descend and
ascend the steep and harrowing canyon walls was like watching a beautifully orchestrated acrobatic dance. Wearing prim-
itively constructed sandals fashioned out of old car tires, they
slid, twisted, scrambled, and hurled themselves down jagged
and treacherous rock faces with extraordinary nimbleness.
One slight misstep along this sheer topography could prove
catastrophic, yet they moved through it like mythical spiders
patrolling their own web.

Watching the Rarámuri expertly traverse the vertical terrain of the Copper Canyon, it would be hard to ever imagine
a horse keeping up or even being coerced into attempting
such precipitous descents. Given the Rarámuri's incredible
agility and speed in navigating this mountainous landscape,
it was clear that no foreign enemy in pursuit could possibly
match their tempo in these craggy canyons. They could outrun anyone, anything. It was also apparent that the quickest

and most efficient way to communicate information throughout the region would not be on horseback, but on foot.

Perhaps tellingly, the clothing they wore was similar to that of the ancient hemerodromoi. Consisting principally of a simple white cloth shirt and wraparound shorts, the emphasis was on breathability and lightness. Whether by intention or not, utility and function were inherently built into the design of their attire.

As for Pheidippides's outfit, he would have run in a very basic tunic, referred to as a Doric chiton. Comprised of a single rectangular swath of linen fabric that hung down to just above the knee, the upper end of the garment would have been draped over his left shoulder and fastened at the top by fibulae (pins). Lightweight and airy as this costume may have been, there were bound to be friction points, and Bodyglide wouldn't exist for another 2,500 years. My suspicion was that chafing pretty much came with the wardrobe, and I resolved one day to test this premise.

To meet my body's nutrition and hydration demands during the run from Sonoma to San Diego, I applied a simple replenishment strategy of 500 kilocalories per hour of activity. Running is a strenuous activity, and maintaining physiological homeostasis requires matching intake with output. Given that I was averaging 10 hours of running per day, I needed to consume an additional 5,000 calories beyond my body's 2,500-kilocalorie basal metabolic rate to prevent catabolism in the form of muscle breakdown. This equated to a whopping 7,500 kilocalories a day!

Thankfully, my support vehicle was stocked with a variety of foods to draw upon throughout the course of the day's run. Some of these items were scientifically engineered energy bars and electrolyte gels, along with specially formulated protein drinks designed to help minimize muscle deterioration. Other foods, like chocolate-covered espresso beans, were a little less technical.

When I needed certain foods to replenish or special rehydration formulas, they were always readily available. Additionally, as any seasoned ultramarathoner can attest, the types of foods you start to crave during long runs can be quite unusual (okay, downright bizarre). No matter what your support crew has on hand, it's never quite what you want. Precisely why I craved pickles one day remains inexplainable, given that I hadn't eaten a pickle in years, or even liked pickles. All I knew is that I needed a pickle, and I needed it now! As fate would have it, there was a convenience store right around the corner, and pickles were handily procured. In another instance, I inexplicably yearned for some sort of cold, frothy coffee drink, even though I'd never had one before. Magically, a Starbucks materialized right up ahead. And it was the best damn mocha, frappe, latte, chai, Frappuccino thingamabob I'd ever had!

Pheidippides would have had no such luxury. In fact, hemerodromoi would have been especially challenged when it came to hydration and nutrition. These men typically traveled alone and had limited means to store excess provisions. At most, they would have carried a small satchel that could hold modest amounts of food, and perhaps a crude goatskin bladder for storing water.

That they were able to sustain themselves for great durations is quite extraordinary. Modern athletes rely on a nearly constant influx of calories to fuel the body's insatiable demands. Back then, however, this sort of instant reliance on food and hydration was impossible. How was it that these early all-day runners could endlessly propel themselves throughout the mountains and hillsides of Greece with limited intake?

To help answer this question, I turned to Dr. Barry Sears, a leading nutrition scientist and author of numerous books, including the *New York Times* bestseller, *The Zone*. Dr. Sears explained that endurance athletes don't require massive calorie intake if those calories are balanced correctly to generate the appropriate hormonal responses.

Ancient Greek athletes were known to eat figs and other fruits, olives, dried meats, and a particular concoction composed of ground sesame seeds and honey mixed into a paste (now called *pasteli*). In Homer's *Iliad*, this energizing sesame-seed-and-honey mixture was referred to as *itrion* and was a favorite fuel among warriors. Early Greeks also cultivated the ancient grain, zea. Low in gluten and containing abundant amounts of the amino acid lysine, zea is a healthy source of complex carbohydrates and was a staple food both for hemerodromoi and average citizens in early Greek times.

In antiquity, the hemerodromoi also consumed handfuls of a small orange fruit known as *hippophae* (sea buckthorn). Thought to be a stimulant and to enhance strength and stamina, *hippophae* would form a significant part of Alexander the Great's army's nutrition. It was they who observed that sick and wounded horses chewed on the plant's leaves to promote healing. This explains the etymology of the word *hippophae* (*hippos* means horse and *phaos* means shiny). Those equine that ate *hippophae* had healthy and vibrant coats.

Turns out sea buckthorn berries are a truly amazing superfood, loaded with vitamins and minerals, fiber, and antioxidants. More than 190 different bioactive compounds have been identified in sea buckthorn. Additionally, it is one of the only known natural sources of omega-3s, 6s, and 9s in a single food. Turns out those horses had pretty resourceful noses!

According to Dr. Sears, the ancient hemerodromoi's food combinations would have created a favorable hormonal balance that helped regulate blood glucose levels and preserve intramuscular glycogen reserves. Using glycogen reserves sparingly helps prolong endurance.

Dr. Sears also explained that if total calorie intake became restricted, as it likely would have during exceedingly long runs, hemerodromoi would draw primarily upon stored body fat for energy. Fat is the body's most concentrated source of energy, and even those with little body fat hold several days' worth of energy reserves. Pheidippides's body would tap into these stores to help propel him through long stretches of countryside where there was no food or water to be found.

Of course, ancient Greece was an incredibly fertile and biodiverse land with wild fig, olive, pear, and citrus trees growing abundantly. Hemerodromoi would be adept at foraging the land for these goodies. As well, given that many of their assignments involved delivering news to surrounding city-states, they could gather additional supplies at these junctures. Although Greece was one nation, the neighboring city-states often feuded with each other. But it was agreed upon by all that heralds were national ambassadors and thus immune from harm. Hemerodromoi were servants of the people and benefited all of Greece's development and protection, so they were considered inviolate and placed under the protection of Hermes, the divine herald. They were guaranteed safe passage and could be provisioned with additional food and water when passing through outside city-states, much the way modern marathoners can stop at aid stations along the course for energy gels and cups of Gatorade.

As Professor Cartledge explained to me, certain hemerodromoi would likely have specialized in certain routes. This would have provided them with a familiarity of the topography and access points to food and water along the way. Given that there were multiple alternatives for choosing a course between a starting point and a destination, heralds would be expert navigators and possess an intimate understanding of weather patterns and of seasonal shifts in winds and temperatures. They would also be attuned to the cycles of the moon and the position of the stars as navigational guideposts. Sometimes following a wider, less severe path might be the best choice, even if it meant running additional mileage, if that route circumvented abrupt climbs and dangerous descents over mountains, especially at night if the moon was low in the sky or dimmed by clouds. Other times, deviating onto narrow and rugged goat trails that shortened the route would be a better option, even if the path were steeper and rockier. A trained herald would be a good judge of not just these external variables but also of his own internal state. Was he feeling fresh and alert, or was he flagging and in a condition of exhaustion and fatigue? All of these factors would be considered when choosing the best path to follow between points A and B.

Running south through the Santa Ynez Valley, I was struck by the many similarities between the area I ran and what I knew of the countryside of Greece. The coastal regions of California are one of the few known areas on earth—outside of Greece—that have a Mediterranean climate. Thus, summertime temperatures are comparably warm and dry, especially as you move farther inland and away from the cooling influences of the Pacific Ocean. Also quite similar is the topography found along the coastline of California and that of Greece, with hilly, mountainous terrain being the norm. Overall elevations of the surrounding peaks, as well as the percentage grades of these inclines and declines, are fairly analogous, too.

The same holds true of the local flora and fauna. California and Greece share related types of foliage as well as a number of the same species of vegetation, chaparral, and low-lying ground coverage. In fact, one of the few known relatives to sea buckthorn grows exclusively in this region of the world. *Heteromeles* (commonly known as toyon berry) is a colorful plant that was used by the local Native American

Chumash, Ohlone, and Miwok for strength and healing (another close relative to toyon and sea buckthorn is the maqui berry of South America, which the Mapuche warriors ate for energy in battle). The Native Americans would consume the ripened, brightly colored toyon fruit directly or sundried. They also prepared a tea out of the leaves as a stomach remedy. Even further connecting California with the Southern Balkans, the indigenous land animal populations and local varieties of aquatic life are remarkably similar between the two regions, despite being continents apart.

Having spent many of my years in the outdoors along this California coastline, I'd developed an intimate familiarity with the subtle nuances in weather patterns and distinctive microclimates of the region. I'd reached a juncture along my current travels where I needed to rely on those instincts, as I had a choice to make between two potential variations in the route. One would take me along a flatter path running parallel to the coastline, while the other would divert farther inland and over the notoriously steep San Marcos Pass. This latter route was 15 miles shorter, but climbed to 2,224 feet along the way. It could also be much hotter compared to running along the immediate coastline.

On this particular day, the prevailing northwesterly winds were unusually strong in the Lompoc region and through the valley of Los Olivos. These winds helped usher in cooler marine air and served to moderate inland temperatures. Such knowledge was an important factor to consider in making my selection between the two alternate routes. Cooler temperatures inland were a good thing to be sure, but a corresponding consideration was that the coastal route would potentially be buffeted by a robust tailwind that would push me along nicely from behind. Even though the total distance required of this route was longer, it was the flatter of the two alternatives, and having a wind at my back would be hugely advantageous. However, there was a counterintuitive weather phenomenon that I sometimes observed when the northwesterly winds were exceptionally strong in this region, as they were on this particular day. During such instances the directional airflow could sometimes abruptly shift once south of Point Conception, which is where the coastal route would take me. Referred to as the Catalina eddy, the effect is created when the adjacent offshore Channel Islands redirect the powerful northwesterly winds back upon themselves, thus creating a counterclockwise vortex. It doesn't happen often, but if it did on this day, it would mean an obnoxiously vexing headwind instead of a pleasantly uplifting tailwind along the coastal route.

My gut instinct said to avoid the coastal route, and thankfully I did, because the Catalina eddy was in full force. Once upon the summit of the San Marcos Pass, I could detect the counterclockwise twist in wind patterns by the refraction of sunlight upon the water. Had I chosen the coastal road, I would have spent 15 miles battling a demoralizing headwind directly in my face.

I tell you these things as though they are just as important to you as they are to me. In all likelihood you're sitting here reading this passage wondering why the heck this guy cares so much about these obscure atmospheric phenomena. None of this is need-to-know information in today's modern world. Weather.com tells you if it's going to rain, and that's all you need to get through most days. Yet these were the things that captured my imagination. I could question why this was so, as I had on many occasions, but I couldn't change my internal hard-wiring. Running down the California coastline was the sort of adventure that enlivened me. I found it all fantastic, enthralling. I could either psychoanalyze why this was so, or I could stop at the wild raspberry bush growing along the road-side and fill my belly. What's in your DNA cannot be altered—that's a battle not worth fighting. And so I stopped at the wild berry bush to eat and left it at that.

A handful of days later I arrived at the starting line of the Rock 'n' Roll Marathon. The journey had been a long one—there was no denying that—but it was not yet complete. Rest could wait another day—there was still one more race to be run. And with that I departed on a final marathon, knowing that it soon would all be over, but not stopping until that point, 26.2 miles in the distance.

9

THE PERSIANS
HAVE LANDED

B lack as the night, there were no finer horses on earth
than the Arabian stallions of Babylonia. Invincible in battle, the early Median and Lydian military forces effectively
used these prized animals to quash the pesky Persian upris-
ings and greedy, expansionary land grabs of their neighboring adversary.

But the Persians were a resourceful and crafty lot. After
years of being thwarted by the almighty Lydian cavalry, the
Persian leader, Cyrus, noticed something peculiar. Those
regal stallions had never seen camels before, and they were
repulsed by the strong odor the hideous beasts exuded. In
fact, the stallions were so overwhelmed by the stench that
they would naturally veer away from the camels, not wanting
anything to do with these vile monsters.

Cyrus took this as an omen and mounted many of his
men on camels. He put the camel-mounted cavalry on the
front line and sent them into battle. The results were beautiful. The Babylonian stallions refused to go anywhere near
these foul-smelling creatures, thus forcing the Lydians to dis-
mount and fight on foot. The vastly outnumbering Persian

forces slaughtered them easily, and soon Babylon belonged to
Cyrus and the Persians.

King Darius took control of this massive, combined
empire in 522 BCE. A mighty ruler, Darius had aggressive
expansion plans for his kingdom, and Greece was one of his
prey. It was only a matter of time until he set about destroying this nascent republic with their absurd notion of collective
governance by the people. And for their part, the Greeks
didn't take such threats lightly. The Persians were greatly
feared. Among the many tools of Darius's war chest were his
elite fighting force known as the Immortals. Thought to be
invincible, the Immortals wore long robes, high felt caps, and
leathery armor vests of interlocked thorny scales, like the
skin of a crocodile, into battle. Equipped with lightweight,
reinforced wicker shields, bows and arrows, short throwing
spears, and scimitar-hooked swords for hacking, they were
quite a formidable sight to behold. Well-trained and superbly
disciplined in battle, they fought in a distinctive way. Quick
afoot, they would rush to within bowshot of the enemy, then
hold up and dispatch a quiver of arrows in rapid-fire succession using their advanced Scythian bows. Given their ability
to volley enormous numbers of arrows skyward and with terrific force, the effects were often devastating, killing or
wounding large numbers of their enemies on first strike.

Once the initial damage was done, they would set aside
their bows, take up their shields, and charge forward with
their spears, hurling them at short range. After this second
wave of killing was unleashed, they would finish the job with
their hacking swords in hand-to-hand combat.

The other important component of the Persian armament
was their cavalry. The Persians bred large numbers of horses
for use on the battlefield to complement their ground troops.
They worked together in concert, and no enemy they faced
had ever been able to withstand this concerted attack. Working in this way, they were able to roar through all of western

Asia, conquering, destroying, and capturing nation after nation, and in so doing they garnered a reputation of being formidable and supreme warriors, completely unstoppable.

The Greeks feared and revered the Persians, both for their fighting prowess and for certain elements of their culture. Young Persian men were purportedly taught three basic skills in life: to ride a horse, to shoot a bow, and to tell the truth. This simple and righteous upbringing was something the Greeks respected. But they also perceived a subversive element in the authoritative Persian system of governance. Were these young Persians taught to be noble or were they brainwashed into becoming subservient trolls of the government, incapable of independent thought and action? As much as Darius projected the image of a virtuous leader, his actions suggested that of a character far more sinister. After all, he routinely ordered the wholesale slaughter of entire populations. In many respects he was little more than a bloodthirsty murderer.

In 494 BCE Darius decided it was time to roil Greece, and his initial invasions were devastatingly successful. The Persians handily sacked the Grecian city-state of Ionia, ruthlessly destroying divine sanctuaries and laying much of the Ionian landscape to ruin. The young Ionian boys were castrated, while the young girls were taken captive and turned into pleasure slaves.

Once in control of this region, the Persians used Ionia as a staging ground to strengthen and fortify their military presence, eventually amassing a huge naval fleet of some 600 trireme warships and tens of thousands of infantry and cavalry. They then set sail for the Greek island of Naxos. When the Naxians saw the magnitude of the military power approaching, they didn't even bother putting up a fight. Instead, they fled to the hills for safety. The Persians showed no mercy and burned the entire city to the ground, leaving only ashes and ruin in their wake.

Next, the Persians made their way to Eretria. The Eretrian

people tried to put up a fight, but they were simply no match. The Persians quickly seized the island and loaded the captured inhabitants onto vessels bound for Asia, where they would face the austere wrath of King Darius.

By all accounts, the Persian campaign to overtake Greece was going splendidly. In 491 BCE Darius sent emissaries to mainland Greece demanding earth and water, the formal tokens of surrender. Most of the Greek city-states realized that they were no match for Darius and bowed in submission. Nobody wanted to see the Persians in control of Greece, but the strength of their military was too daunting an adversary to oppose. The choice was either to capitulate and pray for mercy, or attempt to put up a fight and face almost certain death or enslavement. All of the Greek city-states surrendered.

Except for Athens and Sparta. They were not so quick to submit. The idea of giving up their homeland to a foreign tyrant didn't sit well with them. In a show of solidarity, the Athenians and Spartans entered into a mutual defense pact, or *epimachia*, vowing to remain united in the face of a Persian attack. When Darius's emissaries arrived and demanded earth and water from the Spartans, they did something unthinkable. In a brazen act of defiance, they flung the Persian envoys into a well, telling them that if they wanted earth and water, they could find it down there. The Spartans effectively "killed the messenger," reasoning that the treaties protecting heralds from harm were an ancient Hellenic accord and the Persian butchers should be granted no such quarter.

Needless to say, Darius was none too pleased, to put things mildly. He immediately ordered the Persian fleet to set sail for mainland Greece, and in August of 490 BCE they crossed the Euboean Channel and landed strategically inside the sheltering Kynosoura Peninsula along the northern edge of the sweeping Bay of Marathon. Here they established a massive encampment and set the stage for the greatest military battle the world had yet to see.

Coming ashore where they had was by no means coincidental. Their landing spot offered a large degree of tactical flexibility along with easy access and egress. The broad coastal plains of Marathon were ideally suited to the deployment of the superior Persian numbers while providing ample space for their cavalry to maneuver. The bay was well protected from the prevailing *etesian* winds, and unlike much of the rocky and treacherous coastline of Greece, this landing area offered a gentler shoreline. From Marathon, they could either fight a land battle or set out around Cape Sounion and the Attic Peninsula and launch a seaborne attack.

How did they possibly know to choose this particular spot? It turns out they had some help. An ex-autocrat by the name of Hippias, who'd been exiled from Greece for his domineering, totalitarian ways, was out to seek retribution. Once defected to Persia, he'd fallen in with Darius and dreamed of one day returning to Greece to avenge his democratic banishers. Cunning and embittered, Hippias apparently had relatives in Athens and maintained a cadre of associates who served as paid informants. These were equally greedy men who would gladly set aside patriotism and allegiance to Greece in exchange for personal advantage and power, which Darius had aptly promised them.

Hippias conferred with Darius and the other leaders of Persia on battle tactics and logistical considerations, and then accompanied the Persian fleet to serve as an advisor along the way. He knew Marathon offered an ideal landing spot, one that was protected from the powerful winds that incessantly whipped down the Aegean, and so he helped guide the massive Persian armada to this precise location. At Marathon the Persians would be able to easily establish a sprawling military encampment, which they promptly did.

Word quickly reached Athens that the Persians had landed, and in terrifying numbers. By some estimates there were upward of 50,000 men, perhaps more. The Athenians were badly outnumbered and they knew it. They needed

help. So they dispatched a herald to Sparta to seek reinforcements. Now, Sparta was no short distance—some 140 miles
from Athens across rocky and mountainous terrain—but the
Athenian herald they sent was one of their finest, Pheidippides. A personal friend of General Miltiades, he was trustworthy and capable, perhaps the greatest hemerodromos
Greece had ever known. He would need to execute his mission with exacting precision as the fate of Athens, and perhaps all of Greece, depended on his ability to cover this vast
distance as swiftly and efficiently as possible.

Once Pheidippides had departed for Sparta, the Athenians debated their options. They had two viable alternatives: They could play defense and man the city walls
awaiting their enemy's arrival, or they could deploy for Marathon and attack the Persians where they stood. Led by the
encouragement of General Miltiades, they chose the aggressive move and prepared to depart for Marathon to confront
the interlopers head-on.

Miltiades impassioned the Greeks by reminding them
that although they were badly outnumbered—perhaps five to
one against a highly skilled enemy—they had something more
meaningful at stake. After all, it was not only their homeland
they were defending but also their system of governance, one
in which all had equal political participation and voice.
Unlike the Persians, who were driven into battle by the whips
of their commanders, the Greeks were citizen militia fighting
side by side as neighbors and brothers willing to risk everything for a democracy they all equally belonged to. This system of *demos* sovereignty—self-rule by the people—and political
equality (*isegoria*) gave them something worth fighting for
and, if need be, something worth dying for.

This passion was reflected in the participation rates of
the military. In an unparalleled showing of civic pride and
duty, nearly every single able-bodied male of fighting age
joined the brigade. The egalitarian nature of the Athenian

system made each man feel as though it was *his* estate under attack and *his* interest at stake. This was something worth defending, to the death if need be. To the Greeks, the battle was personal.

Before departing, General Miltiades instructed those inhabitants remaining in Athens to direct Pheidippides, upon his return with the Spartans, to Marathon. The women, children, and elderly citizens staying behind in the city agreed to do so.

With the possibility of never returning again looming over them, the Athenian hoplite forces said goodbye to their friends, family, and loved ones and prepared to depart. And on that August day in 490 BCE, they began their march of some 25 miles to the coastal plains of Marathon.

When they arrived, what they found wasn't a welcoming sight. Scores of Persian warships had already beached upon the water's edge, and hundreds more waited just offshore. The foreign invaders had long since disembarked, and many men and cavalry were securely established in a position that couldn't easily be attacked. It was no use trying to drive them back now. The Persians had arrived, and in no small way.

Seeing the disturbing imbalance in sheer numbers and in the quantity of military equipment the Persians possessed, the Greeks decided to hold their position in the foothills of the Pentele mountain range, which overlooked the Bay of Marathon and was well protected above the enemy encampment. Here they would sit in wait for the Spartan reinforcements to arrive. There seemed no way to take on this immense Persian army without Spartan help. Godspeed, Pheidippides. Godspeed.

10

ORIGINS OF
A CLASSIC

A student of history, British Royal Air Force Wing Commander John Foden was fascinated with early Greek writings. A prodigious reader, he enjoyed delving into the mysterious yarns and torrid tales of the ancient Greek record and exploring the colorful accounts of pre-Christian Hellenic lore. Such was the stuff that captured his fancy.

Commander Foden also happened to be an avid runner, and in 1978 he completed his first marathon. He found the experience entrancing and began running competitively, eventually going on to win a silver medal in the marathon at the World Masters Athletic Championships in New Zealand in 1980.

This accomplishment spurred a simple inquiry into the meaning of the word *marathon*. Thumbing through the *Encyclopedia Britannica*, he came across a rather esoteric reference to *The Histories* and the writings of Herodotus, the "Father of History," as he is known. Intrigued, he pulled A. R. Burns's translation of *The Histories*, which was published by Penguin Classics in 1970.

As he read through this modern translation of Herodotus's

writings, one excerpt in particular jumped out at him. This passage spoke about the prelude to the Battle of Marathon and stated:

> And first, before they left the city, the generals sent off to Sparta a herald, one Pheidippides, who was by birth an Athenian, and by profession and practice a trained runner.

Wait a minute, he thought, the story everyone was familiar with was that of Pheidippides running from the battlefield of Marathon to Athens to announce Greek victory, a distance of 26.2 miles. A run from Athens to Sparta was something altogether different, much more than a single marathon, more like six marathons stacked one upon the other. Such a distance would be appropriately classified as an ultramarathon, not a marathon. Athens to Sparta represented some 140 or more miles; how was it possible that one man could have done this?

What he read next intrigued Foden even more. Herodotus wrote that Pheidippides completed this journey *"the day after he set out,"* meaning he covered such a distance in under 2 days' time. Impossible, Foden thought. He dismissed the notion as fantasy.

But his fascination with what he'd read did not fade. Could it be true? Herodotus was also known in some circles as the "Father of Lies." Was this one such tall tale, or did Pheidippides really run all the way from Athens to Sparta and arrive the day after setting out?

The hook was set.

It wasn't easy obtaining a formal RAF expedition grant to do what Commander Foden intended to do. In fact, the presiding Physical Education Officer in charge of authorizing such grants thought the whole proposal little more than a

harebrained excuse for a holiday in sunny Greece. Thankfully, one of the PhDs on staff was also a runner and took an
interest in Foden's project. He helped usher the funding
request through the system, and eventually it got green-
lighted to proceed. The expedition was scheduled to commence on October 8, 1982.

Foden was able to successfully recruit a team of RAF companions. In total, there were five runners and six support-crew
members to provide assistance along the way. They were all
set to go, but the trip didn't get off to a very smooth start.
The flights they'd booked from their station in Germany to
Athens got cancelled indefinitely. Being a resourceful lad,
Commander Foden hired a minibus to transport the group
instead. The long drive to Greece was a harrowing adventure
in its own right, as the route passed through what was then
Communist-occupied Yugoslavia.

Much of the time they'd set aside for reconnaissance in
Greece was eaten up by the lengthy and time-consuming
drive, so the run was forced to commence without much
advance scouting. With a resplendent sunrise silhouetting the
Acropolis in the background, five men set out to prove the
stated purpose of the enterprise, that Herodotus's telling of
Pheidippides's story in *The Histories* was not a myth.

The men tried their best to follow as close an approximation to Pheidippides's route as they could using the obscure references made by Herodotus and a modern map, but for
necessity of logistics and van support they needed to rely on
established roadways for much of the journey. Some of the
trails Pheidippides might have followed were now likely paved
over, while other sections were covered in thickets and brushy
overgrowth, but the group's intention was to run to Sparta on
a route that as closely as possible mimicked the footsteps of
this fabled Greek hemerodromos, all the while not having
much detailed information on precisely what this route was.

They encountered innumerable challenges along the way.

First was the unexpected nightmare of having to deal with
car traffic and billowing air pollution along the overcrowded
roadways of Athens. Greek drivers were unaccustomed to
seeing people running alongside the highway, and very few of
them realized how terrifying a swiftly passing vehicle could
be to a person who was traveling on foot. The five modern-
day hemerodromoi had to contend with dense industrial con-
gestion, belching diesel fumes, and the terrifying blasts of car
horns assaulting them from every direction.

On the climb through the shantytowns of Dafini, numerous stray dogs, some of whom appeared rabid, rushed out
and snapped at them. The five runners initially stuck
together, trying to protect one another and covering each
other's backs. Pheidippides, of course, would have had to
fend for himself in such instances.

Eventually, tarmac yielded to old, potholed roads and
less heavily trafficked gravel pathways. They ran together as
a group for quite some distance, but soon they discovered
that athletes undertaking an ultramarathon tend to fall into
their own unique rhythms. Periods of high energy and troughs
of low energy rarely coincide between two runners. By nightfall the group had split up and become considerably separated, each man running at his own comfortable tempo. This
made it increasingly difficult for the support vehicles to provide aid and assistance at consistent intervals.

Perhaps owing to this fact, two of the runners were
forced to terminate their efforts along a segment of the
Peloponnese coastline. Lacking sustained energy and badly
dehydrated, they could no longer continue. This left just
three runners on the course, and by morning the following
day they had nearly a 60-kilometer spread between them.

Navigating at night and in the gray murk of dawn was
tricky. There were more encounters with vicious dogs, and
at one point Foden diverted his course to avoid a particular
village—out of fear of being attacked by one such creature—

and was forced to navigate through freshly plowed fields, his shoes filling with stones and debris. Complicating matters, radio contact between the two support vehicles was lost in the mountains, and their ability to communicate with each other was severed. Each of the runners took different routes, some truer to the landmarks Herodotus described Pheidippides as encountering, while others veered quite a distance from those markers. Their intention had always been to follow as closely as possible in the footsteps of Pheidippides, but they learned that this was nearly impossible to accomplish in practice, especially given their lack of research and reconnaissance beforehand.

Thirty-four and a half hours later, however, the first of the three runners arrived in Sparta. He had followed a nearly direct course and avoided a rather extreme climb up to the summit of a mountaintop, but in circumventing this rather vexing obstacle, he also bypassed one of the clear references Herodotus made in *The Histories* to Pheidippides being "high above Tegea."

Commander Foden arrived a bit later, in just under 38 hours of total running time. He had likely run a greater distance than the first arriver and contended with more mountainous terrain, but this was an era prior to the advent of GPS, so neither of them could pinpoint their exact route. The final of the three remaining runners arrived about an hour after Foden.

The expedition culminated in the main square of Sparta, beneath the hulking statue of King Leonidas. Despite dehydration and reports of hallucinations, blisters, horrendous sunburns, and a cumulative weight loss of more than 40 pounds between them, the trio had remarkably completed the journey, and they all did so within 2 days' time. At last, Herodotus had been vindicated!

It was quite an amazing accomplishment, and they were rightfully celebrated in the Greek press. "RUNNING IN

THE FOOTSTEPS OF PHEIDIPPIDES!" the headlines
read. What they had done was indeed remarkable, especially
given the hardships encountered along the way. Foden estimated that he ran about 50 percent of the way on tarmac and
50 percent on unpaved surfaces, and the amount of climbing
and descending through the rugged Greek countryside was
inestimable, though no doubt extreme. Vans were eventually
reloaded and off they set back to Germany.

The mystique of the endeavor impassioned Commander
Foden, and in 1983 he cofounded one of the most grueling
long-distance footraces in the world, the Spartathlon, an
annual 153-mile race from, you guessed it, Athens to Sparta.
More than 30 years later, however, this race remains an
obscure, if not entirely unheard of, event even amongst marathon runners.

Is this just? Does not the legacy of Pheidippides deserve
more widespread recognition? After all, his is arguably the
most important run in the history of mankind.

"Yeah, sure," you're probably thinking. It's a good story
and probably deserves greater prominence, but the annals of
history are littered with underappreciated heroes. Fair
enough, though I urge you to withhold judgment until you
hear about what happened next. The story of Pheidippides is
more than this. Much more.

11

TOGA!

In early spring of 1978, a primitive vessel called the *Hokule'a* set sail from the shores of Hawaii on a voyage across the Pacific to Tahiti. Composed of raw materials procured entirely from the land and mounted with traditional *lauhala* sails, the intention was to re-create the accomplishments of the original Polynesian explorers by following their ancient migratory route between the Hawaiian and Tahitian island chains. True to form, the crew would only be consuming traditionally preserved food during the round-trip journey.

It was a bold plan. Some 2,400 miles of raw and exposed ocean needed to be crossed in a vessel that had virtually no modern equipment. This was a reenactment of a voyage that had taken place many centuries prior, and there were inherent risks in attempting such a journey, as many men had perished at sea in those earlier days of travel. But the lure of re-creating this ancient passage was too strong for the proud Hawaiian crew to resist, and on March 16, 1978, *Hokule'a* left Honolulu Harbor on a voyage to Tahiti.

It wasn't long before the ship ran into trouble. Several hours into the expedition, gale force winds started whipping the sea into a cauldron of torrential swells and shifting currents. The boat was stocked with a month's worth of provisions, and soon this added weight created problems. Massive breakers began washing over the gunwales, flooding the starboard compartments; howling squalls tore apart the sails, violently rotating the windward side of the ship while precariously depressing the leeward hull. The panic-stricken crew scrambled about doing all they could to salvage the ship, but it was no use. During one exceptionally strong gust the *Hokule'a* fiercely pitched sideways and capsized, sending the men flying overboard.

The situation had gone from terrible to tragic. There was nothing the men could do but cling to floating remnants of the overturned vessel and pray for a miracle. Nightfall came, and the midnight blackness made it impossible for the crew to see; desperate pleas for mercy could be heard between the shrill cries of the furious wind. Hypothermia, exposure, and exhaustion soon began taking their toll on the weary and waterlogged men. All seemed doomed.

But one of the crew members happened to be a man by the name of Eddie Aikau. A proud Hawaiian by birthright, his ancestors had sailed these very seas for centuries. Eddie was known as a waterman (a Hawaiian colloquial term for a versatile athlete who can engage in multiple forms of water-sports and who is no stranger to intense ocean conditions). A champion big-wave surfer and lifeguard on the notoriously dangerous North Shore of Oahu, Eddie had ridden some of the world's largest and deadliest waves and had saved many swimmers and surfers over the years. He'd brought along a surfboard on the journey that was still strapped to the hull, and he decided that something needed to be done. Eddie was going for help. It was a dangerous idea, but so was clutching a sinking hull hoping for aid that may not arrive. In the darkness of the gale, Eddie courageously set out on his surfboard with the intention of paddling to the island of Lanai in order to alert the Coast Guard and save the crew.

He was never seen again.

I first read about this story[1] while in high school, and the impact it had upon me was profound. The whole notion of re-creating an ancient voyage was fantastic to me, a thing of legend. Learning about the events leading up to Eddie Aikau's heroic death spoke to me. He wasn't just a hero, he was a god. None of us endure forever; fault me if you will, but I could think of no more glorious way to go than alongside one's forefathers in a brazen act of heroism.

You can thus imagine my fascination when, many years later, I learned about the true story of Pheidippides. The romantic notion of running in his footsteps was the stuff of dreams. Here was a chance to realize my ultimate destiny. John Foden and his party had done a reasonable job attempting to reenact Pheidippides's journey, but I wanted to plunge deeper, become entirely and wholly immersed and experience something that not only put me in his footsteps, but united me with him in mind and body as well. This was something I needed to do, something I had to do. Just as Eddie had sailed in the *Hokule'a*, I needed to be one with Pheidippides.

But I didn't launch into my mission boldly. Instead, I started with baby steps.

State Street in Santa Barbara is the bohemian epicenter of this freewheeling coastal town. An eclectic assortment of unusual shops and restaurants, State Street is the place to go if you're looking to find avant-garde and funky things, and Bizerk is a boutique that excels in this department. Specializing in wardrobe items from Hollywood movie sets, the store is a treasure trove of ostentatious and obscure outfits and costumes ranging from the glitzy to the gaudy.

As I entered the store, it smelled musty and sweet, like mothballs and vanilla incense. I looked around and spotted

---

[1]   Which later became the basis of the book *Eddie Would Go*.

an employee. She was placing a dreadlock wig on a green mannequin.

"Excuse me," I said. "Do you have hoplite outfits?"

She looked at me vaguely. "Is that some sort of hip-hop getup?" Her hair was purple.

"Actually, it's the clothing of the ancient Greek warriors."

"Oh, togas. Yeah, we've got tons of those."

She led me back to a section of the store that looked straight off the set of *Ben-Hur.* There was an amazing array of memorabilia along with a vast assortment of tunics and chitons, massive gladiator helmets and swords, bronze breastplates and shields from the set of *300*, and glimmering artifacts and weaponry from scenes in *Troy*. I poked around looking for the right attire, and there, tucked neatly into a corner as if waiting for me, I found my very own Pheidippides costume.

I thanked the clerk for her help and paid for the outfit. Now that I had the wardrobe, it was time to play the part.

A relatively flat and mellow marathon (if there is such a thing), the Silicon Valley Marathon's one redeeming factor is that the race always corresponds with Halloween weekend. I thought there might be other runners dressed in costumes and that I would naturally blend in with the pack. I was wrong.

There was a guy wearing a Superman T-shirt, though I'm not sure if it was a Halloween costume or not. The looks I got along the way were interesting, to say the least, and a bit unexpected. People seemed genuinely stirred and inspired by the getup. There were fewer jeers and chuckles than what I'd anticipated, and even seemingly disinterested bystanders appeared to acknowledge my presence as I ambled by in a modified bed sheet. I found this warm reception odd, given that I was running down the streets of Silicon Valley half naked dressed as Pheidippides.

Perhaps they felt sorry for me. Even though the outfit was airy and light, there was nothing comfortable about running in this ancient Greek wardrobe, and by the midway point of the race, chafing was developing in places where the sun don't shine. I tried to adjust the fabric, but it was no use. It bound to my skin and mixed with the salty residue of my perspiration to form a gritty brine that abraded any area of skin the clothing touched. Wearing this outfit for 26.2 miles was an insightful experience, though not a particularly comfortable one.

I was extraordinarily pleased to see that finish line when it eventually emerged. Unexpectedly, a group of Halloween revelers had gathered alongside the final stretch of raceway, and they chanted, "To-GA! To-GA! To-GA!" spraying beer in the air as I ran by. It was more like a scene from the movie *Animal House* than one from *Zorba the Greek*.

The 2011 Silicon Valley Marathon provided a taste of what it must have been like for Pheidippides and the other hemerodromoi. But it was just a taste. I wanted more. I wanted to feast upon the marrow, indulge wholeheartedly in the flesh, and relive the true experience, and that just wasn't going to happen on the roadways of Silicon Valley.

12

COMING HOME

A friend of mine has a saying: "Sleep is for wimps." But the past several days of travel had really tested my devotion to that oath. Starting in my hometown of San Francisco, I'd flown to the Midwest for the 2013 Chicago Marathon, driven over an hour back to O'Hare airport in bumper-to-bumper traffic immediately upon finishing the race while still in my running shorts, and then boarded a transatlantic flight to Europe, only to sit idly on the tarmac for the next 3 hours. As would be expected, the delay taking off caused a missed connection, so after the long flight I spent another inglorious 6 hours holed up inside an Amsterdam airport lounge. When my departure to Athens finally left the gate, I hadn't slept in more than 2 days.

This was my first trip to Greece and it had been too long in the making. One thing after another had derailed my plans: kids, work, mortgage payments, trying to spend time with aging relatives—basically, life. Or were these just excuses? Was there more to this than I understood? I'd traveled the world extensively. I'd been to Europe on many occasions, toured Italy—Greece's next-door neighbor—extensively, and flown directly over Greece on my way to Alexandria, Egypt. I'd visited countries to the west, east, north, and south of Greece, but for some reason I'd delayed half a lifetime before finally making the pilgrimage to my ancestral homeland. It made no sense. Or did it?

Whatever the case may be, I was hoping to arrive in a bit more refreshed and energetic state. Instead, after the exhausting travels, all I could think about was crawling into my hotel room's bed and passing out. It was late in the afternoon when the plane finally landed, and the jetlag, sleep deprivation, and soreness—from just having run a marathon and sitting on my butt for the previous 40 hours—wrecked me. Sleep was the only thing on my mind, and I fought hard to keep my eyes open while I checked into the hotel and eventually dragged my luggage up the stairs to my room (the elevator was busted).

Drawing the hotel blinds closed for some darkened slumber, I glanced out the window briefly, and what I saw sent shivers down my spine. I know that sounds cliché, but that is exactly what happened. For there, in the background, perched prominently upon a high, rocky plateau, sat the gleaming white pillars of the Acropolis.

Suddenly, everything changed. I no longer wanted sleep. A rush of adrenaline coursed through my system, a miraculous vivacity washing over me like an incoming wave. When a place calls to you like this, you must answer its summons. Lacing up my running shoes, I slipped out the door.

The rise up to the Acropolis was steep, yet labor I did not. No longer were my legs heavy with fatigue, but instead they felt remarkably renewed. The air was warm, though not too warm, humid, but not too humid. It was perfect, really.

Just slightly did the sun still grace the sky, the final stages of its unhurried descent into the western horizon well under way as I made my way through the entrance of this majestic edifice perched atop all of Athens. Upward still to the Parthenon I climbed, head lowered, hearing only the sound of my breathing, my feet advancing soundlessly forward. Reaching the apex of these hallowed grounds, I turned toward the setting sun, and the gods spoke to me.

Zeus split the clouds and cast thunderbolts of piercing
light into the heavens above. The sky was awash in fiery
orange, with streaks of buttery yellow, searing red, and flow-
ery lilac all coalescing into a kaleidoscopic ballet, the burning
scarlet sun easing into the wine-dark sea on one horizon counterbalanced by the iridescent lobe of a full moon ascended skyward over Mount Hymettus on the other. It was as though
God held the sun and the moon on puppet strings and was
playing the two together perfectly. I stood there, alone, no one
in sight, mesmerized by the surroundings, when I was
strangely overtaken by an uncanny sense of providence, as
though I had stood there before, as though I was somehow
meant to be standing there, now, at that precise moment in
time. What was going on? For a suspended instant, time didn't
just stand still but seemed to move in reverse, like the sand in
an hourglass flowing upward, history rewinding. What was
causing these remarkable sensations? Then, abruptly, it all
became crystal clear. An unmistakable conviction serendipitously emerged from the tumult, and I knew, with all certainty, the root cause of these intensely rousing feelings.

I had come home.

It's hard to explain what it feels like when you arrive at a
place where you were always meant to be. One thing is for
certain, however: When it happens, you know it.

In my 5 decades of existence I had never experienced
such a spiritually impactful moment before. I doubt many
people *ever* feel such a divine sense of destiny, and I am fairly
certain that had I not come to Greece, I never would have felt
it myself, either. I had come home.

It took a few days of exploring and running around the city
before I came down from this mystical awakening atop the

Acropolis. When my eyes eventually cleared, what I saw was not entirely pretty. Greece was in the throes of a gripping recession, and I could now see the true impact of this economic collapse. Athens was a conflicted place. There were great works of ancient Greek historical significance on public display while directly around the corner there were alleyways filled with graffiti and homeless beggars digging through trash bins, searching for scraps of food. It was a tragic situation to behold. This was a country that had once been so proud and prominent, the cradle of democracy, and now it was in a desperate state of hopelessness and ruin. Many held opinions on how things had gotten to this point, but few offered options for fixing them. No easy answers existed, and in some ways, as I would come to learn, these problems had begun 2,000 years earlier.

The next morning I was roused early for a press conference. I had come to Greece for a newly conceived sporting event called the Navarino Challenge. It was an inconvenient time of year for me to be traveling to Europe, but this trip was mostly about helping Greece, not about me.

As a boy I remember one summer attending basketball camp. I loved the game, though I was never very good at it. I was just too compact and short to be a very effective player. I couldn't get rebounds around the taller boys, and my shooting wasn't very good, either. I wanted to help my teammates, to contribute in some meaningful way, but it seemed impossible to do much of anything. I felt helpless and didn't know what to do.

The camp I was attending was named after the legendary basketball coach John Wooden, who had led UCLA to 10 national championships in a 12-year period. Coach Wooden personally attended the camp. He saw what was going on and pulled me aside. I'll never forget what he told me. "You've got talent," he said, "but you'll never be good at getting rebounds, but don't let what you can't do discourage you from doing what you can do. You're a scrappy defensive player and quick with the ball. Do what you can."

This made sense to me. I took Coach Wooden's advice and started hustling like crazy. I made a lot of steals and was like a hornet in the backcourt, buzzing around endlessly, impossible to swat. After Coach Wooden's pep talk I changed my approach, focusing only on doing those things that I could do. At the end of camp I was awarded the Most Inspirational Player prize by Coach Wooden and given a commemorative plaque of his "Pyramid of Success." Basically, I won this award because I took two or three steps for every other player's one, running around chasing the ball down, never slowing to catch my breath. That was something I could do, and that is what I did.

The Greek economic situation was a massive, complex problem, one that would require extreme reforms. While it hurt me badly to see the country in such a sorry state, I certainly couldn't fix the situation myself. But the Navarino Challenge was something I *could* do.

Tourism is one of the largest contributors to the Greek economy, and sports tourism is a fast-growing subsegment of this industry. The Navarino Challenge was a way to showcase the best Greece had to offer. It would help promote sports, fitness, and the benefits of a Mediterranean diet, so when I was offered the role of being the official host and ambassador of the event, I jumped at the opportunity. It was the one contribution I could make to help Greece climb out of this mess.

The Navarino Challenge was conceived both to bolster the Greek economy and to improve the health and well-being of all those who participated in the weekend of fitness and sport. Designed for athletes of every age and ability, the event was the brainchild of Greek-American Peter Poulos along with his Greek partner, Akis Tsolis, and had the backing of prominent Greek businessman Achilleas Constantakopoulos. The running distances were not excessive, covering a marathon over a couple days, but the intention was not to make this an elite endurance event. The idea, instead, was for the event to promote inclusiveness and to encourage citizen participation, not unlike the original Greek Olympic movement.

Consistent with the egalitarian Olympic theme, there were a variety of sporting activities available. Pilates classes were led by professional instructor and entrepreneur Mandy Persaki; there was swimming with Olympic and World Champion Spyros Gianniotis and Taekwondo instruction by two-time Olympic medalist Alexandros Nikolaidis. In many ways the Navarino Challenge was one of the most progressive sporting events in the world, yet it was being held in a country that had fallen well behind the world in other ways. Again, the bipolar nature of Greece was evident.

The press conference that morning was well attended. Most of the major media outlets covered my presence, which seemed a bit peculiar to me. I'm hardly that well known outside of the running community in America, but in Greece I'd somehow become something of a celebrity figure. They asked me questions about my athletic achievements, training, and nutrition. The usual stuff. Most of them spoke English, but I had an interpreter by my side for those who didn't.

One of the reporters asked what I would do if I could no longer run. It was a question I got often, and I was never quite sure how to answer it. I didn't know what I would do if I could no longer run. Running defined me; it's who I was. I couldn't imagine living if I could no longer run, and truthfully, I was afraid of what I might do to myself should that day ever arrive.

"I'm not sure what I would do," I answered. "Probably open a gyro stand."

That brought a round of laughter from the crowd and seemed like a fitting closure to an unsettling question I hoped I'd never have to honestly confront.

Then one of the reporters asked what I thought about the Greek economic situation.

"I think it's tragic."

"What do you think about the politicians handling the crisis?"

"Look," I explained, "I don't mix politics with running. I'm just a runner."

"But you *did* meet with George Papandreou[1] and Bill Clinton, did you not?"

"Well, yes, but we talked about diet and exercise."

"You met with these two world leaders and that's *all* you talked about?"

"That's it. Listen, I'm not qualified to talk politics. I talked to them about the importance of cutting sugar from your diet and eating fewer processed foods."

Just then Akis jumped in, "Dean isn't here to talk about politics. He's not running for office, he's running a marathon."

The others in the room seemed to agree, and the conversation shifted back to where it belonged, though I'm not sure that one particular reporter was satisfied.

Truth be told, my interests in Greece were not entirely altruistic (though they had nothing to do with politics). Perpetually "dreamin' and schemin'," I confess there were ulterior motives in my personal agenda. It was nothing that would interfere with my duties at the Navarino Challenge, but during my stay in the homeland I planned on doing a little wandering of my own, of going "peripatetic," if you will.

When Peter Poulos—mastermind behind the Navarino Challenge—first contacted me, I had a feeling my personal *Hokule'a* had just sailed into town. The Navarino Challenge would be held on the Peloponnese Peninsula, along a region not far from the Greek city of Tripoli. That meant, in order to get there, we would be driving from Athens through Corinth, across Arcadia, clipping Laconia, and then on to Messenia. The destination interested me, and so did the

---

1   George Papandreou was Greece's controversial prime minister from 2009 to 2011.

route. These were the same mountains, valleys, and plains
Pheidippides had traversed. And as much as I was looking
forward to the Navarino Challenge, I was also there to do
some snooping around, to scope out the landscape. After all,
this was Greece, a place where things were never quite as
they seemed. As far as dreams and schemes were concerned,
I could be every bit as conniving as the gods, concealing
agendas and chasing clandestine ploys. When it came to realizing one's dream, I was *kyrios* (a master).

*Former Greek Prime Minister George Papandreou and former President Bill Clinton
with Dean.*

13

WELCOME TO GREECE

A thens is a sprawling metropolis, just like other big cities around the world, but on the day the race organizers and I drove from Athens through the countryside to the Navarino Challenge, about 175 miles across the Peloponnese Peninsula, I wasn't struck so much by how greatly things had changed over time, but by how little they had. While there were signs of progress, they were incongruous and puzzling.

We were traveling on a wide thoroughfare called the Trans-Peloponnese Highway E65, or the Moreas Motorway A7 (there were signs stating it was both). Regardless of what it was called, this roughly 130-mile monstrosity of a freeway cut a swath straight across the Peloponnese Peninsula stretching from just west of the Isthmus of Corinth to Tripoli and then on to its terminus in Kalamata. Although this modern feat of engineering was constructed more than 2 decades ago, the surrounding mountains and ancient ruins tucked away in the nearby hillsides remained largely untouched and in the same nascent state they'd been in for the past thousand years.

The roadway was broad, with multiple lanes in both directions, but there were very few vehicles using it.

"Where is everyone?" I asked Akis as we drove west

along this great highway toward Costa Navarino, the site of
the Navarino Challenge.

"What do you mean?"

"I mean, where are all the other cars?"

"What other cars?"

"That's what I mean, there are none."

"There've been a few."

He didn't find it odd that on this massive freeway there
was only a limited amount of traffic. Nor was he overly troubled that our automatic toll-payment transponder didn't seem
to be working at the tollgates. The entire route is a tollway,
and the sheer number of collection stations seemed asinine to
me. Every 10 miles or so there was another tollbooth, and
none of the fares were ever the same. Nor were they in standard increments. One fare might be 82 cents, while the next
was 94. The first three booth operators promised Akis the
transponder would work at the next tollbooth. Finally, after
half a dozen failed attempts he gave up trying and instead
dug through his pockets to pull out the correct amount of
change. Soon, we were all doing the same.

There were four of us traveling together: Akis, Peter Poulos, Peter's new love, Mark, and me.

"It seemed weird to me at first, too," Mark said.

A Southern Californian, like me, Mark had been living
with Peter in Greece for the past several years. But he was all
too familiar with the infamous 405, a freeway in SoCal about
the same breadth as the A7, but perpetually snarled with traffic. A recent construction closure on the 405 had triggered
what the media coined Carpocalypse, a complete gridlock of
the entire downtown LA metro area. There was talk of a
forthcoming Carmageddon if there were ever to be a seismic
event (news speak for earthquake) that impacted the 405.

"It just seems bizarre to me that the Greeks would build
this enormous highway when there's nothing out here," I

said. "I can't see rows of condos and track housing popping up anytime soon, yet there's a freeway the size of the 405."

"Welcome to Greece," Mark smiled. "Things don't always make sense here."

"Since its construction 20 years ago has the roadway led to *any* new growth?" I asked.

"They installed a gas station along the way," Peter offered. "And they're going to build another one on the opposite side soon."

"Wow, a hundred and thirty miles of freeway and two gas stations," I muttered incredulously.

"The construction is top-notch, too," Mark added. An architect by training, he had an eye for such things. "The tollbooths are exquisitely designed, not like the eyesores you see in many other parts of the world. The Greek engineers were ahead of their time."

"Yeah," I'm thinking, "like a few hundred years ahead." There wouldn't be any shopping malls or Walmarts arriving anytime soon, or ever. But hey, the tollbooths are handsomely designed.

Indeed, welcome to Greece.

There was an additional dimension to this place that remained concealed beneath the surface. During the protracted drive to Costa Navarino something unexpected happened. Instead of the extended duration of the cooped-up transit culminating in a fierce bout of road rage, the opposite transpired. We rolled down the windows and let the fresh, warm air blow in. Peter instructed Mark and me in Greek. We laughed and joked about how different things were here from in the United States, where everything is structured and designed to have a purpose and meaning. Akis had this ridiculous ringtone on his phone, "Get Lucky" by Daft Punk. Every time his phone would ring, which was about every 5 minutes, we'd all start swaying our heads, waving our hands in the air and singing,

"We're up all night to the sun/We're up all night to get some/We're up all night for good fun/We're up all night to get lucky . . . " If there had been any other drivers on the road, they would have thought we were all crazy. But there weren't any.

We stopped at several points along the way, which enabled me to survey the landscape a bit. It was hard to imagine anyone running out in these ancient hillsides and over those steep and rocky mountaintops. From what I could see, there were absolutely no trails or paths to follow and much of the terrain appeared rugged and covered in thick brush. We would delve deeper into this territory during the Navarino Challenge, but from what I could decipher along these roadside vantage points, very little of it looked penetrable.

After exiting the expressway outside Kalamata and transitioning onto a smaller coastal roadway, we stopped to refuel. The sun was just setting, and an explosion of colors set the western skyline ablaze. The evening air was warm, still, and pleasantly fragrant. I decided to walk over and take a peek into the service station. What I saw was absolutely bewildering.

Inside, there was an entire gourmet food section with exotic spices and local specialty items beautifully merchandised on driftwood shelves. Bushels of herbs hung upside down drying above the windowpane. And, get this: There was even a fresh produce section! I'd never seen a gas station that looked so much like Whole Foods Market on the inside.

In the produce section (I still can't believe I'm describing the interior of a gas station in these terms) there were wicker baskets filled with all sorts of fruits and vegetables. The labels and prices were in Greek, so I had no idea what some of the items were. One of the baskets contained something that looked like small plums. I picked one of them up and inspected it.

Peter had come in. "What is this thing?" I asked him.

"It's an olive. They're good. Let's get some."

"A what?" I asked him again. I was holding something the size of a golf ball.

"An olive. This region's known for them."

He put a handful in a paper sack and paid for them. We left.

Once back in the car I offered to repay Peter. "Are you kidding?" he said. "That whole thing was 37 cents."

"What, that's it?" I said, dumbfounded.

"It's hard to sell something when you can walk across the street and pick them off a tree for free. Here," he said, "try some."

He handed me one.

"What do I do with it, just put it in my mouth?"

He looked at me oddly, "That's how most people eat, isn't it?"

Funny thing with Peter, he wasn't being cheeky or satirical, he was truly curious if there might be some alternative way to eat.

I stuck the thing in my mouth and started chewing around the pit.

"Oh my God," I blurted, "that's not an olive, that's a religious experience." The taste was amazing.

Never had I eaten an olive that was so flavorful. It had bouquet, character, and dimension to it, just like a fine wine. As I chewed further, the tastes kept multiplying and intensifying.

"They're good, aren't they?" Peter asked.

"They're unbelievable. How do they get an olive to taste like that?"

He laughed. "Welcome to Greece. It's a combination of things that all come together to make food taste good here. These are ancient trees from small traditional groves, and they've never been crossbred or mixed." He went on to explain that the soil is pure and unadulterated by fertilizers or pesticides and that the mineral and salt composition is unique to this region. The air temperature, air quality, and humidity also play an important role, as does the intensity and duration of southern Mediterranean sunlight throughout the year and the amount and timing of rainfall. "All of these factors come together to produce an olive like that. It seems complicated, but it's really quite simple," he said.

"Hand me another, will ya?"

I stared gnawing on a second one. It was even better than the first.

"The Chinese really love Greek olives. The import fees are excessive, though, so a group of enterprising Chinese businessmen thought they'd ship some trees from Kalamata back to China and plant them locally. But their plan backfired. The olives those trees produced weren't the same. There's no way to emulate the conditions that exist here in this region of Greece."

The road we were now on wound along lazily and was even less traveled than the carless superhighway. It meandered gingerly into the countryside, passing through small townships along the way. The sun had long since set, and it was getting late in the evening.

"This area has been hit really hard by the economic crisis," Akis informed me.

Yet the later it got, the more the little towns and villages along the way seemed to spring to life. We passed local roadside taverns and outdoor restaurants, and there were people everywhere, of every age. Kids were playing along the sidewalks, laughing and chasing each other while the older *yia-yias* and *papous* (grandparents) watched over them. Music could be heard, and people sat together, drinking, telling jokes, laughing, and eating. Young couples sat romantically staring into each other's eyes. It was like a scene from a Hollywood romance movie, only it was real. These people might be poor, I thought, but their lives seemed richer than those of a lot of the multimillionaires I knew back in the States.

"Are you hungry?" Akis asked.

"Sure; I could eat." I was starving, actually.

We stopped at a local diner for some food. The menu was entirely in Greek.

"Do you want fish or meat?" he asked.

"I'd love some fish."

"Okay, follow me."

He walked me back toward the kitchen, where there was a cooler on the counter filled with crushed ice and the day's haul.

"What are you in the mood for?"

"You mean just pick one?"

"*Nai.*"

"So what do we do?" I asked.

"You just pick one."

"But I thought you said no."

"What do you mean?"

"I mean, I asked if you just pick one and you said no."

"I said *nai*. That means yes."

I stood there scratching my head.

"That's a nice-looking snapper," he said, pointing to a reddish fish. "And here's a good-looking rockfish if you're in the mood for something meatier." He held it up by the eye sockets for me to inspect.

"They both look pretty good to me, I guess."

"Okay."

In Greek, he ordered them both.

The food arrived maybe 10 or 15 minutes later, tops. Straight from net to table, the fish had been lightly grilled over an open flame with a bit of locally pressed olive oil, fresh lemon, crushed oregano, and some coarse Mediterranean Sea salt sprinkled atop. Along with the fish they served a large platter of steamed greens, perhaps spinach.

The fish was another divine experience, the skin crispy and flavorful and the meat inside soft and moist. And the greens they served with it were like nothing I'd ever tasted before.

"What is this?" I asked.

"They call it *horta*."

"*Horta*? What does that mean?"

"Weeds," Peter responded, shoveling another serving onto his plate.

"Weeds? I'm eating weeds!"

"Yeah. They're pretty good, aren't they?"

They were delicious.

"You know all that underbrush covering the hillsides? That's *horta*. The *yia-yias* walk around all day collecting it."

I surveyed the countryside. "Looks like there's no shortage of supply. It's everywhere."

"Yeah, and it grows quickly, too."

Most weeds do, but who cared? It was one of the most flavorful meals I'd ever eaten. Simply prepared, the food tasted so good that it didn't need to be disguised under heavy sauces or buttery gravies. I laughed, thinking how different the culinary experience is at a roadside diner in America. Could you imagine someone foraging around outside Denny's collecting weeds to eat?

It was very late in the evening when we finally arrived at the Costa Navarino development. The moon was full, and a soft breeze gently rustled the leaves of the abundant groves of olive trees dotting the property. There were no doors at the entrance to our hotel, just a towering stone archway that opened onto an expansive slate foyer.

I made my way to the reception desk to check in. The young lady helping me had amber eyes clear as honey and a warm, mischievous smile. "Is this your first time?" she asked.

"Here at this hotel?"

"Yes, and also to our country?"

"Yes. I mean no. Er . . . I mean *nai*."

She giggled at my bumbled Greek. "Well, *yasou*, Kostas. Welcome to Greece."

Welcome to Greece. I'd heard that expression several

times that day, and it was beginning to grow on me. There
was something wild and wonderful about this place. I didn't
profess to understand any of it, but somehow all these disparate and seemingly incongruent elements coalesced into an
effervescent tonic that soothed the soul and nourished the
spirit. I'd been in Greece for just a day, and I was already
starting to like the place. Why I'd spent most of my life trying
to run away from my Hellenic heritage made no sense. It is
who I am. I now saw that more clearly than ever.

14

VILLAGE IN
THE HILLS

The next morning we all met for breakfast. Akis, Mark, and I sat drinking coffee when Peter came walking up. He looked a bit ashen and disheveled.

"I just had the weirdest experience," he said.

We all looked at him, like: *And??*

"Well, I was taking a shower when a maid walked in."

"Did she take one look at you and slam the door?" Mark joked.

"No, that was the weird thing. She started cleaning my room."

"Did you say something?" Now *I* was curious.

"Yeah, I asked her what she was doing."

"Did she answer?"

"Yes, she told me she was cleaning my room."

"'But I'm taking a shower!' I yelled at her."

"'It's okay, it's okay,' she assured me. 'Don't worry about it. I've got a son. Besides, you look fine.'"

"So I'm standing there completely naked having a conversation with this woman like we're old friends."

"Did she leave, then?" Mark asked.

"No, she started vacuuming."

Wow . . . welcome to Greece. I made a mental note to deadbolt my hotel room door the next time I was taking a shower, unless I wanted to meet some new friends.

Over breakfast we discussed our schedule for the next several days. We'd be heading deep into the mountainsides for some running and exploration. It was early October, but temperatures were still rather balmy, and we'd need to plan our food and gear accordingly. After breakfast we'd be driving to the little village of Silimna, near Tripoli, where my grandfather, Gus Gibbs (i.e., Constantine Karnazes), hailed from. Vans were packed and away we went.

We traveled along the coastline of the Southern Ionian Sea, which was a warmer and more saline body of water than the Adriatic to the north, which serves as a collection basin for a third of the fresh water flowing into the Mediterranean from Central Europe. These differences in temperature and water salinity create the unique microclimates found along this region of Messenia. A southern-facing hillside could be windless and 25 degrees warmer than its blustery northern counterpart.

The region's topography also plays a big role in influencing the climate, as the great mountain chains along the central part of the country create tremendous atmospheric pressure gradients which serve to direct and accelerate air masses moving north from the moister central Mediterranean Sea or south from the cooler European continental landmass. Local winds are often compressed by surrounding mountain ranges and intensify as they get squeezed through narrow valleys and canyons (referred to as the Venturi effect). These gusts are quite capable of blowing a man over, while outside of the gorge it may be entirely windless. All of these local, regional, and continental factors come together to create weather that is sometimes predictable and other times completely erratic and unexpected, not entirely unlike Greece itself.

In today's world I can use my smartphone to pinpoint the weather down to the very movement of individual cloud formations using real-time Doppler radar. At least in the United States this is possible. In Greece, things are different. Weather.com is a bit less specific with its forecast, and local news sources are generally unreliable as they consolidate broader weather trends over Southern Europe as a whole, more so than offering specific climatic conditions in the local region.

Hemerodromoi must have been highly attuned to the weather. They didn't have hydration packs and stash pockets to store large quantities of extra supplies and clothing. They likely developed an acute sense for forecasting weather through years of close observation. When your life depends on the weather and climate, you tend to pay better attention to it.

We humans have moved increasingly away from our ancestral roots in this regard. Most people are clueless about the weather unless they reference their phone, tablet, or TV. We've all but lost our innate sense for detecting and forecasting the weather and have become increasingly disconnected from Mother Earth in the process. Many people in the developed world spend almost no appreciable time outdoors. We shuffle from subways or automobiles to office buildings, eat our meals inside covered structures, and then return at night to the sanctity of our protected homes. This man-made environment is far removed from our origin.

Many people rarely, if ever, spend an entire day in the outdoors, from sunup to sundown. Yet the outdoors is where we came from. We haven't lost the primordial ability to connect with the earth's rhythms, and those people who spend a significant amount of time outside have largely retained these ancient instincts to detect and predict weather. Ultramarathoners fall into this category, as do surfers, mountain climbers, sailors, backcountry skiers, hunters, and fishermen.

Having once run across America—from Los Angeles to

New York City—I spent the better part of each day outside for
2½ months straight. In doing so, my body learned to detect
subtle nuances in humidity, wind speed, cloud formation,
refraction of sunlight, temperature variations, and barometric
pressure changes. Remarkably, I was able to fairly accurately
predict the weather each day without ever looking at a
screen. It wasn't like I consciously tried to catalog and quan-
tify each of these telltale elements and then crunch the data
to come up with a prediction. Instead, it was done more
through an innate feel, a sixth sense, if you will, by uncon-
sciously detecting the way the air felt on my skin, the way
tension built or dissipated in my joints, how dryness or moisture condensed in my nose, and the way various smells and
aromas wafted through the air. I won't take credit for having
some special or unique talent in this regard; these are nothing more than the evolutionary gifts all of us possess, though
few of us engage them these days.

Hemerodromoi wouldn't necessarily think anything was
extraordinary or superhuman about their abilities to read the
weather. To say they would take such capabilities for granted
is overreaching, because they wouldn't have thought twice
about it. Knowing what the day's forecast entailed was an
autonomic response that just happened, like breathing or
laughing.

The drive to Silimna, high in the hills above Tripoli, was sop-
orific, rendering me sedated and in a groggy trancelike state.
The car was warm and cozy, like a mother's womb, and once
we'd arrived, I didn't want to get out at first. But the moment I
did, miracles happened. My senses immediately sprang to life.

From the instant the car door opened and I left the vehicle, I was swept over by a providential enchantment. The air

was pleasantly perfumed with the aromas of wild rosemary and tangy, vine-ripe lemons hanging from the trees. The sky shone a lustrous sapphire blue the likes of which I had never seen. My pulse sharpened and my body tingled with life. Though I was in a foreign land, I felt an immediate attachment to the place.

There were a few structures around, though most were fairly dilapidated or in a state of disrepair. There was also a bell tower and a church, and plenty of trees. Trees were everywhere, of every imaginable height, age, variety, and fullness. Young trees, old trees, fig trees, walnut trees, blossoming trees and leafless trees, pine trees, citrus trees, pomegranate trees whose branches bent to the ground with fruit, olive trees of every height, stalk, and maturity, red apple trees and green apple trees, miniature pear trees and gargantuan peach trees; trees sprang from every available inch of soil and most of them bore some kind of fruit, nut, or berry. Some were tiring and their limbs hung frail and low, while others were youthful and perky, stretching skyward with rambunctious energy. Rosemary, basil, sage, thyme, and lavender grew abundantly, along with other native herbs and wildflowers. Vines twisted and entwined around fence posts and over old rock terraces. Some were laden with berries, while others produced gourds or small, hanging melons. There were also spiraling threads of vines resting on the ground bearing massive ripe watermelons. And, of course, there were groves of wild grapevines, most being entirely overloaded with plump red fistfuls of fruit. In any patch of unoccupied earth sprang great bushels of *horta*; it covered the nearby hillsides and valleys, blanketing them in a lush carpet of green. These fields emitted a pungent, earthy odor as the sharp rays of sunlight penetrated the damp, dark soil, steaming the moist green leaves into a bubbling cauldron of aromatic vapor that wafted sweetly upward.

There were also bees. Honeybees. Everywhere there

were honeybees. So fat and happy were these bees that they had no interest in us and seemed perfectly content zigzagging around drunkenly suckling the syrupy and swollen blossoms that abounded so plentifully. The place was teeming with life, wild life, natural and raw, the way it was supposed to be, unadulterated by the meddling hands of humans and our mechanized agricultural machines. What little gardening that had been done had been done many years before.

The official census lists the population of Silimna at 119, up from 118 in 1980. It didn't feel like there were even that many people in town on this day. In fact, it didn't feel like there was anyone else there—it was as though we were alone. Perhaps some of the town's inhabitants lived in the nearby hills, or maybe they only lived part-time in Silimna. It was a dreamy place, a place the world had long since passed over.

And that was its magic.

Places like this didn't exist anymore. Not for most of us, at least. Maybe you needed to be submersed and drowned in the cataclysm of Western society to appreciate dawdling old Silimna. That, I don't know. And maybe if this were your birthplace, you'd want nothing more than to escape from it and move far away. I don't know that, either. All I know is that right then, at that moment in time, it felt pretty doggone perfect to me.

Then relatives began mysteriously appearing out of nowhere. *Theías* and *theíos* (aunts and uncles), dressed as though it were 1950 yet somehow looking quite dignified, were suddenly walking next to me. The women wore dark wool dresses and shawls, some with scarves pulled tightly across their heads. Some of the men were in suits, and many were adorned with long, thin mustaches sculpted into fine pencil tips at their ends. These people weren't athletes, but they still had calves that looked like hulking, inverted papayas. Some said our family had located here from nearby Laconia, by Sparta, seeking more fertile land and settling in

Silimna for the richness of its soil. They led me down a dirt path to my grandfather's house, feeding me freshly cracked walnuts and ripe, tree-picked pears and apples as we made our way down the earthen trail.

I bit into one of these apples; it was exceptionally flavorful. Juice ran down my chin. "Wow, this is delicious. Who planted all these trees?" I gurgled.

One of the older men looked at me in amazement. "Planted? What planted? Spit out a few seeds and you have trees, no planted."

When we arrived at my grandfather's house, there wasn't much to it. An aging, white, single-story stone structure with splintering timber girders and cracking support joists barely holding things together, it was simply constructed and primitive by today's standards, and it was showing its years. Still, I wanted to go in.

The townspeople cautioned me against it, advising me that it was unsafe to enter. But I was determined to see the inside, to experience the place in which my grandfather and Aunt Helen had grown up. Against their warning, I made my way in. It was the wrong thing to do, but I did it anyway.

Of course, they were right. The roof was bowing downward so badly it looked as though it might collapse at any moment. The floor, composed mostly of dirt and hay, was uneven and rocky, and there were just two simple rooms with a crumbling dividing wall between them. It was clear that no one had lived in the house for many years, nor had anyone been inside for quite some time. The back side of the house was opened to the air and spilled out onto an elevated outdoor porch. I looked around briefly—now a bit concerned that the roof might indeed cave in—when all of a sudden, near the far corner of the house, I spotted an old, rusted bell sitting on the floor. I carefully made my way over and fetched up this antiquated chime, placing it over the outside ledge onto the floorboard of the back porch.

I watchfully crept back across the room and out through the small exterior passageway of the front door. It was a relief to see daylight when I exited the structure, though it had been quite exhilarating viewing the interior of the house and imagining what it must have been like living there in my grandfather's time. The group waiting outside welcomed me back to safety and asked me what I saw.

"Here, come take a look."

I walked them around the back of the building to the porch and picked up the bell I'd found inside. Its metal was decaying and thinning along the edges, but it still had life. I jiggled it several times, and it let out a rickety clank that made everyone smile and laugh. "*Opa!*" someone called out.

Ksádelfi Vasiliki, a cousin, speculated that this could have been the very same bell my great grandmother had used to summon my grandfather to dinner. "That Kostas, he was an adventurous one, always up to some sort of mischief," she told me.

One could only imagine the fun and frolicking a young boy could get up to in this endless playfield of fruit trees and wild berry thickets that stretched to the horizon. This was a time before paved roads and automobiles, and children could laugh and play and wander as freely and as far as their imaginations would carry them. Part of me was from this place, and I could feel the connection deep within, real and eternal. My great grandmother had held this very bell eons ago, just as I had held it on this day, and I could sense her pride and her loneliness in knowing that her only son was leaving to seek a better life, probably never to be seen or held again.

I thought about bringing the bell home with me, perhaps displaying it on my mantel as a prized keepsake. But it didn't belong in America. Its lineage was in Silimna, in its hills with the memories and the bones of my ancestors. So I returned the bell to the place where I found it, setting it back gently upon the ground. I made my cross and touched my hand to my chest. Perhaps one day I would reunite with this bell, perhaps not. It really didn't matter, for the memory was engraved upon my heart for time immemorial.

When we got back to the center of town (if you can call it that), there were a number of other runners gathered for the day's event, along with a cadre of press. It was the opening day of the 3-day Navarino Challenge, and we would be running a 10-K from Silimna to Tripoli, not a great distance by my standards, but challenging nonetheless, certainly, for many of the others. As I have mentioned, the Navarino Challenge wasn't designed to be a competitive race, but rather to encourage people to get outside and participate in sport, just as the original Olympic Games had been conceived thousands of years earlier. In this regard the event appeared to have succeeded wildly, as there were soon hundreds of runners gathering at the start, of all ages and abilities. The town probably hadn't seen such a crowd in years.

Off we went.

The road to Tripoli twisted and turned as it wound its way down the mountainside. The afternoon sun cast lengthening shadows across the roadway, and although the route was not closed to traffic, not a single car passed us for the entire duration. We runners tended to clump together in groups based on pace, everyone seemingly finding their groove as the miles accumulated.

Entering into the township of Tripoli, we were greeted by hordes of children who had just gotten out of school. At first they just stared at us curiously, but kids being kids, they naturally loved to run (or at least loved to chase and to be chased), and in no time there were hundreds of kids running alongside us through the cobbled backstreets of Tripoli. People sitting in outside cafés yelled and cheered as we ran by. "*Opa!*" they shouted. Shopkeepers clapped, and people stopped what they were doing to come take in the spectacle making its way through their town, inevitably getting swept up in our collective passion and contributing hoots of encouragements and praise as we passed, "Bravo! Bravo *su!*" It was another cinematic moment, as though we were on set at Universal Studios. But this was no scene from a movie; this was a little rural village in the Peloponnese on a random weekday.

The main square was filled with people. The mayor was there, along with many local leaders and representatives of the church diocese. How so many of them knew about this run was puzzling, but all were present and all seemed to be having a good time. When we reached the *agora* (town center), so much enthusiasm and energy had built up that it couldn't simply dissipate peaceably. That's when the music started and the Greek dancing spontaneously ignited. We runners interlocked arms and formed a huge semicircle, swinging our feet to the rhythm and swaying our hips. Kids chased each other all around, laughing and screaming; butchers came out of their shops, stripped off their aprons, and joined in the dancing. Tavern owners emerged with towering bottles of ouzo. Young and old danced together and sang and laughed. Food appeared, great platters of savory dishes and homemade Greek pastries, baklava, *loukoumades, finikia,* and other Hellenic delicacies, all dripping with honey and nuts. It was a regular fall Friday during just another ho-hum week, in a place that was struggling with economic hardship and facing an uncertain future, yet those were hardly sufficient reasons to forgo celebration. These people were all willing to put aside what they were doing and join together, rejoicing in the moment. For better or for worse, the Greek spirit lived large in each of us that day.

Someone handed me a shot glass filled with ouzo. I usually don't drink, but that day I did.

"*Opa!*" I chortled.

Welcome to Greece.

If we always made decisions with our heads instead of

our hearts, we'd probably live much more orderly lives, but they would be much less joyous. I learned a lot in Greece, mostly about myself. It fundamentally changed the person I was. Sure, life was to be taken seriously, but not too seriously. No matter how dire things become, no matter how bleak the situation appears, we should never be beyond a shot of ouzo and some Greek dancing.

How many people spend their entire lives striving for something with their nose to the grindstone, only to wake up one day and realize they haven't really lived at all? You can never surf the same wave twice; you only get one shot at it. Yesterday is not coming back. Sure, I had my goals and aspirations, but I wasn't going to let tunnel vision prevent me from celebrating the struggles and tribulations I encountered along the way. Reaching a finish line can be gratifying, but it's the journey where life is lived. And today had been a wonderful journey.

The inaugural Navarino Challenge proved to be a wildly successful event and went on to become an important annual occasion, with me continuing as the official host and ambassador. It didn't change all of Greece, but it did change some of Greece. The Greek people needed something positive, and the Navarino Challenge provided a glimmer of hope. Enough with the hardship and austerity for a moment, let's run together and celebrate the goodness of life. It was my small contribution to this country I'd come to love, my way of doing what I could, and it made me proud.

The Navarino Challenge also gave me a chance to wander deeper into the sinews of the land, exploring some of the byroads and back trails of Ancient Greece and working on a plot to launch my own *Hokule'a*-like re-creation of an ancient odyssey. Still, there was much research and investigation yet to be done to arrive at the start.

And the one person who could get me there was an aging professor living in the countryside of England.

15

GIVER OF THE
WATERMELON

There's only one person who knows more about Pheidippides's travels from Marathon to Sparta than Pamela-
Jane Shaw, and he died 2,500 years ago. Other than the man
himself, she is the world's foremost authority.

Preferring to go simply by the moniker "P-J," Shaw first
became interested in the topic as a student of history and has
since gone on to become the preeminent expert on ancient
hemerodromos routing. As the expedition leader of a group
that explored and mapped a large portion of the ancient passageways used by Pheidippides during his epic run from Athens to Sparta, she guided this 5-day trek across the Greek
countryside, cataloging and surveying important physical
observations pertaining to the landscape and distinctive topo-
graphical landmarks Pheidippides could have relied upon to
navigate this vast stretch of unmarked terrain without the
use of a map or GPS. In 1997, P-J published an article that
appeared in the periodical *Geographia Antiqua* entitled, "Message to Sparta: The Route of Pheidippides before Marathon."
To this day her research remains the most authoritative work
ever published on the subject.

Professor Cartledge introduced the two of us, and we corresponded frequently, P-J and I. She was remarkably forthright and helpful, always willingly sharing with me great volumes of research material, historical photographs, and detailed notations from her work. While she wasn't a runner herself, we shared a mutual passion in the history of this particular ancient Greek athlete, and that common thread formed the fabric of a bond that developed between us. She was passing along her legacy to me, and I was honored to take the torch and run with it.

My interactions with P-J were occasionally adventures unto themselves. At times I would receive answers to my questions in a matter of hours, yet other times weeks or even months would pass without a response from her, and I would start to worry. Then an eloquent, thoroughly researched, articulate, and thought-provoking reply would arrive in my in-box that completely upended my previous thinking on the topic I was researching.

P-J's mind assembled information in fantastic ways. She had cataloged and archived so much historical record and firsthand observation that she was able to cross-reference inferences and minor passages from disparate ancient sources to draw conclusions that were entirely novel and unique. It continually astounded me that this 21st century Brit had amassed more intelligence on the topic of Pheidippides's travels from Athens to Sparta than even Herodotus had.

In my ongoing dialogue with her, one thing became evident: If I were ever to approach any sort of re-creation of Pheidippides's historic run, I would need to revisit Greece, this time in the sweltering heat of summer, as the Battle of Marathon took place in early August.

And so I returned to Athens in the summer of 2014 and set about my work. Hitching a ride, I headed for the hills of ancient Greece to do some reconnaissance and exploration. I needed to hit the trails and survey the landscape more deeply.

Greece in the autumn can be quite warm, as it had been during the Navarino Challenge, but the heat of summer elevates things to an entirely new level. It smelled as though my hair was singeing as I worked my way along the rocky, exposed hillside. There was a certain raw savagery to the searing beams of solar radiation bombarding this particular stretch of pathway I ran upon, and it seemed to be further concentrated and intensified by the curvature of the landscape. I scurried along quickly, like a bug trying to escape the deadly rays of a magnifying glass held by some sadistic child. The heat was just unbearable, and it was only nine o'clock in the morning. It reminded me in some ways of the Badwater Ultramarathon in Death Valley, or running across the Sahara during the 4 Deserts Challenge, but the shafts of light cast by the Greek sun seemed to be more piercing in certain ways, more intense and focused.

Not only had P-J previously traversed these paths herself, she had scoured the surrounding passageways as well, searching for potential alternative routes that Pheidippides could have used during his travels to Sparta. In her *Geographia Antiqua* research paper, she plotted numerous courses that he may have followed.

Sparta was a powerful and important Greek city-state, and the Athenian leaders would have chosen their most noble and physically able herald to interact with the Spartans. Not only must this individual have possessed godlike athletic prowess, he must also have been a wise diplomat and a gifted orator, even after running hundreds of miles.

In all likelihood, Pheidippides had traveled to Sparta many times prior to his historic run. Given Sparta's prominence, communications with this city-state would have been frequent. Using a single herald to interact with the Spartan leaders would allow a greater level of familiarity and trust to develop between the parties. The Greek city-states were not always on the best of terms with each other, to put things

lightly, yet they all seemed to realize the importance of band-
ing together in unity, especially in the face of a threat such as
the Persians posed. Given that a mutual defense pact, *epimachia*, was in effect between Athens and Sparta at the time, an
Athenian messenger would have been welcomed. Pheidippides would have probably specialized in this particular route
from Athens to Sparta and would therefore have an intimate
familiarity with the terrain.

Having participated in the renowned Western States 100-
Mile Endurance Run on a dozen occasions, including once
during the wintertime, I was aware of a certain intimacy one
develops with a particular stretch of geography after multiple
passages across the same ground. Traditionally held the last
weekend of June—summertime in the Northern Hemisphere—
the Western States Trail is located in California's Sierra
Nevada mountain range and proceeds from the Squaw Valley
Ski Resort near Lake Tahoe to Auburn, just outside Sacra-
mento. A rugged wilderness trail, it has remained largely
untouched since the time of the early settlers.

People may think the mind grows dull after prolonged
periods of intense exertion and that one would easily lose his
bearing, but just the opposite is true. The senses become
more acute and attentive, almost as though the physical
threat compromising the body forces the mind to take up the
slack. A protracted fight-or-flight response ensues in which
awareness progressively sharpens while the body and muscles increasingly weaken and fatigue.

I can remember, with great clarity, events and locations
from nearly every single Western States race. The people
whom I interacted with, the conversations we had and the
emotions that came as a result, are etched upon my memory.
I can describe their faces with vivid detail, the color of their
hair, what they were wearing, and even the types of shoes
they had on. Specific geographical landmarks stick out with
equal clarity. Certain rocks along the path become familiar;
particular trees, abrupt rises or descents in elevation, and the

views afforded by various vantage points all get mentally imprinted and cataloged like data on a computer chip.

A hearty scent of pinesap emanates in certain regions of the trail, while the pungent odor of sagebrush pervades others. The crackling of the earth underfoot is sharper in areas where crumbly granite sands cover the pathway, while in other sections of trail one's feet land in a soft powder of dark silt from the decaying bark of nearby pines. The damp, cool dawn air grows increasingly drier and lighter at higher elevations, while the warmth of twilight's lasting gleam lingers thick and dense well into nightfall, when the stillness of the daytime silence gives way to the sounds of clicking crickets and croaking frogs as the nocturnal phase of the earth's rotation becomes the new reality, the day's hazy blue skies fading into complete blackness bejeweled by a million twinkling stars.

There are points during the 100-mile crossing when the midday sun relentlessly scorches the earth, with little protection to be found anywhere. But I remembered things: On the left-hand side of a particular stretch of trail there is a slight shadow cast by the nearby trees that provides a sliver of shade to run under. A creek at the bottom of a particularly deep canyon offers a refreshingly cool place to reconstitute and hydrate, which is good because a long, arduous, and brutally hot uphill section follows, an area where a windless vacuum of stagnant air hangs thick and heavy, like a Turkish bathhouse. Even during the inaugural wintertime traversal of the Western States Trail, these familiar guideposts were clearly identifiable, if not mentally more than visually (since many of them were buried under several feet of snow).

This phenomenon of developing an intimate knowledge of a section of landscape is not unique to me. I've talked with plenty of other long-distance runners who have reported similar experiences. Perhaps it is a remnant of our primitive survival skills, but during periods of intense physical duress, we catalog information meticulously and store it in a cerebral databank that is both permanent and immediately accessible.

To recall every single step of a 100-mile footrace that transpired more than 2 decades earlier is quite extraordinary,
though it occurred entirely without intentionality, like some
intuitive homing device.

A glaring difference between running a 100-mile sanctioned footrace in present-day California and running an
ultramarathon in 4th-century-BCE Greece is that there would
have been no reliable rehydration and refueling stations along
the remote mountains and countryside of ancient Greece. At
the Western States 100-Mile Endurance Run there are numerous aid stations set up along the course; athletes are not only
familiar with their whereabouts but rely on them for nourish-
ment and the resupplying of fluid. Orienteering solo through
remote Greece, as I was now doing, was an entirely different
proposition.

Yet I was pleasantly surprised by the abundance of water
and streams I came upon during these exploratory treks.
Even in the scorching midsummer heat, there was water to
be found. One side of a ridge might be stony, scorched earth,
dusty and barren, devoid of life and inhospitable, while on
the other side would lie a lush, green oasis. Some of the sub-
terranean upwellings were thermal pools, while other areas
of greenery were fed by cold spring water. I imagine if one
traversed this region frequently enough, they would learn the
precise locations of these outlets and could pace themselves
accordingly.

During my investigative training runs I would stop at
many of these sparkling emerald waterways and wet my
clothing or splash some cold water on my face and neck. I'd
also refill my water bottles with the cool liquid.

Several of these waterways led to enchanting little water-
falls with spiraling tendrils of moss dangling off the cornices,
like long strands of Medusa's hair. The turquoise pools below
were surrounded by a shoreline of colorful lichen and velvety
sphagnum. Bizarre-looking toadstools of fairytale-like propor-
tions sprouted everywhere, some having stalks as sturdy as

tree trunks; they were colorful, many being rusty red or tangerine orange, while others sported vibrant latticework arteries of dazzling purples and blues interwoven throughout their bell caps. Frogs and turtles abounded. They appeared totally unfazed by a human's presence, as though they'd had no prior contact with such a freakish species and thus nothing to fear. Dragonflies the size of hummingbirds lazily danced about, sometimes landing on nearby tree branches, some times sunning on one of the elephant-car-size leaves that sprung from the foliage in every direction. The entire scene was magical, as if it were a ride at Disneyland. But this wasn't a theme park, because the fruit wasn't made of plastic.

I was amazed to find an abundance of wild foodstuff growing along these creek beds. There were berries and pomegranates, and fig, pear, apple, and plum trees. Apparently because of the reliable and consistent source of groundwater, nearby vegetation was able to thrive even during the intense summertime heat. Foodies rave about the goodness of field-to-table foods, but I had it even better—branch to mouth.

Sea buckthorn grew in certain regions, too, though a bit less abundantly than some of the other shrubs and plants. The prized fiery-orange berries were easy to spot as the shrubs tended to grow in large clusters. I thought about the ancient hemerodromoi plucking berries from the thorny branches as they went by and chewing on them as they ran along. The fruit tasted astringent and peppery, with notes of citrusy sweetness, and it gave my body a pulse of energy when I ate it, though I'm not sure if that came as a result of some bioactive components in the fruit or on account of the sharply acerbic taste explosion on my palate. Either way, chewing on sea buckthorn definitely puts a kick in your step!

In the process of re-creating Pheidippides's historic run, I and others have found that the general direction in which he would have proceeded from Athens was not difficult to ascertain, for he would be heading due west toward the Isthmus of

Corinth and needed only to follow the trajectory of the sun. That was an easy course to follow. The difficult part for anyone trying to reconstruct his path today is the rat's nest of intertwined roadways and pavement in every conceivable direction, along with the noxious miasma of sooty exhaust choking the air and making it nearly impossible to decipher where a plausible footpath from Athens to Corinth may once have existed.

As I proceeded deeper into the hills and on to the more remote rural sections, attempting to navigate a likely path went from being complex to being entirely bewildering. P-J's research had been conducted many years earlier; since that time new roads and developments had sprung up. Some areas had changed considerably, though others had remained largely untouched since ancient times. The number of potential choices for plotting a course magnified the more pastoral and rural the geography became. After the Greeks, the Romans had once been there, and later medieval Byzantines, and then the Germans during WWII. All had passed through these parts, and fragmented remnants of their presence remained. Not only was there a variety of possible dirt paths to follow, there was a matrix of jeep roads and ancient stone passageways to choose from, and there was an almost incomprehensible multitude of divergent routes that appeared to be goat trails or paths cut by wild animals, of which I spotted plenty during my travels.

On several of my exploratory outings I had encounters with such animals, especially in the deeper brushy areas where thick shrubs and tall, grassy reeds largely concealed the ground. Wildlife seemed to be everywhere. I saw untold numbers of snakes, big snakes, snakes the length of park benches and fat as eggplants. They slithered along silently, totally camouflaged by the thickets and ground cover. Often spiderwebs would net my face. It was unavoidable. And like the snakes, these were no small spiders, but gargantuan furry spiders whose ensnaring webs seemed capable of halting a charging rhino. There were plenty of turtles, spiny porcupines, and the occasional fox, which seemed to appear most frequently toward the evening hours, as did swift-flying birds of prey with their sharp talons at the ready to pounce on an unsuspecting groundhog. There were also reports of bears in these areas, though I didn't see any of those, thankfully.

Another thing I didn't see any of were other humans. I'd run all over the world, and these were some of the most captivating and enchanting hills I'd ever wandered. Had this been California, the trails would have been filled with runners, mountain bikers in colorful spandex outfits, hikers with cameras and binoculars, and kids chasing butterflies with nets. There'd be signs warning about snakes, and rangers would frequently patrol the area to keep things safe. But this wasn't California; this was a place where time has stood still for the better part of the past millennium. The only human encounters I had were with the occasional goat herder tending to his animals.

It was probably dangerous for me to be running out there alone. What would happen if I were to encounter a bear? Should I be carrying a gun or at least pepper spray? Even if I did, it wouldn't help if I were to be bitten by a snake or were to tumble down one of the many cliffs I traversed. I carried a cell phone, but there was no reception to be had out there. No one would find me for days, or even weeks, if I were to injure myself and couldn't go on. Yet strangely enough, I wasn't worried at all and set about my explorations without concern.

Near the junction of the roadway where I'd exited from the trail was a small market. I stopped in to grab something cold to drink. When the aging shopkeeper behind the counter spotted me coming through the entrance, it was as though Jesus Christ had just walked in the door. Her eyes widened and her face grew ghostly white; I thought she might pass out. Then, when she finally regained a bit of composure, she began frantically making a cross upon her chest and mumbling something incomprehensible in prayer. I could see tears welling up in her eyes. Did she think I was there to bless her or to rob the place?

When she eventually gained her composure, she began talking to me in an endless rambling stream. Her English was nonexistent, and my Greek was atrocious, so I didn't understand a word of it. Then I noticed an old television above the counter, and from what I could gather from her Greek, I surmised that she'd seen me on TV. I could tell she wanted to hug me, but she was too polite and respectful to do so. She was going on and on, and I felt so bad because I had little idea what she was saying. Finally, she put up her hand as if to say, "Wait . . . wait just a minute," then she slipped out the back door.

When she returned a minute later, she was carrying a big watermelon, which she presented to me proudly. The thing was still warm from the sun, and I was pretty sure she'd just picked it from her garden behind the shop.

"*Efharisto,*" I said, thanking her. I wasn't sure what to do at that point, so I walked out the door, drinkless, carrying a huge watermelon.

Now what? My hotel was still a few miles away, but I couldn't just leave that watermelon on the side of the road. There was no choice but to haul it back with me. It was brutal trying to run while carrying this outsize gourd, as it must have weighed 25 pounds. I tried tilting my head forward and supporting it along the crook of my neck; I tried cradling it against my belly like a big plump baby; and I tried holding it under one arm or the other like a lead rugby ball. Nothing was easy; there was simply no painless way to carry this beastly melon.

When I finally got back to my hotel room, I thought I might need traction.

The next few days of reconnaissance in these hills and valleys yielded more questions than answers. In certain instances it was hard to know whether Pheidippides would have followed a shorter, more direct, albeit waterless, path or instead opted for the security of traveling a longer distance with a greater certainty of encountering hydration along the way. Even with my perspective as a fellow ultramarathoner, many

of his decisions would have been improvisational depending
on the temperature that particular day, the state of his thirst or
hunger, and whether he was feeling vigorous or fatigued at the
time. But for someone attempting to re-create his route, these
things were not only unknown but truly unknowable.

As I explored areas nearer to Sparta during my scouting
missions, the scenario became even more convoluted. Given
the high alert at the time of Pheidippides's run, undoubtedly
Spartan interceptors would be patrolling the area and would
have spotted him incoming. At the point of contact, Pheidippides would have simply followed the patrolman back to
Sparta on a route so chosen by this man. It was impossible to
determine at what juncture this interception might have happened, which presented yet another unknown variable.

The other challenging element to my work was that no
matter how stealthily I tried to tiptoe back to my hotel, there
was no way of getting around that little shop on the side of
the road. By the end of my stay, I'd amassed half a dozen
watermelons in my room. That precious old shopkeeper simply wouldn't have me pass without bestowing upon me
another of these colossal fruity gems.

On the final night of my stay, I summoned a bellman
and we carted all of them to the hotel kitchen, where I shared
the juicy bounty with the entire staff. As with all of the other
foods grown in this region, their plump flesh was pure
ambrosia, like nectar of the gods. I've never tasted watermelon quite so delicious.

On the flight back to San Francisco I began to analyze
the notes I'd compiled during my exploratory treks in the
hillsides and mountains of Greece. PJ's research had proven
invaluable, but I still couldn't piece together how it was that
I could possibly re-create Pheidippides's journey accurately.
That's when it became abundantly clear: I couldn't.

Too much had changed in 2,500 years; too many unknowns
couldn't be resolved; too many factors were beyond recon-
struction. Reenacting Pheidippides's actual pathway would

be impossible. It was a most disappointing and heart-wrenching verdict to reach, but it was the honest truth. All the work that had been undertaken, all the effort and planning that had gone into the endeavor had only led me to the forlorn conclusion that my dream of re-creating the actual route of this ancient Greek messenger could never be realized, that I had set about doing something that couldn't be done. I had such grand intentions, but I now knew with certainty it was never to be.

I wasn't good at failing. Who is, really? We talk about picking up the pieces and moving on, but this was more than a temporary setback to me, this was everything. "Fuck!" I pounded my fist on the tray table. The gods give to us and the gods take away, and that sometimes joyous, sometimes cruel balance we're left with is this thing we call life. Things don't always go as planned, I reminded myself. Dreams don't always come true. Deal with it.

Unexpected spring in the hills of Greece.

16

SIGN ME UP

B ut deal with it I could not. Upon returning home to San Francisco I entered into a state of funk. My final correspondence with P-J stamped a chilling permanence on my hopes. "It would be impossible to accurately re-create Pheidippides's endeavor," she wrote, "for we will never know with certainty the route that he followed."

The *flokati* (rug) had been yanked out from under my feet. My sense of purpose and bearing was inexorably undermined; I drifted about, rudderless in a swirling sea of despair. Where once there was meaning and a clear sense of purpose in my life, now there seemed only emptiness and the hollow anguish over having failed. I spent the better part of a month moping about, licking my wounds and wallowing in self-pity.

Perhaps this was somewhat of a dramatic overreaction, but I couldn't just throw my hands up in the air and shrug, "Bummer, it didn't work out," and then carry on. Hey, I'm Greek; we don't keep calm. Trying to repress my Greekness was like a man trying to run from his own shadow. No matter how far I journeyed, it would chase me down and remind me that you can never outrun yourself.

Keeping things in healthy perspective wasn't (and still

isn't) my strongest quality, nor was moderation. The oracle of Apollo at Delphi got it mostly right, except for *Meden agan* (nothing in excess). Runners overall tend to be a compulsive bunch, ultrarunners all the more so. Many are downright obsessive, teetering on the verge of irrationality. Moderation bores us. Personally, I exemplified these fine qualities. For me, it's either 100 percent fanatical commitment or nothing at all.

In our world, there are no shades of gray, only black and white.

Maybe this is why some are drawn to ultramarathoning. When running an ultra, the rules of engagement are crystal clear. There is a starting point and there is an ending point. If you make it from the starting line to the finish line, you succeed, and if you don't, you fail. Simple as that. The distance between the two points might be daunting, but at least you know from the outset what's expected of you. In life, the rules are never quite so neatly defined. Sometimes you think you're moving in the right direction, only to have the rules changed and the finish line shifted to a different location, or hidden altogether. Our modern society is filled with this sort of permanent ambiguity, yet for those with a simpler, more linear outlook, this unceasing vagueness can be intolerable.

I have always held that life is essentially a series of setbacks and obstacles. Living is overcoming them. One morning I woke up and finally had the sense to realize how pathetic and self-absorbed my thoughts and actions had become. "Is this how Pary would want to see you living? Would you be making her proud?" The sad answer was, no, it would not. It was time to mend these wounds and do something about it. It was time to overcome this obstacle and start living again.

Sure, my fairy-tale script for the future had crumpled into ruin, the goal of re-creating Pheidippides's pathway proving unattainable, but no amount of sulking and self-pity could alter the reality of the situation. Coach Wooden had taught me to not let what you can't do stop you from doing what you can do. True, I couldn't reenact Pheidippides's actual run, but I could do the next best thing and attempt the Spartathlon, which was the closest approximation that existed in this modern day. And that is what I intended to do: run the Spartathlon.

The game of life was back on. The Spartathlon is one of the most grueling endurance contests on earth. To prepare for the challenge, running 100 miles a week or more became the norm. Lengthy overnight forays once a month became standard affairs, and entering 50-mile and 100-K races to help maintain my competitive edge augmented this training. Additionally, extensive cross-training sessions in the gym occupied nonrunning days. The Spartathlon demands this type of rigorous preparation.

After Commander Foden and his two comrades ran from Athens to Sparta in 1982, he went on to establish the Spartathlon, which, in its present-day incarnation, is a 153-mile footrace between these two Greek cities and nearly a perfect 10 on the intensity scale. Not only is it an insanely long distance to run, but the rules also impose strict cutoff times between checkpoints and an aggressive total finish time to complete the race. For instance, racers must cover the first 81 kilometers (50.22 miles) in fewer than 9.5 hours or face disqualification. They must hit 124 kilometers (76.88 miles) within 16 hours or be yanked from the race, and all must complete the entire 246-kilometer (153-mile) course in fewer than 36 hours to officially finish the race, which was in accordance with Herodotus recording that Pheidippides reached Sparta the day after he set out (i.e., started in the morning of one day and finished before sunset on the next).

The Spartathlon now attracts a global field of the most elite ultramarathoners from around the world. Still, in some years, less than a third of the entrants are able to complete it.

In many ways, the Spartathlon stands as the ultimate test of physical stamina and mental fortitude. Only with dogged tenacity and gritty resolve is one able to persevere and stand at the finish beneath the towering bronze statue of King Leonidas in the town center of Sparta.

Even though the modern Spartathlon has become an international event that attracts athletes from all over the world, in many ways the Greeks still own it, one Greek in particular. When Tripoli-born runner Yannis Kouros reached the finish line of the inaugural race in 1983, there was nobody else there. He was more than 3 hours ahead of the more established field of elite runners. So he recorded his results himself, a mind-boggling 21 hours and 51 minutes.

Some were suspicious of Kouros's achievement, believing that he had certainly cheated. How could it be that some unknown runner from the small village of Tripoli was able to accomplish this feat and trounce a field of globally renowned competitors in the process? It seemed dubious. Until the next year when he bettered his finish time, completing the course in an unfathomable 20:25. It is a record that has stood since 1984 and one that may *never* be broken.

Maybe I'd be able to tap into an inner Yannis Kouros to help me get to the finish line. But first, I needed to make it to the starting line.

You see, my already insane schedule had taken on a life of its own these past several months, burgeoning into a rapidly metastasizing tumor that was threatening to kill the very host it depended on for its survival. It wasn't that I didn't enjoy what I was doing, because I did. It was just that the breakneck volume of nonstop commitments was suffocating me. I found myself on the road nearly constantly, and not just making long stays in single locations but endlessly crisscrossing the country and the globe. Two days in Toronto, a day in Dallas, 4 days in France, 3 in Tokyo, then on to Australia, and finally Brazil. Some 70 percent of my time was spent traveling, which made it increasingly difficult to maintain consistent training blocks in preparation for the forthcoming Spartathlon.

My shoes logged tens of thousands of airline miles, traveling with me everywhere I went. I also developed a bodyweight training program that I could whip out during any brief period of downtime, thus helping to preserve my overall strength and musculature. The sleep deprivation and jetlag were the most difficult elements to overcome, but I did my best. The other harsh factor to deal with was illness. Because I was interacting with hundreds of people each week, in multiple geographical locations, I found myself with a nearly continuous case of the sniffles. Who knew what I was being exposed to out there, and if a bug was circulating in a particular region, I was certain to come in contact with it.

In an effort to be as authentic as possible, I was hoping to complete the Spartathlon using only those foods that Pheidippides would have eaten: figs, olives, *pasteli,* fruit, and cured meats. Also, I would be relying only on plain water during the race, not the typical electrolyte replenishment beverages. It was as close an approximation to running in Pheidippides's footsteps as could be undertaken, so I went for it. In preparation, I trained with these ancient foods of Greece in hopes of conditioning my body to adapt to this unusual diet. Plenty of lessons were learned along the way. Olives tasted great when the temperatures were warm, though they weren't so appealing for breakfast during morning runs. Cured meat provided hearty sustenance, but could be unsettling if overconsumed and would leave plenty of gristle stuck in your teeth along with acid indigestion. *Pasteli* was sweet and delicious, though the honey could liquefy if temperatures got too warm, resulting in a goopy, syrupy mess. And figs were terrific on the way in, but dangerous on the way out, if you catch my drift.

When September rolled around, I felt as though I'd done all that I could to prepare myself for the upcoming challenge.

I'd maintained a weekly mileage of between 50 to 200 miles (the wide variation being due to my travel schedule) and had completed several 80-mile, all-night training runs. I felt fit and strong, ready to give it a go. However, to say that I felt confident and assured would be untrue. Truth is, no matter how good of physical shape my body was in, I still remained anxious and uncertain. Hardly a day would pass when I didn't think about the Spartathlon. Sometimes not even an hour would go by without a thought. It's not the kind of thing that easily escapes your mind. Often I would lie in bed at night staring up at the ceiling wondering what my fate would be. Just lying there, staring at a blank ceiling and wondering. I've always been of the belief that we control our own destiny, that we hold the keys to our future. If it is to be, it is because of me. But I had a sense that the Spartathlon would require something more. What that was, I wasn't sure. I'd never felt like this before a race, and I didn't know what it meant. But I was about to find out.

17

HAND ME THE CONTROLS

The North Face Endurance Challenge is a series of races that take place across the United States and Canada. These events attract thousands of racers and spectators. One of my duties as the conceiver of this event, and also as a member of The North Face Global Athlete Team, is to attend each of these races and meet with the runners, sign posters, present trophies and medals, and generally mix and mingle with folks over the course of 2 days of running and racing.

There are seven different race distances to choose from during the 2 days of competition, everything from the 5-K to our flagship 50-miler. Usually I'm a cheerleader at these races and see it as an opportunity to give back to the running community and support others. For the 2014 event in Madison, however, I asked The North Face if I could participate in the 50-mile race myself, to which they agreed. The race happened to be held the day before I was scheduled to leave for Greece; it would serve as a good final training run before the Spartathlon. That's not to say I'd be shirking my other duties and obligations at the event. After finishing the 50-mile race I still hung around for many hours signing things, presenting awards, and chatting with people at the finish festival until well past dark.

If you've ever been to the finish line of a running event, you know that they're not the most hygienic of places. We runners are a sweaty lot, and stuff comes out of our noses, too. But this hardly dampens one's enthusiasm for congratulatory hugging, high-fiving, and handshaking, and we swap plenty of bodily fluids in the process, knowingly or otherwise, all at a time when the immune system may be compromised due to the intense physical exertion our bodies have just endured. A postrace finish festival is quite possibly a germophobe's worst nightmare. Every job has its risks, and being exposed to potential pathogens is something I have come to accept as an occupational hazard in this line of work.

That night after the race I felt fairly exhausted. I'd flown across the country from the West Coast just the day before, risen early to make the predawn start, run 50 miles, and then spent the balance of the afternoon and early evening on my feet chatting with other runners and fans. When my head finally hit the pillow, it was nearing midnight.

The next morning I awoke at 5:00 a.m. to attend the second day's festivities. Now I know that I sometimes talk about running 50 miles the way others talk about fetching the morning paper, but running 50 miles is, well, running 50 miles. No matter how many times I've run that distance, and much farther, running 50 miles still takes its toll. Rolling out of bed that morning wasn't easy, as I was tired and sore. Getting through the rest of the day was quite taxing. Despite feeling great satisfaction at the sight of so many happy runners attending our race, handshake after handshake slowly ground me down. I'd lost nearly 10 pounds training for the Spartathlon using the ancient Greek foods, and I was beginning to wonder whether this dramatic decrease in body mass was perhaps compromising my immune system.

My flight to Greece that afternoon was tight, and I made

it to the airport just as they were concluding the boarding process. I didn't even have time to wash my hands. "Perfect," I thought, "I'll put my earplugs in and get right to sleep."

We sat at the gate without moving for more than an hour. Finally, the captain came over the loudspeaker and announced that there was a slight weight imbalance and they'd have to rejigger some of the luggage. That's odd, I thought. The only previous time I'd had to rearrange luggage during a flight was on a snowboarding trip to Lake Tahoe in my buddy's small prop plane. After moving a board or two around, the problem was solved and away we went. But this was no prop plane; this was a 747 jumbo jet capable of transporting herds of stampeding elephants. The cargo hold was nearly the size of a football field. It seemed like a really strange announcement to me.

After another hour of silence the captain came back on the loudspeaker. This time he announced that the rejiggering effort had been unsuccessful and that they were now going to have to remove *all* of the luggage and reload it back into the hold, presumably much better this time. I couldn't believe what I was hearing.

Another hour passed. Then the captain came on once more. Finally, I thought, we're ready to get going. Instead, he announced, "Air France-KLM is now on strike," and the mic went dead. That was it, nothing more was said.

Now I was pissed off. What the heck was going on up there? Did the captain make that announcement and then walk off the plane? Was the whole cargo rejiggering thing just a ploy to buy time? I needed answers. But the flight crew was just as clueless as we passengers were, which was even more unnerving. Nobody seemed to know what was going on. I was fuming, though strangely enough, I seemed to be the only one who was upset. None of the European passengers on the flight reacted as though anything was amiss. I wanted answers, but there was no one to ask.

Another hour of radio silence went by, and then all of a sudden the jets fired up and the plane started moving. There was no announcement, nothing. We just started rolling down the runway. I could see the flight attendants scurrying around frantically trying to get everybody back into their seats. Before we knew it, we were throttling up and preparing for takeoff.

"HOLY SHIT!" I was thinking to myself. "Who's flying this thing?" Did some kid near the front of the plane notice that the cockpit door was left wide open and sense opportunity? The flight simulator on his mom's iPad was kinda cool, but this, *THIS* was the frickin' mother lode!

Despite my best efforts, I didn't get much sleep on that flight. I was a little too nervous to fully relax, to be honest.

When we arrived at Charles de Gaulle airport in Paris the next morning, picket lines had already formed. A full-blown labor strike was now under way. I had long since missed my scheduled connection to Athens and was hoping I'd be able to somehow take another flight later that day.

Finally, after hours of anxious waiting, I caught an Aegean Air flight to Greece. Akis and Peter met me at the airport, as the 2nd Annual Navarino Challenge was set to get under way the week prior to the Spartathlon. My parents had flown in from Southern California to join us. They had arrived earlier in the day and were already at the hotel. It was late in the evening when I arrived at my room, and I barely made it to the bed before blacking out.

It wasn't a long night's sleep, for we'd planned to meet in the lobby for breakfast the next morning. Seeing my parents in their homeland was about the most heartwarming sight a son could ever wish for. We embraced. "How'd you guys sleep last night?" I asked.

"Okay," my mom replied.

"I slept like a rock," I said. "Was everything all right?"

"A *skylos* came into our room and crawled into bed with us."

"What! A dog got in bed with you?! Did you shoo it out?"

"No, but I probably should have. He was a real bed hog."

"Mom! This is a four-star hotel."

"I know, but it's Greece."

I had to chuckle at that. It wasn't my first time in Greece, nor was it the first time I'd heard that line.

Yeah, this was Greece all right, and despite all the trials and tribulations involved in getting here, it still felt pretty darn good being back.

It also felt good spending time with my parents. None of us were getting any younger, and I'd heard too many people who'd lost their parents say that they wished they'd spent more time together. I was determined never to let that happen to us, so I brought my parents with me wherever I went whenever possible. It helped that I genuinely enjoyed their company and that we got on well together, though they did possess two very different personalities. My father could be tense, and intense, at times. An exceedingly prompt man, if he told you he'd be somewhere at a certain time, not only would he reliably show up, he'd arrive half an hour early. Nick had strong opinions and maintained rigid positions on certain subjects. Although principally a fun-loving man, he had an obstinate streak within him and could become slightly ornery on occasion.

My mother, on the other hand, was a carefree and whimsical soul. Very few things rubbed her the wrong way. Nothing, actually. She pretty much rolled with the punches and was unfazed by much of anything. Mary Francis, "Fotini," had a slightly looser relationship with promptness than her husband. Meetings and appointments were viewed more as rough approximations, nothing particularly fixed or rigid. So long as you arrived within a general range (i.e., some time that same day), all was good.

I traced this lax mannerism back to her Ikarian roots. Few clocks are synchronized on Ikaria. In fact, few clocks even exist. None of the shops or stores have them; neither do the restaurants. They somehow magically open when people get hungry and close when everyone's done and decides to go home.

Time is immaterial on this sun-kissed Mediterranean island, deadlines malleable. Everyone casually runs behind. *Argamisi*, as the Ikarians like to say (late-thirty). Attitudes remain carefree and life stretches along merrily without measure. People forget to die.

But they don't forget to live. Family gatherings and get-togethers mean everything on Ikaria, and celebrations are frequent, though they sometimes get off to a late start. I was told a story of a young Ikarian who arrived at a wedding a day late (her own). But that didn't matter because the guests had already started celebrating (I guess you could call it a prenuptial commemoration). Eventually she joined the merriment herself, because the priest didn't show up for another day after that. Once vows were finally exchanged and the marriage officially consummated, the celebration continued for another 3 days until all the revelers decided it was time to walk back to their villages and have some rest.

When my *yia-yia* (my mother's mother) was a young girl, she remembers her mother sending her brother down to the store for some eggs. Apparently, along the way, he met a group of friends who were heading to the other side of the island for a party, so he decided to join them. He showed up back at the house 4 days later, and the first thing their mother said to him was, "Where are my eggs?"

Summertime visitors speak of the Ikarian "Golden Triangle" (i.e., from bed sheet, to beach towel, to napkin). There's no need to keep track of time for regulating such movements. The lazy flow from one to another of the trio occurs naturally when things seem right; there's no need for annoying buzzers or alarms. So long as you remember the suntan lotion, all is good.

The euphoria of seeing my parents and reliving some memories over breakfast was preciously short-lived. Almost immediately the procession of activities commenced. There were speeches to give, press conferences to attend, talks to be made at local schools, and sponsor appearances planned for that evening. By the time we finally finished dinner, it was well past midnight. We capped off the day with a shot of ouzo, though for me it was less of a celebratory toast than a tranquilizing agent so that I could get some rest.

Unfortunately, throughout the course of the day, I'd grown progressively ill and was now feeling like a festering petri dish of contagion. Brushing my teeth, I glanced in the mirror. I didn't look like my normal, vibrant self. There was no sparkle in my eyes; rather, there were dark circles and bags. I looked washed out and haggard. This wasn't good. It was the worst imaginable time to be getting sick. The next 12 days would be a whirlwind of nonstop commitments and activities culminating with the Spartathlon. Getting sick wasn't part of the plan.

The last thing I recall before nodding off was a comment a friend once shared: "Wanna make the gods laugh?" he smirked. "Tell them your plans."

The incubation went like clockwork, and in the morning the green monsters crawling out of my nose looked angry and possessed, like something Odysseus battled during the Odyssey. How was I possibly going to get through the day, let alone the next 12 days?

Sometimes you've got to fake it to make it. Throughout the course of the Navarino Challenge I did my best to put on a happy smile and retain an upbeat and cheerful demeanor. These people were so excited to see me, and I, in turn, was genuinely glad to be seeing them. My state of mind had nothing to do with the external setting and everything to do with my compromised health. When you don't feel your best, a dark cloud hangs over your head wherever you go. I'd slipped down a few rungs on Maslow's hierarchy and was now more concerned about survival than self-actualization.

Although the Navarino Challenge involved a couple days of back-to-back running, the longest distance was only 21 kilometers (i.e., a half-marathon). I could schlep my way through that relatively short distance no matter how horrible a bug I harbored. There may be a few unsightly snot rockets ejected from my nostrils along the way, but a half-marathon is something I knew I could get through, despite being ill.

And I did.

By the conclusion of the first week in Greece, my condition had steadied. It hadn't worsened, though it hadn't gotten much better, either. It had reached a plateau and stabilized. The most troubling repercussions from this illness were that my body clock refused to reset. Usually I'd adjust to a new time zone in a matter of days, but I'd now been in Greece for a week and still hadn't adapted. Things had better change quickly, as the Spartathlon was right around the corner. For that race I knew I couldn't fake it to make it.

18

FOR GREECE, FOR HOME

As we have seen from my trials and tribulations in the backcountry of Greece, the exact distance from Athens to Sparta is impossible to know given the vast number of potential routes and detours Pheidippides could have taken. Greek historian Isocrates says it was 1,200 stades, while Pliny fixes it at 1,140. And then there is the issue of the length of a stade itself. Most take a stade to be 200 yards, but the ancient stadiums were closer to 180 yards. Thus, the likely distance Pheidippides covered between Athens and Sparta is somewhere between 136 and 142 miles.

What sort of condition might Pheidippides have been in at the time of his departure? Could he have been nursing an injury? Did he get a good night's rest the evening prior? Was he at the top of his game, or had his training been slacking off prior to being called to duty? These things will never be known with certainty, though we can assume that as a trained professional and the chosen one to undertake this critical mission to Sparta, Pheidippides was in a constant state of readiness and fully prepared to carry out his duties at any time should the need arise.

What did the man look like? Did he have a solid physique? What was his age? According to the *Suda,* an ancient Mediterranean encyclopedia, hemerodromoi would have been beyond *ephebos* (adolescence) and more mature. It is likely that Pheidippides was a bit older and more senior than the average hemerodromos, probably in his late twenties (remember, life expectancy was much shorter back then). The supposition that he was an elder herald is based on the fact that it would have taken time to develop the navigational skills, physical experience, diplomatic poise, and familiarity with the Spartans necessary to earn their trust. Because he would also travel through many other city-states on his journeys, having solid relationships with those entities would assure his safe and expedient passage.

Regarding his physical stature, Pheidippides was probably firmly built. From modern analysis we know that high-impact weight-bearing exercise—including running—helps develop bone density. The belief that Pheidippides had a muscular physique is further validated by excavations of the necropolis at Eleutherna in which anthropological data showed the people living there to have had extremely strong lower legs, likely in response to the never-ending physical demands of their duties and lifestyle. (Eleutherna is in a mountainous region of Crete that was home to an abundance of trained-athlete militia.) Running great distances over prolonged periods of time in uneven and challenging hilly terrain recruits many of the body's major muscle sets in the legs, core, upper body, and arms. It can therefore be reasonably presupposed that Pheidippides and the other hemerodromoi maintained a high strength-to-weight ratio, with a thick and sturdy skeletal structure.

Yet, having a strong body is only part of the equation. Having a strong mind is equally, if not more, important. There is a saying at the Western States 100-Mile Endurance Run: "The first 50 miles are run with the legs, the next 50 with the mind." There comes a time when the human body is fully tapped out, depleted, and spent. Even the mightiest cannot go on forever; this is where mental fortitude comes into play.

Mastering the mind is a complex process. A warrior has confidence, yet is not blinded by foolhardiness. He knows that victory is never assured, regardless of one's abilities. Mastering the mind requires an intimate awareness of one's weaknesses and shortcomings as well as the mindfulness to mitigate and overcome such vulnerabilities. A warrior is humble and unassuming, knowing that despite possessing great strength and discipline, triumph must be earned each and every day.

In the period leading up to the Spartathlon, my mind was cluttered and overwhelmed with outside stimuli. After the conclusion of the Navarino Challenge, the pace never slackened. Once I was back in Athens, more invitations and requests flooded in, things that were important to me like visiting local schools, attending charity fundraising events, supporting Greek economic development, and touring historical sites and museums. There were more interviews and press conferences, which were challenging, along with a dizzying array of new people I met and was introduced to along the way, many of whom had equally challenging names to pronounce. There were Aiketerine and Vasiliki, Panagiota and Evangelia, Alexandros, Calliope, Demetra and Panagiotis, Elias and Theodoros, Athanasios, Spiros, and Charalampos. Most of these people were associated with the media, I think, or an institution, or an event, or something? To be honest, I was never actually sure. But there were hundreds of new faces every day, some speaking English, some not. I continued feeling sick and broken down, though I did my best to conceal it. I didn't want attention or sympathy directed my way. This wasn't about me; this was about doing my best to give back to the people and the country that had welcomed me as one of its own. *Sto kalo*, as the Greeks say, to the good.

But an introvert needs quiet time to digest and process unfamiliar settings and situations, to catalog and make sense of new occurrences and put things into a logical perspective. There was no such solitude to be had, the procession of frenetic activity continuing unabated, finally climaxing in an invitation to tour a museum in the small township of Marathon, where I was to meet the mayor and be recognized for my contributions to the sport of running during a press event.

This was something I would have loved to have done *after* the Spartathlon. The thought of driving hours to Marathon and back to attend another ceremonial affair so close to the start of such an intense physical test lacked the appeal for me that it otherwise would have held, though I kept these sentiments to myself. For now, I simply resolved to smile graciously and try my best not to sneeze or cough on anyone (or to get sneezed or coughed on!).

Naturally, we got lost trying to find the museum and ended up on some country road along the outskirts of town. The houses we passed were simple one-story structures, with dirt yards and laundry drying outside, hung by wooden clothespins. Chickens and goats wandered the roadways, appraising us curiously as we passed but in no great hurry to move out of the way. Round and round in circles we drove. Our GPS kept misdirecting the route, almost as though our destination didn't exist.

"Akis, are we lost?" I asked.

"I'm not sure; these roads aren't on my GPS."

Just then we came upon what looked to be a warehouse, where a large group had gathered outside. Apparently we'd arrived. There were about 75 people in front of the building along with the mayor, who stood at a makeshift podium. All of the attendees appeared to be affiliated with this event in one way or another; there didn't seem to be many museum-goers walking around, and the nearby parking lots and streets were entirely devoid of cars, even though it was peak visiting hours.

The front of the building itself was fairly understated. An abandoned elementary school, it lacked any massive neon signage or billboards to announce its presence; rather, there were a simple bronze statue of a runner in front and some flagpoles. The mayor turned out to be a really cool guy. A radio DJ and media personality, he was completely new to politics and pledged both to end corruption and balance the budget, no mean feat in these parts, apparently, as he'd learned the day after being elected that the town was 25 million Euros in debt. His speech was funny, poignant, engaging, and powerful, even though most of it was in Greek.

After he presented me with the certificate and award, it was time to enter the museum. I wasn't expecting much. What I found inside absolutely obliterated my expectations. There, before me, was the most extraordinary display of marathoning and Olympic memorabilia on the face of the earth. It was a stunning, world-class exhibit complete with remarkable staging, dazzling architectural design, and beautiful natural lighting throughout. Every detail was breathtakingly attended to with meticulousness, taste, and flair. How this forgotten municipality situated on the outskirts of time could contain such a vast collection of priceless historical artifacts was yet another juxtaposed Hellenic paradox.

The Marathon Run Museum was largely the work of Dimitri Kyriakides and his sisters, Eleni and Maria,[1] and was a tribute to their father, Stylianos. The youngest of five children born into a deeply impoverished farming family in a small mountainous village, young Stylianos left home at the

---

[1]   It must be noted that Maria Polyzou, the Greek women's marathon record holder, also played an instrumental role in the development of the museum.

age of 12 to find employment. He eventually landed a job
working for a British Medical Officer, who noticed the boy's
athletic talents and encouraged him to take up running. Stylianos excelled, eventually competing for Greece as a marathon runner in the 1936 Olympics, finishing eleventh overall.
Not a medal, but respectable, especially considering the
Olympic training program in Greece was nothing close to
that of larger developed nations. These Games were held in
Berlin, and in an ironic twist of fate, Stylianos was the athlete
chosen to present Adolf Hitler with a sprig of wild olive from
Mount Olympus, which he gave to him during the opening
ceremonies, telling Hitler that it represented a symbol of love
and peace. Improbable as it seems, it was actually Adolf Hitler who conceived of the modern Olympic Torch Relay as a
way to spread friendship and unity among nations.

The irony is that Stylianos's athletic career was brought
to an abrupt halt by the Nazi occupation of Greece. In 1942,
he and a group of friends were captured and taken prisoner
by German soldiers. Stylianos was recognized as an Olympic
runner and thus released, but all of the other men were executed. Enraged, Stylianos joined the Greek resistance movement and spent the next several years fighting to drive the
Nazis from Greece. The allies succeeded and the Nazis were
eventually defeated. Finally, he could run again.

But it was not to be. After fighting the Germans in World
War II, he began fighting in the Greek Civil War in 1945.
The entire time he yearned to resume his running career, and
his dream was to one day participate in the famed Boston
Marathon. Then, in 1946, an American friend named John
Kelley secured an entry for him. Because Stylianos arrived in
the United States frail and emaciated from battle, race officials
protested that he might not survive. But he had given everything he had to travel to the United States, and eventually the
officials relented and allowed him to enter the race.

It didn't go well for him. He languished near the back of
the pack for most of the race. Nobody expected much from

this obscure Greek runner, so his poor showing came as no surprise. Boston, after all, was the world's preeminent marathon, and he was competing against an elite and established field of the world's best. Besides, Stylianos was weakened from years of fighting. But when he heard the cry of an old man shouting from the crowd, "For Greece, for your children!" pride and passion took over and he ran like he had never run before, passing runner after runner until he eventually caught the leader, who was none other than John Kelley. The two men locked strides for a period, each vying for victory. But in the end it was "Stelios" who prevailed, hailing jubilantly as he crossed the finish line, "For Greece, for home."

He had done the unimaginable and won the Boston Marathon. Nobody thought it was possible, but Stylianos Kyriakides was used to overcoming staggering odds. A tough life had created a tough runner and one with an indomitable spirit. He was honored by President Truman at the White House and spent the rest of his life humbly dedicated to public service.

The inspiration for the museum came when Dimitri discovered some dusty cardboard boxes in his father's attic. It had been a decade since his father's passing, and it was time to clean things out. Inside these forgotten boxes he found a treasure trove of historic memorabilia. There were trophies and medals, news reports about his father's remarkable accomplishments, and presidential decrees. Most of these were unknown to his family. Stylianos was an unassuming man who didn't speak much of his successes. Had Dimitri not discovered these tattered old boxes gathering dust in the attic, his father's legacy would have largely passed by without recognition.

The museum now houses some 6,000 artifacts from around the globe. Organized into 3,100 exhibits, the museum showcases the history of the marathon race from 1896 through the present day, with every Olympic Marathon spectacularly memorialized with its own unique tribute. In all of my global travels, I had never seen anything even remotely close to this incredible exhibit. Yet we appeared to be the only visitors at the museum that day, and I think they may have opened the place solely for our function, even though it was during regular business hours. Normal everyday attendance must be too low to justify opening the doors.

I could have spent hours, if not days, wandering these hallowed corridors, absorbed in all the lore that was on display in this fantastic cathedral of running and sport. As it was, I had scarcely an hour before my crew started prodding me to go. We were due back in Athens for another function and were already running late.

The last vision I saw as we drove off from the Marathon Run Museum was that bronze statue of a runner on display in front of the property. Fixed in midstride, he seemed to be calling out to me, *"Stay. Don't go. Run with me . . . "*

We drove off, but I would run with this figure again, for its replica is the bronze sculpture we runners pass in Hopkinton at the 1-mile mark along the Boston Marathon course. The statue of Stylianos Kyriakides lives in two places, and his enduring spirit lives on in the many athletes who have run past it.

As I was lying in bed that night before the Spartathlon, my mind raced through all the places I'd been and all the people I'd met over the past several days. There wasn't enough time in each day to fully appreciate the value and richness of these experiences in the moment, so at night I would lie in bed and replay these events over and over again so I could properly acknowledge them and store them neatly in my memory. This is what an introvert does. If deprived of quiet reflection during the day, the mind will activate at night. People might think introverts are a subdued and drowsy bunch, but such is hardly the case. Extroverts tend to be more vociferous and outspoken, gregariously flitting about in active conversation and chatter. But an introvert's mind can be an extremely hyperactive space. At night my mind would restlessly course through the day's episodes, cross-referencing and triangulating them with prior events and experiences, seeking connections and logical inferences, trying to make sense out of the chaos of a fast-paced life that was inconsistent with who I am.

This night was no exception. At a time when I most needed sleep, I lay in bed wide awake. The harder I tried to quiet my mind and slip into slumber, the less tired I became. Was I trying too hard, putting too much effort into it, like a chameleon attempting to force a color change instead of just allowing nature to do its thing? I thought about that question, too.

I wondered how many other competitors were lying in their beds that night staring wide-eyed at the ceiling. Perhaps every single one of them was. Or perhaps none of them were and I was on my own. I tried not to think, which made me think more. I tried to count down from 100, but only made it to 60 before determining that the exercise was frivolous and contrived, totally ineffectual. Finally, I just went with the flow. I allowed my mind to wander freely, to do what it needed to do without any obstructive conscious intervention. A glorious procession of recollections and memories played out before me in a grand theatrical presentation. I smiled and cooed, contentedly watching the episodes unfold in my mind's eye. Unexpected characters emerged and dissolved into the milieu; locations and settings moved quickly from one scene to the next, yet retained all of their original clarity and rich contextual associations. It was 2:30 a.m. when I last looked at the clock and 5:30 a.m. when the alarm went off, though those several hours of contented bliss were deep and restorative.

I rolled out of bed, splashed some water on my face, and looked in the mirror. Morning was here. It was time for battle.

Award from Mayor of Marathon

Crew from Navarino Challenge

Talk at Public School of Palaio Faliro in Athens

19

THE RACE IS ON

Three hundred and fifty warriors huddled in the predawn mist at the foot of the Acropolis anxiously awaiting the starting gun to splinter the morning stillness. Athletes had hailed here from 46 countries; some made crosses on their chests, others pranced and stretched, while others hugged loved ones in a final embrace of farewell. Each individual standing at the starting line held the same dream, that of touching the feet of King Leonidas before sunset the next day. Sparta was 153 miles, and untold perils, away. But every person wearing a race jersey was determined to make it there.

For me, the quest was deeply personal. I'd been waiting a lifetime to be standing in this place, and at that moment I saw this more clearly than ever. I would finally run alongside my ancient brother, Pheidippides, albeit $2\frac{1}{2}$ millennia in his wake. I felt better this morning than I had in the past week, as though my body had cleared itself of illness and risen to meet the challenge ahead. This was my hour to shine brightest, in full honor of the intrepid adventurer who had brought me to this place.

In the crowd there were some familiar faces, along with some new ones. There were acquaintances I'd met at various venues across the globe, and there were people I'd heard of but never met. We were all kindred spirits now, standing there together before the start. No matter how competitive we were, all held a mutual respect for our fellow athletes, for each of us was acutely aware of the sacrifice, commitment, dedication, and courage it took to be toeing the line that morning. Whether one's intention was to win the race or simply to finish it, these same qualities were a shared prerequisite among us, a commonality that cut across borders, religions, ethnicities, and socioeconomic status and bonded us together in a sacrosanct union of blood, sweat, and honor.

That was the emotional context of the starting line experience. The practical consideration was that it had started to rain, making one's gear choice during this initial stage critical. Due to the unusual rules of the race, the first opportunity we'd have to modify our outfits wouldn't come until 26 miles after the start. The Spartathlon was somewhat unique in this regard. During many ultramarathons, especially ones taking place primarily on roadways (versus wilderness trails), there are designated points at which a runner can access his or her support crew for food and supplies, and to make gear changes. While there were many aid stations set up along the Spartathlon route—places where an athlete could obtain hydration and nutrition—there were strict rules as to when a runner could potentially interact with an outside crewmember or accept outside aid to change clothing or footwear.[1] My crew would be driving to sanctioned spots along the course to meet me. There were a very limited number of places where I could see them, so most of the time I would be running alone or with other

---

[1]   Along the course are 75 aid stations, or checkpoints, provisioned with food, liquids, and other refreshments. Certain checkpoints served as drop stations for athlete's kits that had been left at prerace registration the day prior to the event and which were delivered to specified locations on the course.

runners, while my crew drove up ahead to junctures where I was allowed aid.

This crew consisted of a team of Greeks. I had some acquaintance with them, but none of us knew one another all that well. Over the course of the next couple days we were sure to gain an intimate familiarity with each other, whether we liked it or not.

With the rain, it was an unusually cool and cloudy morning, though it wasn't expected to stay that way for very long. At some point the forecast called for clearing skies and warming temperatures, but when this transition would occur was anybody's guess. The tactical consideration was that you wanted to be wearing enough clothing at the start to remain warm and dry, yet not so much clothing as to become overheated when skies cleared and temperatures warmed. I decided to go with a lightweight waterproof shell to remain dry. I could always tie it around my waist should the sun make a premature appearance and I didn't need it, but I would have it at the ready should the rain resume farther down the road.

Amid the swirling commotion and restless anticipation of the starting-line countdown, I glanced up one last time to take in the towering white columns and sweeping broad arches of the Acropolis. That single glance sparked what appeared to be a chain reaction of the other runners and spectators doing just the same. A silence swept over the group, and for a frozen moment in time all seemed awestruck by the magnificence of the setting. It was humbling to think that 2,500 years earlier a man stood in this exact location with the intention of doing precisely what we would be doing today, running to Sparta, only his hopes were not to earn a finisher's medal but to save Greek civilization. In all my many years of running and racing across the planet, nothing compared to the emotional force of that moment.

"*Trri-ia . . . the-e-o . . . ena,*" the countdown concluded; the starting gun went off, and away we went.

The send-off was ceremonious to be sure, though a bit less so than in other ultramarathons, especially those run in the United States. This crowd seemed slightly more subdued, a bit more introspective and focused than at other races. Perhaps it was owing to the composition of the group. There were many athletes from Japan competing on this day, and they seem to engage less in overt rah-rahing and chest-pounding than do their Yankee counterparts. The Europeans, too, skewed toward the mellower spectrum on the bravado scale. Or perhaps the solemnity was on account of the intensity of the race that lay before us. The Spartathlon is considered one of the most grueling physical contests on earth. The qualification standards for gaining entry into this event are set high—only the most elite athletes are eligible—yet no matter how many ultramarathons you'd previously completed, no matter how fit and experienced you were, the odds of finishing this race were no better than the odds of not finishing, perhaps worse. We set off through the streets of Athens not so much in a frenzied flurry of unbridled enthusiasm, but in more of a contemplative awareness of the contest that lay ahead.

One of the reasons this race is so demanding is the aggressive cutoff times between checkpoints. For instance, runners must reach the Ancient Wall at the Hellas Can factory—50.22 miles from the start—within $9\frac{1}{2}$ hours or face elimination. For comparison, many 50-mile ultramarathons have cutoff times of 13 or 14 hours to complete the race in its entirety. Spartathlon runners have to better this pace by many hours, and then run another 103 miles on top of that. And this merciless cutoff to cover the first 50.22 miles of course isn't an isolated thing; such accelerated milestones continue unabated the entire duration of the race, which leaves little margin for error. If an athlete experiences a setback or physical decline at any one point along the course, it could spell imminent doom. This knowledge taxes one's psyche from the very first step.

Setting out from Athens, I was keenly aware that a fairly aggressive clip needed to be maintained in order to ensure reaching the various milestones with an ample buffer of time to feel secure. Of course, knowing that I needed to maintain a fairly aggressive clip to feel secure made me feel insecure. Was my pace too fast, too slow, or just right? Was I placing undue stress on my system, or holding back too much? Should I try to hang with the experienced frontrunners, or should I follow my own instincts? These questions kept turning over and over in my mind.

One thing I was absolutely sure of, however, is that I didn't want my feet getting wet. Although it wasn't raining hard, it was coming down at a fairly steady rate, and creating standing puddles of water in the roadway. Larger pools, some deep enough to swallow a foot up to the ankle, were beginning to accumulate in many of the low-lying areas. You invariably alter your footsteps when the ground is wet and slippery. Your muscles and micromuscles make calculated adjustments to help stabilize your body, whether you perceive these subtleties or not. Muscles that may not normally get utilized during dry running conditions are recruited, and this extracts greater effort and increased exertion.

Attempting to avoid getting my shoes and socks too wet, I exercised caution in navigating around these waterholes. From previous experience I knew that running in wet socks could be a recipe for disaster, especially when temperatures got warmer. Feet that are kept in a perpetual state of dampness become pale, puffy, and plump, with distended fissures and deep crags developing between skin folds. If you've ever stayed in a Jacuzzi or a warm bathtub for too long, you know what I mean.

Skin that is softened and swollen in this way tends to be more susceptible to irritation and trauma if subjected to repetitive microabrasions, such as the grating that can occur from a seam-stitch or flap of fabric jutting slightly outward from inside the cavity of one's shoe. This point at which an irritant contacts skin is often referred to as a hot spot because of the heat such friction inevitably generates. Waterlogged tissue is extremely sensitive to this dynamic and easily develops boils and blisters in response—not a condition you want to perpetuate in the first few miles of a 153-mile footrace.

Other runners appeared to be exercising care as well, but some were not. They were trudging straight through the waterholes without trepidation. I wondered how their feet would fare farther down the road. It would be several hours—a full marathon's distance—before there was any possibility of changing into dry socks. This provided ample time for blisters to build up.

Dodging puddles wasn't my only concern. The streets of Athens were becoming crowded with morning traffic. Policemen were stationed at most of the main intersections to stop vehicles, but after crossing the street, we runners had to run along the sidewalks and fend for ourselves. These sidewalks were filled with all kinds of obstacles, from overflowing trash cans to meandering pedestrians to stray dogs. On top of that, the periodic motorcycle or moped would come careening down the pathway in an effort to skirt the blocked intersections, nearly taking out unsuspecting runners like bowling pins. There was yelling and screaming and the honking of horns, both by frustrated motorists who were angered by our presence and by enthusiastic commuters who were expressing their support. Gestures were extended from car windows, mostly congratulatory, though some otherwise. Many of the older shopkeepers appeared to be aware of the race. "Bravo! Bravo!" they shouted. Many others, however, like those just walking down the street or waiting at a nearby bus stop, seemed to be oblivious to what was going on. They looked at us with unease, as though we were a horde of criminals who had just busted out of the local penitentiary. The whole scene was a chaotic and disjointed puzzle, a perplexing amalgamation of fear offset by elation, along with unnerving disorganization improbably paired with a grand atmosphere of celebration. I'd come to expect nothing less in Greece, and it strangely served to heighten the mystique of this legendary race in its modern-day incarnation.

Greece was a paradox, an unsolvable conundrum. In the bad there sometimes could be found good. In the darkness there sometimes appeared light. In the midst of desolation and despair, hope could spring anew. It was in this swirling ambiguity, this impossibly illogical riddle of contradiction, that everything suddenly made perfect sense. Life could not be understood, and Greece elevated this truth to its surface. As we ran down the congested streets of Athens, cars and trucks zooming by just inches away, what we runners were doing made no sense at all. Yet it made all the sense in the world.

Drizzly walk to Spartathlon start with Dimitris Troupis

Start of Spartathlon

20

IT'S IN THE AIR

As historical records show, when word arrived in Athens about the Persian incursion at Marathon, the Athenian generals wasted no time in summoning their greatest herald. Recruiting the Spartans into battle was of critical importance, and the sooner they could arrive, the better. Speed was of the essence, and Pheidippides was the right man for the job.

His departure from Athens would have been quite a different scene from our modern-day exit. With little fanfare, except perhaps some encouragement from a few fellow hemerodromoi and the leaders of Athens, his send-off was likely a somber affair. Pheidippides was tasked with a momentous undertaking, the outcome of which was quite uncertain. Yet the future of Greece depended on his success. The stakes were high, mortally high, thus it was hardly an occasion for revelry.

He likely would have left earlier in the morning than we had, owing to the fact that the days were longer in early August, when he made his heroic run, than they were roughly 7 weeks (and 2,504 years) later, in the last weekend of September, when we attempted ours. Longer days meant more sunlight, but also more heat. Leaving under the coolness of dawn would provide some reprieve from the oppressive heat, at least for a short while. Greece in the summertime was inevitably hot, and it was impossible to completely avoid the intense midday solar radiation. The more miles he could accumulate in the early morning hours, the better. Money in the bank, as ultrarunners say nowadays.

Pheidippides would have been under intense pressure to perform at his *aristeia* (bestness). He knew that every wasted step meant the invading Persians would be able to further fortify their position at Marathon and build their strength. While we Spartathletes had artificial cutoff times to reach certain milestones along the course, Pheidippides's time constraints were very real. The consequences of his failure were unthinkable. The young boys of Athens would be castrated and made into servants, the women raped and enslaved. Older men would be seen as offering little value and would be disposed of without hesitation. Any surviving Athenian hoplites would be slaughtered wholesale, and all the treasures of architecture, art, and science would be looted or destroyed. Worse, the Greek system of democracy would be lost forever to a tyrant who ruled men not by consensus and collective accord, but through fear and intimidation. Darius had little sympathy for the Greeks. He wanted complete and total revenge for their defiance. Fools they were for not surrendering to him immediately, and now they would pay dearly. No mercy would be shown. Persian victory would spell the end to everything the Greeks had worked so diligently to construct. Pheidippides was well aware of all of this. He knew he mustn't fail.

I didn't think much about Pheidippides during those initial miles of the Spartathlon. I couldn't, really. There was too much to watch out for, too many distractions and potential hazards. I needed to direct the entirety of my attention toward avoiding the many perils and pitfalls that running down congested city streets presents. But as the miles progressed and the chaotic traffic of Athens faded away, my thoughts again returned to this mighty hemerodromos.

Knowing intimately the situation and the consequences of his actions, what must have been going through his head? Imagine rushing home to save your family from an oncoming hurricane. There would be few extraneous thoughts passing through your mind other than reaching them as quickly as possible. Your heart would be racing, adrenaline flooding through your system; the pituitary would release cortisol, inducing the so-called fight-or-flight response. The mind would be stimulated and intensely focused, constantly analyzing and processing every split second of motion. All of these physiological reactions evolved as a survival mechanism to ready the body for immediate action against clear and present threats. This is how our bodies rise to the occasion when confronted with an urgent, life-threatening matter, giving us a burst of quick energy that enables us to put up a fight.

But such would be a heavy burden to carry for 153 miles of continuous running. Pheidippides knew the ensuing storm was brewing, but being supreme commander of his body, he was also grand master of his mind. Learning to quell anxiety and to channel this emotional electricity into long-term storage for steady release over a prolonged period of time is an essential skill for any endurance athlete, and Pheidippides is the father of us all. Who knows? He may have had a family of his own, children, and a loving partner. Certainly he had parents who could have been alive and living in Athens, as well as brothers and sisters. Thoughts of the Persian military laying their filthy hands on his family could paralyze a man with anger. But such unchecked emotional discord would have been demoralizing and counterproductive to the fulfillment of his mission. Pheidippides must have repressed such thoughts and remained focused on the task at hand. As I've witnessed in myself and other ultramarathoners, we tend to be a hopeful and optimistic lot. Rather than fixating on the consequences of failure, we project forward and concentrate on the elation that will ensue as a result of accomplishing our goal. Pheidippides must have harbored the belief that if he were to succeed in his conquest, all would be good. The Persians would be defeated and driven out of Greece, and his family and all of Athens would be saved. Such positive self-talk would serve to reinforce his determination and unwavering resolve to reach Sparta as quickly as he could.

We had made a rather long and gradual climb across the shoulder of Mount Aigaleo and then dropped down through a wooded area and on into Skaramangas, along the coastline. The route we followed was the Sacred Way, a path the ancients used to travel to the verdant agricultural district of Elefsina, and farther to Delphi. Although just 10 miles into the race, the once-concentrated pack of runners had thinned considerably, most running individually or in pairs.

American ultrarunning champion Jon Olsen came running past. He looked strong and composed, as usual, but it was still very early on in a very long race, and most runners looked relatively fresh. We chatted for a bit, and I noticed that his feet looked wet, which called to my attention, for the first time since trying to dodge puddles earlier in the morning, that my feet were wet, too. Jon bid me farewell and bolted off into the distance at a pace that was too aggressive for me to sustain. Sure, I could have locked strides with him, though so could have anyone else at such an early point in the race. Maintaining a faster pace was something well within the ability of every runner in the field. The question was, what toll would maintaining such a hastened pace at this initial stage extract during the later phases of the race? Jon was a seasoned professional, and this was hardly his first rodeo. Although it was his inaugural attempt at the Spartathlon, he was an expert at pacing himself for long durations, as he had skillfully done on many such previous occasions, winning races and setting records in the process. You don't accomplish these things without a complete mastery of body and mind. I wished him luck and settled back into my comfortable cadence, taking the opportunity to inspect my feet.

I'd chosen to wear white knee-high compression socks from the start. At least I thought they were white. When I looked down at them, I saw only a saturated oily muddle of sagging gray fabric spackled liberally with gritty particles of loose road debris. The runoff we'd trodden through along the byways of Athens had been a grimy cesspit of drippings from the undercarriages of a thousand poorly maintained and rusting vehicles. The puddles and small streams were a veritable rivulet of greasy mechanical pollutants, and my shoes and socks were soaked in it. I'd need to change them, but the earliest opportunity wouldn't come for another 12 miles, at the 26-mile mark, when I would see my crew. So I continued running.

The road along the coastline was pretty in places and grossly industrialized in others. With the cobalt Mediterranean glistening beside us as a backdrop, we ran past aging shipyards, crumbling barracks with massive lots of broken and parched concrete, gigantic corroding rebar matrixes openly exposed like the skeletal corpses of rotting leviathans. Urban decay was rampant all around us. Now an apocalyptic wasteland, 30 years earlier the area had been a highly productive center of manufacturing and commerce. Forgotten and past its prime, the region was abandoned and left to decompose. The Greeks weren't always so good at cleaning up their own messes.

Although slightly thinning now, a layer of clouds still blotted out the sun. I'd experienced clouds in Greece before, but these clouds were different. The summertime clouds I'd encountered were towering cumulonimbus formations created by the earth's radiating warmth. As these clouds developed and mushroomed outward, they would sometimes release intense downpours. But this rain was always localized and transient, soaking the ground for an instant and then vaporizing into the heavens, the clouds disappearing as

quickly as they'd formed. The clouds on this day were more
of a low-lying blanket that stretched from one horizon to the
other. This type of cloud coverage can be a double-edged
sword. While it affords some level of protection from direct
rays of sunlight, it also causes temperatures at ground level to
elevate. This may sound counterintuitive, but as the warmed
air near the earth's surface rises, this smothering layer of
cloud coverage creates a barrier which prevents the heated
ground air from escaping upward, thus trapping it down low.
Not only does this greenhouse effect elevate surface temperatures, it also raises humidity levels. Humidity is a runner's
enemy, because it renders our body's normal system of evap-
orative cooling less effective. In drier conditions, perspiration
on the skin's surface evaporates quickly, which serves to cool
the body. As humidity rises, the sweat we produce doesn't
evaporate. Instead, it sticks to the skin's surface and accumu-
lates into a salty crust, which only exacerbates the situation
and raises the body's internal thermometer even further. I'd
take higher temperatures over higher humidity any day, as
would most runners.

I soon encountered another downside to this extensive
low-lying cloud coverage. There were a series of refineries
and tanker docks near the roadway, and they were all billowing thick, foul-smelling fumes into the air. These noxious
vapors were being trapped down low by the cloud coverage,
and since there was no way to avoid breathing in this tainted
air, I was left feeling queasy and light-headed. I wasn't the
only one affected by it, either. I spotted another runner vom-
iting near the roadside. The guttural sounds of his retching
made me feel as though I might do the same. Who knew
what kinds of toxins and pollutants were being spewed out of
those smokestacks? There was no way around this caustic
fog, no alternate path to follow, so we runners had no choice
but to inhale the unwholesome discharge.

Running through the putrid murk rekindled a memory

of a high school surf trip I'd once taken to Baja with some buddies. As we were driving down a remote dirt road, our truck had struck a concealed boulder, severing the vehicle's gas line. Using some mechanical tape, we were able to construct a makeshift patch, but not before the gas tank had been drained of its contents. Thankfully, we'd brought a spare gas can that we'd filled prior to leaving, as the guidebooks advised us to do. But there was no nozzle on this can and thus no way to get the gasoline into the vehicle. We did, however, have some spare plastic tubing, so my buddy decided he would siphon the gas from the can into the truck by inserting one end of the tube into the opening of the gas can and then sucking on the other end to start the flow of gas moving upward. Once the flow started, he'd simply insert the tube into the truck's tank and the contents of the can would be transferred. He tried several times to no avail. The liquid that he'd sucked upward didn't sustain enough momentum to initiate an ongoing stream and quickly receded back into the gas can once he pulled his mouth off the tube. On his next attempt he drew in even deeper to ensure success. But he didn't manage to remove his lips from the tube in time and accidentally inhaled a mouthful of gasoline. Almost immediately he violently discharged the contents of his bowels and collapsed on the ground, convulsing and heaving spasmodically in the dirt. None of us knew what to do. He was flipping and flopping on the ground like a gaffed fish, violently dry heaving, his face hideously reddened, mouth wide open with his tongue dangling outward, a viscous purple-black sputum dripping off his chin like ink from a squid. We stood there watching in utter horror, completely unprepared to deal with the situation. Our festive surf trip at once had become a horrible nightmare. We didn't know if he'd live.

Fortunately, we were rescued by some local fishermen who happened to pass and told us to rush him home immediately. There were no hospitals deep in Baja at the time, and only one paved road. It was a long, sleepless drive back to Southern California, and even with all the windows rolled down, the vehicle reeked of vomit, feces, and gasoline the entire way. Our friend spent several days in the hospital but eventually recovered. That deathly smell, however, lingered in my nostrils for months. I hadn't thought about this experience in years, but the stench of those refineries along the Greek roadside reawakened the disagreeable memory.

Earlier in the day, I'd eaten a couple of figs, a handful of olives, and a mouthful of *pasteli*. I'd grabbed a few glasses of water from volunteer-staffed checkpoints along the way, but that was all I'd consumed thus far. My hunger had been mounting prior to reaching the refineries, but now my appetite was entirely gone. After breathing in that nauseating effluence, I couldn't eat. As we came running into Megara, at mile 26, all I could think about was changing my socks.

Megara marked the first crew access point along the course, and it couldn't have come soon enough. The growing warmth of the asphalt underfoot was becoming problematic, and my feet were at risk of blistering if I didn't change into dry socks. My crew had driven from the starting line and would be meeting me here, so now was the opportunity to change into a fresh pair.

Flanked by Mount Pateras, Megara is home to many ancient landmarks, including the temple of Artemis, which contained the statues of the 12 gods of Olympus, the gold-plated statue of the goddess Athena, and a consecrated temple to the god of gods, Zeus. It seemed tragic that all these treasured ruins were within spitting distance of a row of hideous oil refineries, but I would try to forget that reality and relax in Megara for a moment and think happy thoughts while I changed my socks.

Only 127 more miles to go.

21

ENCOUNTERS OF THE ULTRA KIND

M egara was hardly the quaint seaside enclave I'd expected, at least not when the Spartathlon was passing through town. Instead it was a bewildering suburban maze replete with gridlocked traffic, honking horns, crews frantically jockeying for parking places, and pissed-off locals cursing at the unruly interlopers who had invaded their otherwise peaceful community. Everyone seemed to be yelling or arguing with someone else, gesticulating wildly with their hands and overemphasizing the direness of the situation with exaggerated eyebrow raises and fancifully animated facial expressions. Remember, they're Greeks; they don't keep calm. After all, this was the birthplace of drama. The Greeks invented theater along these very byways. Tragedy, comedy, and satire have been forever intertwined into everyday existence in Greece. Whether during the Dionysia festival in the 5th century BCE or during a traffic jam in present-day Megara, we Greeks remained richly steeped in the theater of life.

In an unexpected theatrical twist, my support team was nowhere to be found. Apparently they'd gotten delayed in the traffic backup and had been unable to make it to me as planned. What to do? Should I wait for them or keep going?

Just then I saw one of my team members, Dimitris, sprinting up to me. He was sweating and out of breath. Dark-olive-skinned, at 6'2" or 6'3" Dimitris was one of the tallest Greeks I'd ever known, and he had spindly long limbs, which may have been one of the reasons he was such an excellent runner.

"We could not . . . " *pant, pant, pant* "get here in time," he gasped between breaths.

"Okay, where's the car?"

"It's back . . . " *more pants* "down the road."

"What should I do?"

He looked at me queerly. "Run back down the road?"

I wasn't about to run in the wrong direction, so I thanked him and told him we'd meet at the next crew station, forgetting that it wasn't for another 25 miles. They were required to leapfrog to Corinth, so I wouldn't be seeing them for several hours' time.

It was a hasty, amateurish move on my part, and I knew better. I didn't have to run back down the road to get those socks; I could have just waited in Megara for my crew to pull up. Sitting for an extra 5 or 10 minutes over the course of a 153-mile run wasn't going to have a significant impact on my performance. But running with blisters on my feet would.

As well, I could have easily left a spare pair of socks at the prerace registration meeting the day prior, to be delivered in advance to Megara should a situation like this arise. Had I done that, my socks would have been waiting for me upon my arrival, and I wouldn't have found myself in such a predicament.

My guidance to newbie ultramarathoners is always to hope for the best, but plan for the worst. Have a contingency plan for your backup plan, I say. Boy, am I a hypocrite! You'd think during such a significant race I'd practice what I preached. But the reality was that I'd allowed my anxiety to interfere with my judgment. I knew better. We're told to learn from our mistakes, but how many of us really do? I should have just coolly assessed the situation and reacted rationally, but instead I got flustered and made a rash and foolhardy decision. Hey, I'm Greek. Keeping calm isn't in my DNA.

A deeper reality, however, was that I didn't really fear blisters all that much. Sure, they might be gruesome and painful, but they would never stop me. I'd once developed severe blisters on the first day of a 6-day run across the Atacama Desert in a remote area of South America. But even with a marble-size, fluid-filled blister festering under my big toenail, I was able to complete the race (winning, actually). Perhaps subconsciously I like pain.

As quickly as my musing had begun, it dissipated. I snapped out of it to once again be swept away by the natural beauty of the setting we were running through. Walled by steep limestone cliffs along the inland side of the highway, the sparkling Bay of Salamis now came into full panoramic view across the seaward side of the road. The rain had stopped and the day was windless and calm, which made the water look like porcelain, the opaqueness of the low-lying clouds reflected like mirrors off the still surface. It appeared as though one could ice-skate across the broad expanse, effortlessly gliding onward with one gentle stroke and then another, *Whoosh . . . whoosh . . . whoosh . . . whoosh . . .*

"KARNO!" suddenly I was jolted from this spell. "Hope it's cool if I call you that."

I turned to see an oxenlike figure, big and broad shouldered, with a bold, booming voice to match. I knew this man, though mostly by reputation. Prior to this roadside encounter, we'd only once briefly met in person. But his lore preceded him, and I felt like I knew him better than our chance acquaintanceship would indicate.

Brash and unfiltered, Dave Krupski wasn't afraid to speak his mind. A standout collegiate athlete at Yale, he went on to attend Notre Dame Law School, graduating magna cum laude. Dave was a true scholar and a polished orator.

"Dude, so howzit going?" he asked.

"Ah, so far so good, I guess. You?"

"It feels hot out here to me," he said. "Does it feel hot to you?"

"Yeah, it feels a bit warm for sure."

Dave was a brawny, muscular guy, which could be problematic for a long-distance runner on several levels. First, working muscles tend to generate and retain more heat, the metabolic processes working like small kilns to provide a constant source of energy. Servicing these active muscle fibers requires a greater flow of blood, which can force the heart to work harder in an attempt to pump additional volume. Consequently, the entire cardiovascular system gets placed under greater demands. I've consciously tried to reduce some bulk myself, for these very reasons.

Dave seemed hardly affected by his brawn, though. This guy was a beast of a runner, despite his barrel chest and twin-cannon arms. His résumé included several dozen sub-3-hour marathons along with an impressive list of ultras, many of which stretched beyond the 100-mile mark. And he didn't just finish these races; he often won them. That same relentless drive he'd applied toward achieving excellence as a lawyer was now being transferred to the tarmac.

Another athlete came running up from behind. He was European, I think, perhaps from the Balkans or Ukraine. Or maybe he was Brazilian. He spoke a language that was completely undecipherable to me; almost no words, or even sounds, could I understand. I'd learned a bit of Portuguese in my travels to Europe and South America, and also I spoke some Spanish, French, German, and Italian, but nothing he said registered.

He was trying to explain something to me, and though I couldn't understand a word, I knew without much effort precisely what he meant, because it was exactly the same thing many people had been attempting to articulate to me over the past few days. He had read my book, at least one of them, and was trying to express this to me. My books had been translated into 16 languages, so runners across the globe now had access to them. Many runners could identify, personally, with the stories of struggle, pain, loss, and perseverance in these books because these are the same experiences they share themselves. We runners are united in this way.

Through my books, I'd become something of a de facto conduit between runners of various nationalities at these international events because I was the one commonly known entity among athletes of various ethnicities, many of whom spoke different languages. Whether one hailed from Germany or Japan, Slovakia or Brazil, the Czech Republic or Korea, New Zealand or Italy, they knew me as the author of those books about running. It was an unintended consequence of publishing my books, and it was quite beautiful.

It was also somewhat confusing. Here was this poor guy going on and on trying to express himself, and I couldn't understand a word of it. Finally, he looked at me and realized this fact. He smiled, laughed at himself, and then gave me a runner's hug. That's the other universal trait we runners share; we're not afraid to hug (even while running). It's a bit awkward at times, but quite touching nonetheless, and probably something the world could use a little more of these days, though I digress.

I'd never let such notoriety go to my head. I'd been largely unaffected by it, never growing impatient with people, regardless of the setting or circumstance, and never taking any of it for granted. I thought of myself as just another runner, part of the clan, nothing more. A passage by Epictetus had profoundly shaped the way I sought to conduct myself in this regard:

> To live in the presence of great truths and eternal laws,
> to be led by permanent ideals—that is what keeps a man
> patient when the world ignores him, and calm and
> unspoiled when the world lavishes him with praise.

Dave had disappeared during my conversation with the other runner (er, *attempted* conversation with the other runner), and in the interim it seemed to have gotten progressively hotter

outside, stifling almost. The road we were running along continued to weave near the seashore, but the air remained thick
and heavy. There were numerous aid stations set up along the
way—nearly every few miles it seemed like another appeared—
but the only thing I was getting at these stops was water. My
appetite was starting to reemerge, but I was relying only on
ancient foods and they were entirely absent at these outposts.
Overflowing with energy bars and electrolyte-replacement for-
mulations, these stations provided plenty of modern athletic
foods, but no figs, olives, *pasteli,* or cured meat were to be had.

I had one fig left in my satchel and I ate it, but it hardly
filled the growing void in the pit of my stomach. We ran past
a tavern called Zorba's and I thought about how nice it would
be to indulge in some flaming *saganaki* and a plate of *tiropita*,
dolmas, and souvlaki, with perhaps a piece of baklava (or an
entire platter) and a shot of ouzo (or the entire bottle) to finish things off. Yes, I was growing hungry.

Dave reemerged. "That guy was cool, but your critics are
not. They're a bunch of jealous whiners," he announced.
"Some of the shit they post [to the Internet] is pathetic."
Clearly, this was a man who didn't mince words.

He was referring to another unintended consequence of my
rising notoriety, though one that was a bit less uplifting. Shocking, really, and a bit disturbing, too. At first I was taken aback
when someone posted a critical remark about me. I took it personally, and it was hurtful. What was I possibly doing that
could spark such ire in a person? The condemnation was generally over a perception that I was in this sport for myself, or that
I'd given away the "Holy Grail" of running by exploiting our
sport and exposing the whole world to the joys of ultrarunning.

Fair enough, I thought. Everyone's got a right to his opin-
ion. Having critics kept me grounded, and that was a good
thing. And, truthfully, I found some of the criticism useful,
and I appreciated the feedback. I made changes in response
and became a better person in the process. Then again, some

of the rants were entirely unjustified and seemed to be poking fun at me, personally, more than anything else. These comments were always left online by someone using an alias like "toe jam" or "butt butter." Never once had anyone come up to me in person and expressed such misgivings. My father taught me that if you have a problem with someone, take it up with him or her directly. Don't slither around behind their back; conduct yourself with honor and talk to them up front. These were the ageless Greek ideals I was raised on. Live life virtuously. Irrespective of outside forces, never compromise your principles. For, as Socrates had recognized, it is better for the soul's sake to suffer wrong than to do wrong.

Perhaps the Internet age had brought out the worst in some people, or at least made it easier for such people to express their opinions publicly. Whatever the case, having malicious barbs lobbed at me was one element of being me that I still hadn't warmed to.

"Haters gonna hate," Dave added. "Don't take it personally. Everything I've seen of you is nothing but positive. You've done more for this sport than anyone else, and you've inspired plenty of people along the way."

"Thanks, man, I really appreciate you saying that. Sometimes it gets to me."

"Look, there's always going to be a few envious sulkers out there who have nothing better to do with their time than sit online and criticize others. Just remember, they're the minority. Look at all the good you've created. Don't let those bastards drag you down!"

"You oughta be a coach. That's one helluva pep talk!"

"I am."

"Legal advice?"

"No, running; branched out from the courtroom into the playroom and started a coaching service."

"I think you oughta offer psychological counseling, too."

"A running shrink, that's good."

"Aren't all us runners a bit crazy? I think there's a market for it."

"Ha! But on that topic, I heard you're following some crazy diet. How are the olives, figs, and sesame-honey mush treating you?"

"*Pasteli.*"

"Huh?"

"That sesame-honey mush you're referring to, it's called *pasteli.*"

"Whatever, dude. I think you're crazy subsisting on that crap during this race. Seriously, ever thought about a shrink?"

"Give me your card and I'll be in touch."

Dave's support about those critics had been soothing, though I'd long before accepted that no man can ever be free unless he learns to forgive. If Prometheus could endure the injustice of being bound to a rock by his evil nemesis, his liver pecked out nightly by bloodthirsty vultures, I could certainly forgive a few vile remarks left online by some loathsome Internet trolls. Their trespasses were forgiven, and I was liberated from any ongoing pain that may have otherwise gnawed away at me. My liver remained intact.

Another aid station appeared ahead, and just as quickly as Dave had surfaced in my life, he vanished into the quixotic opium running great distances inevitably evokes. People appear and then they disappear. Faces emerge but then mysteriously teleport to some future stage of the race or to some future stage of life. We were nearing the 40-mile mark, and the notorious Southern Mediterranean heat was progressively mounting. Skies were clearing, but a certain vaporous, mental ether was condensing within my brain like a brooding hallucination. My mind was adrift, but my legs kept churning ceaselessly onward into the fomenting sepia abyss, the hazy cerebral solemnity broken only by the sound of repetitive staccato footfalls strumming the ground: *tap, tap, tap, tap* . . .

22

STALKERS

There are different theories about food intake during an ultramarathon. Some prescribe eating prodigious quantities and frequently, adhering to a more-is-better school of thought. Eat early and often, the saying goes. Ultramarathoners have been known to consume 60 or 70 gel packs during the course of a 100-mile footrace. Others preach limiting calories or restricting foods to certain types of macronutrients, such as fats of a particular composition (like medium-chain triglycerides, or MCTs). Then there's the 40:30:30 Zone plan (i.e., 40 percent calories from carbohydrates, 30 percent from protein, and 30 percent from fat) and the 4:1 carb-to-protein ratio strategy for fueling the body. Volumes of research are used to support each approach, with some studies being more credible than others, but for an athlete looking for answers, it's all a bit confusing and overwhelming.

Personally, I've always subscribed to the "listen to everyone, follow no one" approach. We are each built a bit differently; what works for others might not work for me (and vice versa). So I'm constantly experimenting with various nutritional strategies and continually tweaking my diet until I hit upon something that seems to work. In the final analysis, what usually works best for me is to simply listen to my body (go figure).

Sometimes during a race I feel ravenous and consume all kinds of food without regard to composition. Other times I crave syrupy, high-carb foods or savory, salty foods. Sometimes I'm not hungry at all and eat hardly anything.

The same holds true for fluid consumption. I've run a sub-3-hour marathon and consumed only half a glass of water the entire way. Conversely, during the Badwater Ultramarathon, a grueling 135-mile footrace across Death Valley in the middle of summer, I've consumed as much as 9 gallons of liquid—more than half my body weight—over the course of 28 hours of continuous running.

My conclusion is that if you feel thirsty, drink. If not, don't. If you feel hungry, eat. If not, don't. The worst thing you can do is to force yourself into following a predetermined plan even if your body isn't agreeing at the time.

My problem at this juncture in the Spartathlon was that the inner workings of my body craved calories, but a lingering nausea had made the thought of eating completely unappealing. The illness I'd been suffering over the past week had diminished my appetite. Consequently I'd dropped a few additional pounds on top of the weight I'd already lost while training for the Spartathlon. I needed to eat, but a pervasive nausea left me incapable of doing so. What was causing this queasiness?

Not half a mile down the road I got my answer. The racecourse passed yet another row of refineries and petroleum processing plants that were spewing more vile-smelling fumes into the surrounding atmosphere. I sucked in a hearty lungful of these repugnant emissions and almost immediately began coughing and choking. A thick, foul-tasting reflux from the pit of my stomach rose into my mouth. It tasted like the putrid backwater sludge of a bayou. I spit out a corrosive

black wad of this acidic goop, and it splattered on the roadside like an oil slick.

The horrendous air quality was not something I'd anticipated having to contend with during the Spartathlon, and I
was woefully unprepared to deal with it, perhaps more so than
any of the other athletes competing in the race owing to the
cleanliness of the air I normally breathe. Where I live in
Northern California, Marin County, the air is remarkably
pristine. The prevailing westerly winds blow in straight across
the Pacific, which serves as a massive cleansing and purifying
filter. The only thing separating my house from the shoreline
is a forest of tall redwood trees, and any pollution generated
farther inland from us is pushed away from my house by these
persistently strong westerly winds. On days when the wind
isn't blowing, which are typically fewer than a dozen per year,
the county declares a Spare the Air Day and prohibits activities that emit airborne particulates, like the use of wood-burn-
ing stoves and fireplaces and certain types of diesel machinery.
Air quality is taken very seriously in these parts, and further
boosting air purity, the region has one of the lowest rates of
smoking in the nation. Inhaling secondhand smoke is almost
unheard of in Marin. The hypersusceptibility to poor air quality I was experiencing now was likely due to the fact that my
body's natural defenses weren't acclimated to it.

I came upon another aid station and had a sip of water to
wash down the tinny, acrid residue still left on my palate, and
my mood was brightened by the cheerful group staffing the
small post. I'd never been to a race before where there were
so many stops along the way. There were legions of volunteers staffing these checkpoints, and they were all incredibly
upbeat and supportive, always quick with a smile and a shout
of encouragement. Many of these people could barely feed
their families, yet here they were cheerfully and dutifully
feeding us. It is the Greek way.

Pheidippides would certainly have had a lonelier time of

it. Rarely would he have encountered a smiling face, if at all. As he passed through the various city-states along the way to Sparta, he'd likely have met with people, though these inter- actions were probably more formal in nature. Although the Greeks universally agreed upon safe passage of messengers, these were troubled times. All the other city-states except Athens and Sparta had bowed to Darius; thus alliances would be strained. If Darius were to learn that one of these city-states offered Pheidippides assistance in his quest to recruit the Spartans into battle, he might no longer honor his vow to spare the lives of its inhabitants for surrendering to him. If the Persians were to prevail in their quest to rule Greece—and odds were pretty good that they would—those city-states that had provided aid to the resistance would likely be annihilated.

It is hard to imagine what Pheidippides's mood must have been like as he approached these other territories. He probably had friends there from his previous travels, but things might be different given the current state of affairs. One absolute certainty: He wouldn't have had 75 well-stocked aid stations set up along the way with cheering volunteers. He also wouldn't have been running on pavement, which 95 percent of the modern Spartathlon is run on. My heel was all too aware of this fact. Because of my hastiness back at Meg- ara, my soggy foot had developed a blister. How big, I didn't know. But the unmistakable tenderness resulting from pro- longed friction was clearly recognizable. I would need to tend to it in Corinth, perhaps lance and tape it if necessary. But that wasn't for another 10 miles.

Dave resurfaced as if from out of nowhere, and we ran together for a bit more.

"Does it seem hot?" he asked again.

"It seems a bit warm, yes."

"It seems hot to me."

I glanced at him and saw that he was drenched in sweat,

his chest and forearm muscles bulging out from under his race jersey.

"Is there ice at the aid stations? Have you seen any ice?"

"Hmm . . . not sure. Haven't been looking, honestly."

"I need to get some ice."

He seemed a bit out of it, not that I wasn't. I couldn't tell if it was he who was losing it, or *me*. Most likely it was the both of us.

"I need to get some ice. And some Coke. Have you seen any Coke?"

"Hmm . . . not sure. Haven't been looking for that, either."

"Oh right, you're only eating nuts and berries and sesame mush."

"*Pasteli.*"

"Huh?"

"That sesame mush, it's called *pasteli.*"

"Oh, right. I still think you're crazy to be eating that stuff."

Another aid station appeared up ahead.

"I'm going to get some Coke."

"Okay," I nodded at him. "And some ice," I reminded him.

I bypassed that particular aid station and kept on running. It did feel warm, though nothing compared to the searing midsummer's heat I'd experienced during my solo reconnaissance missions through the backcountry and byways of Greece. I'm not sure why the race organizers settled on holding the event the final weekend of September, when Herodotus specifically referenced Pheidippides having departed Athens in early August. There were probably a number of practical considerations that were taken into account. But whatever the case may be, the reality is that running in late September was inevitably cooler than it was when Pheidippides undertook his mission.

The narrow, two-lane roadway continued paralleling

the coastline, sometimes down closer to the water's edge
and other times rising up along the cliffs above. Not much
of this section was flat; it was either slightly uphill or
slightly downhill, undulating and rolling the entire way.
There were far fewer cars passing us now that we'd progressed some 45 miles outside of Athens. The runners had
spread out, too. I was now running by myself; there wasn't
another runner to be seen in front of me or behind. There
were no aid stations in this section, and my crew had leap-
frogged to Corinth, which was still seven or eight miles
from here. I was all alone.

Up ahead, at perhaps 200 or 300 hundred meters, an
underpass appeared. It looked as though the road we were
running on crossed beneath it. As I drew nearer, it became
apparent that the structure was quite dilapidated; the concrete edges along the entrance were crumbling, and there
were weeds growing everywhere, even up from the cracking
pavement.

As I entered the archway of the underpass, it suddenly
became very dark inside. There were big chunks of concrete
strewn across the roadway, and I had to be careful not to trip
over them. It looked as though several trucks had tried to
cram their way through the structure but were too tall to fit.
In their attempt they'd scraped their carriages along the ceiling and caused it to disintegrate and collapse to the ground. I
tiptoed and zigzagged around pieces of metal and big chunks
of rubble and rebar. When my eyes started to adjust to the
darkness, I could see that the interior walls of the underpass
were covered in graffiti. It was cool and damp inside the
deeper recesses of the structure, and mushrooms and weeds
sprouted up between the fissures of fractured concrete, as if
nature was preparing to reclaim it.

As I neared the far side of the underpass, the glare of
sunlight from above cast a dark veil across the exit like a
black curtain. It was impossible to decipher anything beyond

that point, and as I crossed through the shroud and my eyes began attempting to readjust to the brightness, I noticed a car parked up ahead. There was a young man standing next to it, staring at me. Was I about to be mugged?

I kept running toward him, unsure of my fate, my vision still not fully adjusted to the glaring sunlight. He kept staring at me. My heart began racing, and I started to get that uneasy feeling like something bad was about to happen. The road was narrow, with a cliff on one side and he on the other, so there was no place to escape. I could see that his eyes remained fixed upon me. This wasn't good. Where were all of the other runners? What was going to happen? Then I noticed he held something in his hand. Was it a knife? A gun? Had I met my destiny?

All of a sudden I realized he was clutching a copy of my first book, *Ultramarathon Man*, the Greek version. Whew, was I relieved. The tension drained. Then I felt incredibly humbled.

"*Yasas*" (hello), I said to him, now feeling safe. He was a trim lad, young—perhaps in his midtwenties—well groomed and nicely clad in a polo shirt, Bermuda shorts, and Top-Sider shoes. I had snot running down my face and pieces of cured meat stuck between my teeth.

"Hello, Mr. Karnazes."

After he greeted me, he just stood there looking at me in a wide-eyed stare. It was awkward.

"Would you like me to sign your book?" I finally asked.

He snapped back to life, "Oh, yes, sorry, do you have time?"

"Sure."

He handed me the book. I could see that his hands were trembling when he did so. The book felt warm and moist from his palms.

"Do you have a pen?" I asked. "I don't happen to be carrying one with me at the moment."

"Oh, yes, sorry." He rummaged through his pockets nervously. "Here you go."

"That was a joke," I said, smiling.

"Oh, yes, sorry, of course it was a joke," he said nervously. My attempts at humor clearly weren't hitting their mark.

"What's your name?" I asked.

"Ah . . . John."

"Yannis?"

"Oh, yes, sorry, of course, my name is Yannis."

I signed Yannis's book and handed it back to him.

He thanked me, and then added, "Oh, sorry, would it be okay to take a picture?"

"Sure, Yannis, that's fine."

"Oh, would it be okay if my girlfriend was in it?"

Girlfriend? I didn't see anyone else around. "Sure, that's fine," I said. "Where is she?"

He ran over to the car. "Nicola! Nicola! *Ela, ela!*"

A stunning, dark-haired young lady stepped out of the passenger-side door. She had a classic Dorian profile with radiant olive skin, a beautifully sculpted nose, prominent cheekbones, indigo eyes, and full, rosy lips. Her features were timeless, like those of Helen of Troy, whose angelic face is said to have launched a thousand ships.

She walked over and said hello in a heavy Greek accent. I don't think she spoke much English, and she was very shy. She was holding a cell phone and handed it to Yannis, who was standing next to me.

"Let's put beauty in the middle," I said to him. They both looked at me blankly.

"You know—the rose between two thorns." Neither of them moved. It was clear they had no idea what I was talking about. My attempts at diffusing their nervousness were backfiring, as they now appeared more nervous than ever. It was awkward.

I moved Nicola in between Yannis and me. "There."

"Oh, yes, sorry." Yannis now understood what I was try-ing to explain. We scrunched our heads together, and he held out the phone and snapped a few selfies. He immediately started inspecting the photos on the phone's screen and smiled broadly. I guess he liked what he saw.

"How did you guys know where to find me?" I asked.

"Oh, yes, sorry. We've been following you."

"Yannis, you don't have to keep saying you're sorry."

"Oh, yes, of course. Sorry."

"So where have you been following me from?"

"From Athens."

I almost choked. "From Athens? You mean you've been following me this entire time?"

"Oh, yes, sorry. There are a lot of people waiting in Corinth, so we came here."

Corinth was a major checkpoint, so I figured it would be a busy place. Still, I was quite stunned that they'd followed me for the past 7 hours.

We stood there for a bit longer in silence. More awkwardness.

"Hey, listen, I'd love to stick around, but I really should be . . . *running along.*" It was a pathetic pun and a feeble last-ditch effort to break the ice with some slapstick American jesting.

They both just stared at me blankly.

"Get it? Really should be '*running along* . . . '" I raised my eyebrows and tilted my head back and forth a couple times for emphasis.

They both continued staring at me blankly.

"'*Running along.*' No?" It was a final desperate attempt to break through.

"Oh, yes, sorry. I understand," Yannis said dryly. I think he was sincere, but any element of humor was clearly lost in translation. It was obvious their heads were in a different place than mine.

I smiled, chuckled at myself, and bid them farewell. They both just stood there waving from the roadside. A hundred feet down the roadway I turned back around, and they were still just standing there, waving.

I gave them one last wave, giggled, then put my head down and ran off to Corinth.

Dave and Dean along the Gulf of Salamis

23

ROLL CAMERA

Corinth was once an illustrious Greek city. Home to the Temple of Apollo and the famous agora, it was a flourishing artistic, architectural, and cultural hub in the 5th century BCE. Situated along a narrow isthmus between the Gulf of Corinth to the west and the Saronic Gulf in the Aegean Sea to the east, its positioning offered a strategic defensive advantage along with exceptional views in every direction.

Unfortunately, Corinth didn't fare well as time progressed. The city was burned to the ground and looted by the Romans in 146 BCE. Along with the destruction, many of the treasured Corinthian vases were lost or destroyed, and much of the classic Corinthian artwork was either pilfered or defaced. Ironically, it was another Roman, none other than Julius Caesar, who eventually restored the city.

Then, in 67 CE, the Roman Emperor Nero had an idea to boost trade and improve logistics by cutting a gigantic channel between the two seas on either side of the isthmus. This newly constructed passageway would significantly reduce travel time and increase commerce by shaving some 430 miles off the journey around the Peloponnese. Using a golden spade to start the digging, he commenced construction.

Nero didn't live to see the project's completion. Nor did his children, or his grandchildren, or their grandchildren, for that matter. It wasn't until 1893 that this engineering marvel was finally completed. Picture this: a 300-foot-deep, 81-foot-wide, sheer vertical parallel cut into solid marble earth and thus connecting the blue waters of both seas. Measuring 4 miles long, it was dug deeply enough to completely avoid the need for locks, even though it connects two massive bodies of water. It is quite an astounding feat of engineering, and quite a remarkable spectacle to behold.

Crossing a 300-foot-high walkway that bridges the two sides, I arrived at the bustling checkpoint in Corinth in just over 8 hours' time. Since it is situated at mile 50.22, many runners struggle to make it here within the 9:30 cutoff period (or they struggle so hard getting here they have nothing left to continue making future cutoff times farther along the course). I still wasn't sure which category I fell into, but I was sure glad to be there.

Corinth couldn't have come a moment too soon, either. It was high time to do some serious regrouping, repairing, and refueling. Mentally, I felt light-headed; physically, I felt weak. The heel of my right foot needed attention, and I knew I needed to force myself to eat regardless of my ongoing nausea. Socks needed to be changed and layers of clothing needed to be removed. There was an adequate buffer left within the cutoff time, so I planned to use some of the surplus to gather myself and start afresh.

Unfortunately, it wasn't to be. A large crowd had assembled awaiting my arrival. People were holding books, posters, magazines, and mementos for me to sign. It was concurrently heartwarming and horrific. There were a number of reporters there, along with TV crews and newscasters. All I wanted was a few peaceful moments to address my foot and choke down some *pasteli,* yet all I was seeing in front of me was a sea of adoring fans and followers (and family, as I would soon learn).

They all rushed me at once, simultaneously asking me to sign things, pose for photographs, and meet long-lost aunts, uncles, cousins, and nephews. The reporters cut a swath through the masses and demanded that I conduct interviews with their news stations first. Nearly all of these requests came flooding toward me in Greek, each person talking progressively louder to overshadow the last. It now occurred to me that when Yannis had said there were a lot of people in Corinth waiting, he meant that they were waiting for *me*.

And so it began. Someone stuck a Sharpie between my fingers and I was suddenly signing books, flyers, and photos for people I didn't even know (but who apparently knew me), as well as napkins snatched from nearby restaurants and loose scraps of paper people had grabbed from recycling bins in their frantic rush over to me. I was surrounded three deep, and it was paralyzing and claustrophobic. The energy of everyone all wanting a piece of me at once fed upon itself like an out-of-control wildfire.

I stood there unable to move, not sure what to do, not sure where to go. I couldn't think for myself, couldn't reason, my mind totally preoccupied with trying to decipher the multitude of requests being lobbed my way from every conceivable direction. The deafening noise and commotion was disorienting, and I just stood there in a daze like a puppet, trying to accommodate people as best I could. Truthfully, my mind was on autopilot; not much of anything was registering at the moment. I'd completely lost all sense of time and place, and I just stood there blankly reacting to one person after the next as though in a dream.

At some point my left forearm was clasped by the strong grip of a hand. It started tugging me away, with some force I might add. People kept following me along as this unknown hand dragged me sideways; all the while I kept signing things with my right hand and smiling for photos as I was being pulled along. This invisible force hauled me some distance

and finally plopped me down in a chair. I was still surrounded by people, but now I could see that my crew was
there. They asked me if I needed anything, while at the same
time I was being peppered with questions from a multitude of
news reporters. They all wanted face time and elbowed each
other in a scrum, attempting to jockey for position. What had
I gotten myself into? All I wanted to do was run the Spartathlon, and suddenly I had media obligations. I'd never signed
up for any of this.

"ROLL CAMERA!" one of the news crew shouted. Next
thing I knew three microphones were shoved in my face and
a series of rapid-fire questions assailed me like incoming
buckshot. I started jabbering incomprehensibly, not sure what
else to do. "Blah, blah, blah, blah, blah . . . "

"Oh, that's beautiful," one of the reporters said. "Ωραιος"
(beautiful).

I had absolutely no idea what had just rolled off my
tongue, but apparently it was to her liking. Then I felt someone unlacing my right shoelace. I couldn't see my foot
because of all of the microphones and equipment in my face,
but I was certain my shoes and socks were being removed.
Then someone shouted in my ear, "Do you want me to pop
it or just tape it?"

It was Nikos Kalofyris, another crewmember. Apparently
I'd mentioned something about a blister on my heel during
the interview, and he'd responded accordingly. An ultrarun-
ner himself, Nikos knew precisely what to do.

"*Oxi, oxi,*" I shook my head, motioning with my hand not
to worry about it.

Sure, it would have been nice to properly take care of my
foot, but I knew that the hounding would be incessant the
entire time. All I had wanted was to get to Corinth, and now
all I wanted was to get the hell out of Corinth.

I couldn't understand why these people were drawn to
me. I was nothing special. We all need heroes, I guess, not so

much for what they do as much as for what they do to *us*. For
these people I'd become a source of optimism; I was a means
of hope that somehow, someway they could move closer to
their idealized selves. They saw in me something they
wanted more of in themselves, and in meeting me they reaf-
firmed that value and perhaps reignited their passion to get
to that place. Ωραιος.

Nikos finished putting on a new pair of socks and laced
my shoes back up. He slapped a pouch of food in my hand
and gave me a fresh bottle of water. He could tell I wanted to
leave; I didn't have to say anything. "*Efharisto*," I thanked him
and started to get up. Reporters kept interviewing me and
people kept asking me to sign stuff, but I just ran away. I had
to. I had nothing left to give.

These sorts of situations usually don't bother me much. I
accept them as part of my duty in trying to be a good ambassador of endurance sports and in trying to be a positive role
model in general. But hullabaloo like this is certainly easier
to deal with when you're feeling fresh and at your best, which
I presently wasn't. And today's particular situation was a bit
more excessive than usual. The Greeks were exceptionally
passionate people, which was both uplifting and draining.
Right now I needed to get into my own head and sort things
out. To think, I'd already covered roughly two marathons
but still had the equivalent of four more to go. I was feeling
pulverized, but my journey had just begun. The Spartathlon
was going to test me in ways I'd never been tested before. I
liked that.

There are always ups and downs during an ultramarathon—high points and low points—that is to be expected. It's
entirely unrealistic to think that a race of this duration will
go like clockwork, no matter how well trained an athlete is. I
was all too aware of this fact. Just as smooth seas do not
make skillful sailors, smooth races do not make resilient runners. Still, the challenges of a new experience, such as the

odyssey I was now embarked upon, posed unique and unfamiliar obstacles. Dealing with the unknown under the best of
circumstances can be trying, but when the mind and body
are under severe strain, these situations become even more
difficult and imposing.

Pheidippides would have been challenged to retain both
his physical constitution and his mental equanimity. When
he came upon each new city-state, it was important for him to
communicate clearly and concisely with the interceptors and
to appear confident and astute. If he gave off an aura of delirium or hopelessness, it would send a chilling message to these
other Greek territories that the Athenians had little hope of
prevailing against the invading Persians, and this was a senti-
ment he wouldn't have wanted to convey.

While scholars and historians have consistently mentioned the deeds of Pheidippides, they've never dedicated
much analysis to the plight of this great hemerodromos,
despite the critical importance that recruiting the Spartans
played in the course of history. Most academics seemingly
take for granted the feat of this legendary hemerodromos and
question it no further. Perhaps this is owing to the way Herodotus so casually mentions Pheidippides being dispatched to
Sparta without further elaboration on what pulling off such
an unfathomable undertaking entails, as though his ability to
successfully run 140 miles nonstop was a forgone conclusion.
In Herodotus's time, the role of a hemerodromos was to run
great distances, no big deal. This guy was just doing his job,
that's all.

Most modern scholars and historians are completely
unfamiliar with modern ultramarathoning and thus lack
much firsthand experience in what it's like to run such a
great distance in so little time. They just take his accomplishment at face value and leave it at that, kind of like
Herodotus did.

Yet, as anyone who has ever attempted to run an ultramarathon can attest, the chances of success are no greater than the odds of failure, especially when you're talking about running farther than 100 miles, in sandals or barefoot, over mountainous terrain and without much access to food, water, or supplies. This perspective with regard to the true difficulties facing Pheidippides is entirely lacking in scholarly depictions of the events and outcomes surrounding the Battle of Marathon.

By competing in the Spartathlon, I was afforded a more intimate glimpse into how Pheidippides must have felt during his run to Sparta and the tremendous pressure he was under to remain composed. Although he would have had no way of knowing the historic significance his undertaking would eventually play in shaping world history, he would certainly have known that if he were to fail in his mission, Athens would fall. If there was to be any hope of overthrowing the Persians and driving them back to their homeland, recruiting the Spartans into battle would be paramount. This knowledge would have weighed heavily upon Pheidippides's psyche, and as the Greeks have shown us, the mind is the master of the body. He must have fought hard to tame the inevitable feelings of fatalism, knowing full well that the odds for his success, and for the future of Greece, were not good.

The highway leaving Corinth dropped back down onto rural byways. Soon, empty roads and rich pastoral farmlands replaced the refineries and the maddening snarl of traffic. The occasional car that did pass puttered along gingerly, seemingly unhurried and unrushed. It was a much different feeling out here. My lungs began to clear and I ran alone, by orchards and vineyards, through great fields of empty earth, past rippled expanses of rock outcroppings spackled with patchworks of greenish blue lichen. It continued to amaze me that the group of runners competing in the Spartathlon had become so isolated. Despite there being more than 300 competitors at the starting line, there was hardly another sign of a fellow athlete anywhere to be seen. A few stray dogs wandered past, but other than their disinterested presence, I ran in complete solitude.

The bag of food that Nikos had given me in Corinth contained an assortment of items, including several figs. Those seemed to be sitting best in my stomach. The once delectable *pasteli* now tasted like maple syrup mixed with talcum powder, chalky and repulsively sweet, and I could no longer tolerate the stuff like I had during my training runs. I tried gnawing on a piece of cured meat, but it was rubbery in texture and the gristle was impossible to chew. Holding the masticated pieces in my mouth like chewing tobacco, I did my best to extract some of the salty residue from the meat juices, knowing that the sodium would help replenish some of the essential electrolytes that were being depleted in my perspiration, then I'd spit out the cuddy remains in the bushes along the roadside.

The smaller townships we runners now passed through were more alive than those we encountered earlier on. Children laughed and played as I sauntered by. They knew that the Spartathlon was passing through their town, and they cheered, clapped, and giggled at the strange outfits we runners wore. Some joined alongside me on bicycles or push scooters for stretches. They seemed to find this practice quite entertaining, as did I. Being around kids always brought me back to life. They occupied a world that was simpler, one more innocent and carefree than ours, and hearing their laughter and watching their liveliness brought with it familial feelings of warmth and joy.

On the outskirts of a village in the Assos District, a group of youngsters clad in traditional Greek clothing were dancing in the streets, acrobatically twisting and twirling to the rhythm, putting on a show for us runners hoofing past. I slowed to watch their graceful maneuvers, marveling at the remarkable agility and skillfulness they possessed. Seeing my interest, they elevated the precision and sharpness of their movements to a new, higher level, their feet whipping with increasing speed and astounding exactness. As the song's beat built to a climactic crescendo, dust swirling in the air, I hailed and clapped, "*Opa! Opa!* Bravo! Bravo!"

They bowed formally to me, panting and drenched with perspiration, expressing their gratitude for my acknowledgment of their routine. To be honest, the pleasure was all mine. I've seen lots of Greek dancing over the years—some by award-winning production companies—and these kids were some of the best I'd ever observed.

As quickly as I'd come upon this festive roadside gathering, the sound faded into the background and I continued along my path. Once again I found myself completely alone and running down a narrow rustic road that drowsily meandered through the pastoral landscape, groves of olive trees casting lengthening shadows across the way as the sun dipped lower into the horizon. The warm afternoon air was nearly motionless, the aroma of wild rosemary and coriander drifting lazily in the stillness. Nectar-laden honeybees buzzed about blissfully; fields of abundant blossoms stretched endlessly. For the first time since embarking upon this journey at the base of the Acropolis, I felt at one with the land. Finally I'd found my peaceful place to recharge.

Then, suddenly, a speeding police car came careening around the corner heading straight for me, its sirens blaring in full alert. My heart skipped a beat, but no sooner than I saw the flashing lights in front of me did I turn to see a late-model blue BMW racing toward me from the opposite direction. It appeared dusty and dented, and the driver looked wild-eyed and crazed. When he spotted the cop car coming toward him, he yanked the wheel around and sent the vehicle spinning 180 degrees into a ditch alongside the road. The police car came screeching to a halt, and two armed officers jumped out, pointing their guns and yelling. Dust flew everywhere as the BMW spewed steam from its crushed radiator, hissing violently. I stood there frozen in disbelief.

Along with the driver, there were two passengers in the car. All of them were young males, and they appeared dirty and disheveled. The gun-wielding officers ordered them to lie facedown with their hands behind their heads, but the men just stood there with their arms jutted straight toward the sky as though they had no idea what was being said. One of the officers grabbed an assailant and threw him to the ground, cuffing him while kneeling on his back. His two accomplices then lay down on the ground, mimicking their friend. They, too, were handcuffed. The whole thing took place in a suspended instant of time.

What I came to learn later was that the men were likely Syrian refugees seeking asylum from their civil war. As the fighting intensified, illegal immigration was becoming a burgeoning problem. The dreadful irony was that the Greek economy was in no shape to handle this influx of new immigrants. In some ways things in Greece were no better than they were in other parts of the world, though at least in Greece there was no one pointing a gun at your head, unless, of course, you stole a car.

While there was no excuse for their behavior, these were desperate men, destitute and displaced, with no hope for a better life and no promise of a brighter tomorrow. At least in a Greek prison they would be fed.

Perhaps most disturbing about the situation was that these young men had likely paid for transportation to Italy. But unscrupulous traffickers had begun dumping refugees from Syria and Afghanistan on uninhabited Greek islands or unloading passengers on the shoreline under the veil of nightfall, claiming it was Italy. The Greeks had fewer resources to patrol their waters than the Italians did, and the trip across

the Mediterranean to Greece was shorter, saving these traffickers both fuel costs and time.

Here I'd been carelessly striding about this rustic countryside on a slow path to enlightenment when the tragic
dichotomy of this conflicted land was thrust upon me like a
kick to the gut. Suddenly witness to the brutal realities pervasive in this world, I found it impossible not to recognize that
in 2,500 years of conflict and warfare between men and
nations, not much had changed. Like an unsettling Homeric
revelation, the unforeseen drama of this episode shocked my
sensibilities, toppling the pillars supporting my worldview to
the ground. The plight of humanity was still as doleful as
ever; we just possessed greater means of exploitation and killing these days.

With this disturbing realization fresh in my mind, I ran
into the setting sun.

Crossing into Corinth

The media circus

24

GEORGE CLOONEY

When I would see my crew again was uncertain. Perhaps they had communicated this information to me during our last encounter, but in the swirling chaos that was Corinth, little had been retained.

Did it matter? Not really. I'd trained myself to be self-reliant. I'd seen too many ultramarathoners' performances suffer when they didn't get their special potion or their secret sauce at a certain juncture. This, to me, always appeared like more of a psychological blow than a physiological one. Anyway, I didn't want to be dependent on anything other than my wits and my own two feet.

The rumble of a car materialized in the stillness behind me. From what I could tell, it was moving quite slowly, but I still gave it a wide berth, moving myself well off onto the shoulder of the road. Given the police chase I'd witnessed earlier, erring on the side of caution seemed warranted.

As the vehicle passed beside me, the driver howled out the window, "*Yasou*, Kostas!"

Startled, I turned to see a lone driver in some funky European brand of car I could not identify. All the windows were rolled down, and the driver dangled his arm casually outside.

"How's my long-lost Greek friend?" he asked. He looked like he could be an Athenian shop owner, wise to the ways of the world, and perhaps a bit hardened by them, too. His English was good, though he spoke with a heavy Greek accent.

"I'm doing all right," I said. "Thanks for asking."

"Hey, I brought you a little something." He held up a paper bag.

"Thanks. What is it?"

"It's a chocolate chip cookie from one of the best pastry shops in Greece!"

"Oh man, thank you, really, but I've been told to never trust a Greek bearing gifts."

"Ha!" he snickered. "That whole Trojan Horse thing was eons ago. Here, take it." He held the bag out to me, "They're heavenly."

"I appreciate it, really, I do, but I'm trying to follow this special Greek diet."

"Yeah, that's what I've heard, but who would ever know?"

I guess he was right. There were no other runners around to witness this act, and besides, it wasn't against the rules to eat a chocolate chip cookie. That was an imposition of my own doing. He was tempting me, like the siren sisters, only instead of promising otherworldly sensual pleasures, he was offering me man's other great vulnerability, food.

"Hey, look, it's really nice of you, but *I* would know."

He gazed at me queerly. My response didn't seem to compute. If I were the only one who knew that I was getting away with something, wasn't that a good thing?

That's precisely the sort of convoluted Greek rationale that had gotten this country into trouble, I thought. Every local merchant knew that the other was running a Greek till, so why shouldn't he do the same? One dollar in the register, one dollar in the ol' pocket. Who would know? The government had tried to crack down on this practice, but they were just as corrupt as everyone else. The buck (er . . . drachma) had to stop somewhere, and my refusal of that cookie was a bold step in the right direction. Or maybe not.

"Sure you don't want it?"

"Thanks, man, I'm sure."

"Okay, suit yourself." He pulled the cookie out of the bag and started to maw on it. "Mmm," he moaned with pleasure, "that's delicious."

Ouch. I'm sure it was really delicious, even heavenly. A lot better than warm olives and leathery cured meat, that's for sure.

He puttered alongside me for a while, eating his cookie. After he'd finished it, he licked his fingers clean.

"Boy, that bakery is really something else," he said. "A true Greek treasure."

I'm not sure he fully comprehended the internal anguish watching him devour that cookie caused me, both physically and emotionally. But one must exercise discipline in order to remain resolute. The economic calamity in Greece and the Greek people's attitude toward it seemed rather undignified to me. National pride had suffered badly as a result; there was no denying this. As the economic journalist James Angelos so aptly put it in his book, *The Full Catastrophe*, "Doomed to perpetually contrast themselves to the unmatchable splendor of their predecessors, Greeks often confront a nagging sense of inadequacy and strain under the weight of their own historical narrative like few other people on the planet." Still, I had an empathetic streak within me, as though the Greek people were trapped inside a powerful undercurrent that callously pulled them down despite their most strident attempts to escape. Just eat the cookie, dammit! Who could blame them?

My new travel companion looked to be in his early fifties. He didn't appear to be especially athletic, and his hair—what little of it still remained—was graying at the edges. He was a few days overdue for a shave, though the peppery stubble was actually quite becoming on him. Despite his unkempt appearance, his eyes still sparkled with a spirited vivacity and he exuded charisma. If George Clooney had a twin, this would be he. The car he drove was an older sedan, and not very well maintained. Several hubcaps were missing, and the paint was scratched and chipping in spots. He may have once aspired to a life of riches, but clearly such ambitions were now of little concern, if they had ever been.

"Do you want to listen to some music?" he asked.

"Sure, that would be nice."

He turned on the car's radio. It sounded like an old CD playing, and the speakers distorted the sound, but it was fine. The light beat of the music reverberated melodiously within the car's interior and then poured out onto the roadway like honey. The tune sounded vaguely familiar, like one of those modern Greek bands playing traditional Greek music, the kind I'd heard as a kid during Greek weddings or at Greek festivals. When I heard the melody seeping out of the car's aging speakers, a gush of nostalgia washed over me like a warm summer's rain. My life was so simple and unrestricted when I was a kid, and the rules got even more relaxed once I entered the precinct of the Greek Orthodox Church during such festive occasions, taking on the flavor of the old country. Supervision was eased as though we were on Hellenic soil rather than in downtown LA. As the music blared and the wedding-goers danced and caroused on the warm outside patios, we kids would slip behind the church altar or hide in the pews taking turns sneaking glasses of wine and eating *loukoumi*, giggling and egging each other on. God pulled on one arm, the devil on the other. "Of all the animals, the boy is the most unmanageable," Plato opined. Once in a while a priest would catch us and shoo us away, though always laughing more at our juvenile antics than becoming angered.

And perhaps reminiscing a bit himself. "Life is trouble,"
Zorba the Greek had said. "Only death is not."

My newfound friend and I moved slowly down the roadway together, I on foot and he puttering along next to me
with all the windows rolled down and the sweet sounds of
music oozing harmoniously out into the air. A crimson tapes-
try ignited the faraway skyline, a vivid mosaic of colors
before us, the buttery sun melting into the cast-iron horizon,
wisps of thin white clouds stretching across the heavens like
the feathery streams of a fiery arrow shot by Apollo.

We roved along the road together for a few more songs,
the sky continuing to put on a kaleidoscopic light show of
dazzling cherry pink, tourmaline, golden-yellow saffron,
plush magenta, and fluffy lavender all majestically coalesced
against a backdrop of deepening cobalt blue, the roadway
ensconced on both sides by a forest of olive and laurel trees
with an occasional spruce or cypress jutting skyward, higher
than the rest.

As he peered through the car's dusty windshield at the
glittering alpenglow in the distance, his mood seemed to
grow increasing melancholy and reflective.

"It's beautiful out here, isn't it?" I said.

He turned to me slowly, his eyes dreamy and distant. "It
sure is."

"Do you ever wonder where we're heading?" he asked.

"You mean to Sparta? Hopefully that's where I'm heading."

"No, I mean after all this. Where do we go?"

The Greeks had thought about this question since the
dawn of antiquity. The great philosophers and theologians
had pondered and contemplated the meaning of our existence, divinity, and the afterlife much in the same way our
high priests do today. It was yet another reminder that not
much had changed in 2,500 years.

"I'm not sure where it is we go," I answered, "but let's just hope that wherever it is, they have chocolate chip cookies like the one from that bakery."

"Amen to that," he chuckled.

We plodded along together for a bit longer, both of us enraptured by the array of colors lighting up the skyline.

"Is there anything else I can get you?" he asked.

I thought about it for a moment. "Do you happen to have a Band-Aid?"

"Let me think . . . yes, I should. There's a first-aid kit in the trunk. I imagine there's one in there."

He pulled over and we stopped to have a look. The box was slightly rusted and looked as though it had never been opened, but sure enough, there were plenty of Band-Aids inside.

I sat down in the dirt alongside the roadway and undid my shoe. The heel of the sock was stained with a pinkish discharge the color of grapefruit juice.

"What happened?" he asked.

"It's just a blister."

Pulling off the sock revealed that the blister had ruptured and the flap of skin that had once covered the area was mostly torn away, only dangling by a thin thread of dermis.

His eyes widened, "Do you need stitches?"

I giggled reflexively, "No, it's fine." He was clearly more concerned about it than I was.

"Does it hurt?"

"It used to, but the pain's gone away."

Over the years I'd developed a means for overcoming pain. Instead of attempting to suppress the pain or trying to cast my mind elsewhere, I delve into it headlong and focus with all my concentration on the point of pain, trying to decipher the origins of the sensation at its core. Pain is ephemeral and fleeting, and the more I focus on the impulse at its roots, the more it dissipates and dissolves away. My belief was that the nerve endings could only accommodate so much stimulation and eventually would become saturated and thus unable to transmit any more pain signals to the brain. Whether this theory held any basis in science, I had no idea. But it was what I believed, and it seemed to work for me.

People think of pain purely in terms of a physical sensation, but there is also a very deep emotional connection to pain. Pain makes people uncomfortable. It hurts and is therefore viewed as a negative thing, as something that must be mitigated and cured. I've shifted that viewpoint and instead assigned positive feelings to the sensation of pain. Pain is good. I welcome pain, because it makes me feel alive. I like feeling alive, though I can't lay claim to being the first to play the pain game. After all, Odysseus's name in ancient Greek means "man of pain."

I yanked that dangling flap of skin from my heel. It stung. I felt more alive.

He winced when he saw me do this, his face pale.

I slapped the Band-Aid across it and pushed down the adhesive on either side. "There, good as new."

He continued staring at me wide-eyed, shocked by what he'd just witnessed.

I started lacing up my shoe. "You a runner?" I asked, hoping to diffuse some of his dismay over seeing what just transpired.

"Ah . . . not any more. I used to be as a kid, but then I started smoking and drinking, and that put an end to it. I just quit those vices a few years ago and have put on some weight since then, but I feel a lot better not waking up every morning hungover with a smoker's hack."

"Maybe you'll start running again?"

"I might, though nothing like this," he joked.

"I might not do anything like this again, either."

"Bah. You can run forever, Kostas. And you *will* run forever. You make us proud."

"I'm not sure about forever. Let's just hope I can make it to Sparta."

"You'll make it," he assured me. "You make us proud."

I'm glad he had such confidence in my abilities, because I was starting to have some doubts myself, one of the chief concerns being a lack of nutrition. I needed to get some calories in my system fast, but the ongoing nausea was problematic. In retrospect, I'm pretty sure that chocolate chip cookie would have sat with me just fine.

Crawling back to my feet, I got up and slowly resumed forward progress. He drove alongside me for a while longer, but I could tell our roadside interlude was about to come to an end.

"I really should be going," he said eventually.

I didn't know where it was he would be going. Back to a wife? A family? And where was it he'd come from? Athens? Tripoli? These questions would go unanswered, and that was fine. We'd shared a moment together and it was good, but now that moment was drawing to a close.

"Thank you for the Band-Aid," I said. "And thank you for the company."

"Pleasure's mine, my friend, my *koumbáros* (distant brother). I pray for you and Pary every night."

Pary? His comment threw me aback. How did he know about my sister, Pary? How did he know about my life? It was yet another upending mystery that would go unsolved, another overwhelming enigma that pried open my heart and left me tingling.

I simply thanked him for the prayers. "*Efharisto,*" I said, "we will all meet again someday."

"Amen to that."

And those were the final words I ever heard from him.

The car swung around and in a slowly rising billow of dust disappeared into the night. Gone was he, in the flesh, at least, though in spirit I knew his memory would live on within me for many years to come, perhaps forever.

The sun had set and the luminous twilight aura faded to near black by the time I reached ancient Nemea, the midway

point of the race. In the process of getting there the course
had elevated some 1,200 feet above sea level, whirling its way
toward the summit of this mountainous pass on which I now
stood. The soil in this region is exceptionally rich and fertile,
and many renowned vineyards are scattered throughout the
terraced hillsides. Grapes that had been recently harvested
for the crush lined the roadway, squished and splattered
about like little burgundy paintballs. Many of the local
townspeople made their own potent village wine, referred to
as *kokineli*, and there was certainly no shortage of fermentable
fuel about. As I ran into the checkpoint, which was set up in
the churchyard of Archea Nemea near the site of the Panhel-
lenic Games, the streets smelled of hardy red wine as if the
entire city were engulfed in a giant cask.

It was here, in ancient Nemea, where Hercules had slain
the mythical Nemean lion that had terrorized the city for
years. Hercules hoisted the crucified beast upon his mighty
shoulders and carried the carcass to King Eurystheus, thus
proving his heroic deed. I should only hope to be possessed
of such strength.

My crew was waiting for me when I arrived.

"You need to eat," was the first thing Dimitris said to me.
"Here."

He handed me a piece of *pasteli*. It still tasted revoltingly
sweet and syrupy, but I forced myself to choke it down even
though I thought I might gag at any moment. Nikos handed
me some water to wash it down, and I took a long, slow swig,
sighing as I finished. They both knew I was struggling.
Accomplished ultramarathoners themselves, they were
keenly aware of these telltale signs because they'd experienced them firsthand. One's energy inevitably ebbs and flows
during the course of an ultramarathon. There are peaks and
there are troughs. But typically at some point during the race
a trend begins to establish itself, either to the upside or to the
downside. Eventually this tendency takes increasing command and the duration of the race continues moving further

in that particular direction. Rare is the ho-hum ultra where things go just so-so. More typically the race is either exceptionally strong, or a complete disaster. Unfortunately, I was trending toward the latter.

"I shouldn't stay here long," I said. "It will be harder for me to leave if I do."

"Can you stomach any more food?" Dimitris asked.

"Not now. When will I see you guys again?"

"In Lyrkeia?"

"How far is that?"

"Twenty-five kilometers."

"How far is that in miles?"

"Fifteen and a half."

I should have known this. I did know this. He wasn't telling me something I didn't already know. My mind was losing its sharpness, which wasn't good. Nikos handed me my headlamp. I would have forgotten it had he not.

"I'd better go," I said, and staggered to my feet.

They both looked at me helplessly, unsure of what to say, feeling my pain but unable to do anything about it. I turned, stared numbly into the murky, dark void, and started slowly moving away into a universe of infinite black.

The road to Sparta

25

THREE DRUNK MICE

Finding my way out of ancient Nemea was like trying to navigate through a labyrinth in the middle of the night with a dim candle. In the darkness, streets crisscrossed and dissected each other with no apparent logic or reason, often doubling back upon themselves or coming to an abrupt end without forewarning. The course wasn't marked very clearly and my mind wasn't operating any more so, this combination of factors could result in big mistakes if I wasn't careful.

My focus was so intent on trying to find the correct pathway out of town that I nearly stepped on something skittering across the roadway beneath me. By the time I saw the furry little critter, it had disappeared into a crevice between two buildings on the opposite side of the road. Then another one popped out from somewhere up the road; it spotted me coming and pulled an abrupt U-turn, scrambling anxiously back to safety. What were these small creatures, field mice? Another one darted out, this time right below me, scurrying about in a haphazard figure eight like one of those windup toys you find at the dollar store. I danced around on my tiptoes trying not to step on the poor thing. When it finally regained its bearings, it went rocketing off headlong into the side of a building. It sat up for a moment, no doubt seeing stars, then toppled over sideways and started rolling down the alleyway. Weird.

More appeared, and now that I was paying closer attention, they all seemed to be acting quite oddly, running into things and into each other and generally flip-flopping about purposelessly like a bunch of drunken sailors. Then it hit me—that's precisely what they were! These little party animals must have been drinking from the small pools of grape juice that had fermented alongside the road in the warm autumn sun. This is why this city smelled so strongly of burgundy. I laughed aloud. Inebriated Greek field mice—*that* was a first. In Marathon, where the fields of wilting fennel ferment into ouzo, the mice must get *really* blasted.

This moment of levity served me well, at least for a stretch, though one needed to pay close attention in this area to avoid getting lost. Abruptly, the course made a sharp left turn off a city street and onto a farm track that was completely unlit and filled with deep ruts and potholes. A wrongly placed footstep could easily wreck an ankle, or worse. Complicating matters, the downward grade progressively steepened, descending dramatically the farther we proceeded toward the Inachos Valley. Every ultramarathoner knows that the downhills are often more torturous on the quadriceps than the uphills.

Mercifully, my leg muscles were faring quite well at this point, allowing me to maintain a steady trot even on the severe and gravelly downhill grade. There had been situations in the past in which just the opposite had been true—my quadriceps were all but shot—and these were not fond memories. On a descending path one should be able to make up some time, not slow down. Who wanted that? There were enough unforeseen factors conspiring to make one vulnerable during an ultramarathon, and weak quadriceps muscles were something that seemed to be under my control, so I had decided to dedicate considerable amounts of effort during training toward strengthening my leg and core muscles to withstand such rigors.

At some distance ahead of me the dim glow of a head-lamp emerged. The shaky beam appeared to be moving up the trail pointed in my direction. As I proceeded toward the bouncing light, however, the faint disk of illumination didn't seem to be getting any closer, or if it were, it wasn't moving very quickly in my direction. Gradually as I grew nearer to this small oval of light, I realized that it wasn't coming toward me at all, but moving away from me. The runner whose head this device was mounted upon was scuffling down the trail backward.

Then I realized there was another runner directly beside him, and that this individual was facing forward. As I drew progressively nearer, I saw that the two of them had inter-locked their arms and were bracing each other as they shuf-fled along. The backward-facing runner was moaning audibly, gazing downward at his feet in an attempt to prevent falling. I don't think he even noticed me as I ran up beside them.

Pulling alongside the two, I said hello to the runner fac-ing in the forward direction. He glanced over at me and nod-ded his head a couple of times. There's a particular technique we night runners use when looking at each other while wear-ing a lighted headlamp. You don't want to look directly into someone's eyes because your light will temporarily blind them, so instead you kind of fix your head off to their side and rotate your eyeballs to make contact. Initially, I thought that's what he'd meant to do. But as we ran along together a bit longer, I realized that his neck muscles were so seized up he was incapable of twisting his head sideways.

"Are you okay?" I asked.

He responded with a couple of grousing yet cordial grunts. Judging from their appearance and from the apparel and equipment brands they were wearing, it was obvious they weren't American. Probably European, I figured, but where exactly they were from didn't matter.

"Would you like some help?" I asked.

He said something in a dialect I couldn't decipher. It was clear he didn't speak English, and after I was unable to offer a response to his statement, it must have been clear to him that I didn't speak his language, either.

Recognizing this barrier to verbal communication, I did the next best thing. Stretching my arm outward in front of us and directing the beam of my headlamp onto my hand, I gestured with the universal symbol of inquiry, a thumbs-up sign (i.e., You good?).

He shook his head back and forth a couple times (i.e., Not so good).

Then he pointed at me (i.e., you?).

I tilted my hand side to side a couple quick times in rapid succession (i.e., so-so).

He sliced his index finger across his neck like an imaginary knife (i.e., we're finished).

I put my hand upon his shoulder (i.e., sorry, man. I feel your pain).

Aristotle had said, "A friend is a single soul dwelling in two bodies." We didn't know each other. We didn't speak the same language, and we may never see each other again. But none of that mattered because for a brief moment in time we had connected on a much deeper level. It was impossible not to feel this union.

We ran together a couple minutes longer, and then I nodded to him that I was going to proceed onward. I shone my headlamp on my outstretched arm once again and continued the hand-mime, waving goodbye (i.e., until we meet again).

He smiled, moved his hand into the beam of light, and gave me a thumbs-up (i.e., Good luck, brother. May the wind be at your back).

With that shared moment I nodded farewell and started gradually peeling off ahead of them, the sounds of moaning and groaning slowly fading to a distant murmur behind me until eventually there was no sound at all, save for the soft tapping of my feet upon the ground.

Until I got closer to Lyrkeia an hour later. The Lyrkeia Taverna was alive with music; I could hear it blaring from miles away. Eventually I came upon this bustling little township of late-night revelry, and as I huffed down its crowded streets, overhead sparkled bright lights that had been strung festively along its cobbled roads and alleyways. When I came running in to the tavern, people cheered and clapped. The sweeping porch of the open-air structure stretched outward like a welcome mat. Music blared from street-side speakers, the smell of souvlaki and grilled meats drifting into the atmosphere. There was sand on the floor, which may have seemed odd because we were many miles inland and up in the mountains, except this was Greece. Every taverna, no matter how landlocked, seemed to have a generous layer of sand coating the floor as though the patrons had just come in off the beach in flip-flops.

Lyrkeia was 93 miles from Athens and a separate galaxy unto itself.

My crew was already there waiting for me. They had a table for us beneath the taverna's thatched rooftop. I plopped down in a chair and looked around. The place was mostly filled with support crew and other runners. Some of them looked ashen and nearly dead, while others were a bit better off, though not much. It was easy to distinguish the support crew and spectators from the athletes because the athletes looked like they'd been through hell. On the tables were platters of half-eaten souvlaki slathered with *tzatziki* sauce and triangular wedges of pita bread with crescent-moon-shaped bite marks out of them. Bowls of Greek salad lay strewn about, with big chunks of feta cheese, olives, tomatoes, and cucumbers coated with glistening olive oil, oregano, thyme, and

other Greek spices. During any other occasion this would
have all been delectable to me, but at the moment I felt as
though I might vomit.

I asked for the restrooms, and a waiter led me through a
narrow hallway to the back of the building where they were
located. I needed to rinse off my face, but the bathroom
wasn't such a pleasant place. The lighting inside was yellow-
brown, and the cramped interior smelled of ammonia and
stale cigarettes. Above the washbasin was a small, cloudy
mirror with badly corroded corners. Through the foggy glass
surface I peered at my reflection, inspecting my constitution
as if seeking answers. My cheeks shone like freshly lacquered
mahogany, and my hair was rumpled like an old burlap sack,
untamed and frizzing wildly at the edges. I splashed some
water on my face and it felt good, refreshing. My trapezius
muscles were aching, and I reached my hand around the
back of my neck and soothed them with the cool, slippery
liquid, rubbing the water all around. It had been a long day,
and it was sure to be a longer night. But these are the
moments I lived for. Life is at its most extraordinary during
the struggle, not during times of idle contentment, and this
was sure to be an epic contest. As horrible as I felt, and knowing that untold adversity still lay ahead, there was still something tugging at me to get going, an inner voice compelling
me onward, back into battle. I swished some water around in
my mouth and spit it in the sink. I glanced at the mirror one
last time, reassuring my own reflection that it could carry on.
Life was waiting on the outside, and it was time for me to get
back after it.

My crew reminded me that I hadn't consumed anything
in a long time. But as much as I needed to eat, losing your
guts is worse than not eating at all. It was far better to keep
the fluids I had in me, well, in me. I felt that if I ate anything,
everything would come gushing out. I had a sip of water. The
glass was coated with an oily film, the contents warm, as

though the party was over. I nodded to Nikos and Dimitris. It wouldn't be for another 15 miles until we'd meet again, and those were certain to be tough miles as I would need to scale 3,608 vertical feet up Mount Parthenion and cross over the Sangas Pass to reach the next aid station. Much as I wanted to rest, I needed to go. It was after midnight, and the hourglass was emptying. If only I could scoop a handful of sand from the floor and replace time.

Dimitris gave me a shell to wear. "Here, you'll need this," he said. "It's gonna be cold up there." I thanked him, tied the jacket around my waist, said goodbye, and made my way back onto the street.

Exiting the taverna, I noticed a runner lying on the sidewalk near a ditch. He was flat on his back with his hands folded neatly across his chest, like a pharaoh in his tomb. His crew shook their heads as I ran past. It appeared he wouldn't be going anywhere soon, probably not at all. This wasn't the most encouraging parting sight to behold as I set out to confront the toughest section of the course.

There are three capitalized letters no racer wants appearing next to his or her name on any race results, and they are DNF (Did Not Finish). But in a race of this intensity, DNF can take on an entirely different meaning: Did Nothing Fatal. As I started the approach to Mount Parthenion, I wondered to what extreme I was willing to push myself to reach Sparta. How far down was I willing to plunge into the murky nadir that separates consciousness from unconsciousness? How far would I go?

The answer was clear. Pheidippides would stop at nothing, nor would I. Death before DNF.

26

SHADOWS IN THE DARK

A racecourse elevation profile can sometimes be a mislead-ing thing. If you're unfamiliar with an elevation profile, it's basically a graph that marks the various inclines and declines along the route, with distance plotted across the bottom of the graph (known as the X-axis) and the elevation plotted up the left-hand side of the graph (known as the Y-axis). The slope of any climb can be calculated using rise over run. What can be deceiving, however, is that if the horizontal X-axis is compressed, the inclines appear to be more abrupt than they actually are. Normally as you stretch the X-axis farther across the page, the rises tend to taper (i.e., appear less vertical).

Such is not the case with the Spartathlon elevation profile. The climb up Mount Parthenion is so steep that no matter how far you elongate the X-axis, the slope still points directly skyward. It looks more like something mountain climbers would scale with ropes, pitons, and safety harnesses. So how is a runner able to scale such a steep pitch? The answer is that terracing has been cut into the mountainside. Otherwise, you probably *would* need ropes and a harness.

Known as Bey's Ladder, a series of switchbacks has been crudely hacked out of the jagged precipice so that it is possible to scale the peak on foot. The work was done during the Greek War of Independence in the early 1820s and remains largely unfortified since its original construction. As I stood at the base of this towering colossus, in order to see the top I had to tilt my head so far backward my mouth opened. It seemed to jut impossibly skyward, cold and foreboding, almost evil. There were no lights to be seen on the mountain, no dim gleam of a distant runner's headlamp, and I wondered if there was anyone else scaling this wicked, motherless rock.

There was a man sitting next to the trailhead with an antiquated lantern; he wished me luck in Greek (*kalí tíhi*). On I proceeded.

Hardly 30 paces up the mountainside the devil himself lashed out, sending a swirling downdraft of air laced with gravelly pellets hailing over me. The blast peppered my eyes with grit and coated my throat in a dusty powder. I coughed and choked, and blinked several times in an effort to clear my eyes, but blinking abraded the corneal surface and made it sting. Shaking my head, "ARR!" I growled in agony. I couldn't see. "ARR!" Oh, how I loved this shit!

Untying the shell and pulling it onto my body, I plunged into the tempest, hurling myself across stretches of loose scree, ascending serrated boulders, and navigating vast deposits of talus and shale in the moonless dark. The incline sharpened. The route became more precarious, the switchbacks tightening and weaving along the very precipice of the ledge, the pathway underfoot rough and uneven, making it difficult to identify a landing place for my foot that wouldn't crumble and break away under my weight. The pitch was frighteningly sheer, near vertical at points, and one misplaced footstep could send a runner free-falling off the mountainside. They say no runner has ever died climbing Mount Parthenion, but there's always a first.

Upward progress was extremely slow and arduous. Each step needed to be executed with a measure of exactness. Even then it was quite harrowing, especially when you considered the potential ramifications of a stumble. On several occasions I nervously hesitated and slid backward, overcompensated and jerked flat to the ground desperately gripping the earth, heart pounding. I glanced downward, and what I saw was not reassuring. That distant light of the well-wisher's lantern at the beginning of the trail was nearly directly beneath me now, as if I'd risen in an elevator to the top of a tall building and was looking over the ledge at the street below. One stumble, and the resulting plummet would almost certainly prove terminal.

Pheidippides would have had a bit clearer picture of the overall terrain. We know from Herodotus's account that the moon was approaching fullness when he undertook his historic run. Of course, this was well before the advent of flashlights, so he wouldn't have had the direct spotlight a modern headlamp provides.

Another blast of frigid air came hurling down from the darkness above as though the gods were angry. I tucked my head deep into my chest, rolling my shoulders inward, hoping to protect my eyes from the barrage of sand and spray that rained down. Fistfuls of pebbles scattered across the barren rock, popping sharply against the hard surface and ricocheting down the mountainside. My fingertips were growing increasingly numb, and each new gust of the cold, heartless wind seemed to increase the deadening sensation.

Between flurries of wind, I tried to maintain some semblance of forward progress. Each new step was slow, deliberate, and unsteady, but I did my best to remain persistent. I badly wanted off this godforsaken mountain. Step by labored step I plodded onward, confining my focus to the immediate terrain in the 2-foot radius before me, trying not to slip, muscles twitching. It freaked me out to look down at the deadly drop below. Startled, I sensed a presence nearby, as if eyes were tracking me. I turned to my left, and there, sitting on a trailside rock, was indeed a man. His dark and shadowy outline melded eerily into the mountainside. I tried to inspect him as best I could, but his body was monochrome and amorphous, making it nearly impossible to discern. Who was this man, and what was he doing here?

"Is everything okay?" I asked, looking at him sideways like a bird, not wanting to shine my light directly in his face.

There was no response. His eyes were hidden within the recesses of their sockets, and I couldn't tell where his gaze was fixed.

"Do you need help?" I questioned.

The whites of his eyes flashed before me, and the pupils were tiny slivers, like those of a goat. His face appeared angry or annoyed that I was asking him questions. Still, he offered no response.

I felt uneasy, as though I was intruding upon his space and should go. So I said goodbye and continued moving. No salutation was offered in return.

When I eventually reached the summit, there were two volunteers sitting around a small portable heating unit warming their hands. "There is a man down there that may need help," I informed them. They both looked at me curiously. "I tried to ask if he needed assistance, but he didn't respond."

They both just continued staring at me. "Did you hear me?" I asked. "There's a man down there," I said, jerking my thumb in the air pointing down the trail.

"There is no one else down there," one of them finally offered.

"Why, yes, there is. I saw him."

"You are the only runner on the mountain right now."

"How do you know that?" I asked him, puzzled.

He held up a walkie-talkie. "We're keeping track."

"How could that be? I saw someone, I tell you."

They both just looked at me, shaking their heads, saying nothing.

Was that whole thing a hallucination, I thought to myself? Was he not real? Had a contorted outcropping in the rock's surface briefly anthropomorphized before my eyes? Suddenly, I wasn't so sure myself.

"Are you positive there's no one else down there?" I asked one last time.

They both just continued inspecting me, as if looking for signs of exhaustion-induced psychosis, but saying nothing.

I stood there for a moment longer thinking about it, but I knew I had to get down off this mountaintop. My toes had grown numb, and the tips of my fingers were purple and tingly. Perhaps the cold air blurred my vision, or the grit in my eyes, though I don't think so. Maybe it wasn't a hallucination after all; maybe it was a ghost. Who knew how many men had perished on this mountain during the war. All mountaintops are sanctuaries of the gods, but this one was also a grave, with ghostly spirits haunting its crevasses and crags. I wanted out of there.

Quickly I spiraled down off the back side of the summit, following a narrow, rocky pathway that was a bit less relentless than the face of the mountain had been, though still quite unstable and tricky to navigate. The apex of Bey's Ladder crosses the main Artemision Range between Mounts Kaequria and Mavrovouni. The top of the pass peaks in 3,608 feet of nearly sheer vertical rock. Part of the reason the Spartans were able to so successfully defend their territory is that there was no easy way for an enemy to launch an attack. Crossing these mountains on foot was too perilous and impractical for an army to undertake, and the nearest port was 25 miles from the main city and situated in a notoriously hazardous section of coastline. A naval fleet would have to risk their lives just to reach the shoreline and would be in no condition to put up a fight once they got there. Sparta was virtually impenetrable and cut off from the outside world, which ultimately proved to be both good and bad.

Now that I'd been running for more than 100 miles, the steep downslope was utter torture. My once capable quadriceps, those arduously conditioned and thoroughly trained muscles that lined the front of my legs, screamed in agony. I pushed the pace nonetheless, attempting to make up lost time. My accelerated cadence wavered on the verge of destruction. For if a muscle were to cease and cramp at this moment, a severe tumble was the inevitable outcome. It was a reckless thing to do, but truthfully, my mind was becoming fatigued and increasingly careless, which can be a perilous combination during a race of this duration. Slowing would have been the prudent thing to do, but instead I sped up.

In doing so, I passed several runners along this downhill section. Some of them used hiking poles to brace themselves; others shuffled along sideways, like a crab scurrying away to safety. No words were exchanged between us. It was too intense to disrupt the focus of a fellow runner.

In scarcely more than a mile's distance from the summit, the course plummeted some 1,800 feet (that's higher than the Empire State Building) straight down and over fragmented stone and loose gravel. The rugged pathway eventually deposited me in the remote outpost of Sangas and then proceeded onward toward Nestani along an undulating, potholed road that rose and fell over the outlying foothills. My crew was waiting for me there. It had taken nearly 5 hours to cover those 15 impossible miles.

The air was damp and chilly when I arrived. A slight mist hung in the valley, and dew had formed on the surfaces of nearly everything. They offered me a seat, but I didn't want to sit for fear of never being able to get back up. "Beware of the chair," as they say in ultrarunning circles. I took my headlamp off and massaged my temples. The aching was bottomless, inescapably infinite. If my crew harbored any previous doubts that I was unraveling, they now knew with certainty that such was the case. Slowly, bit by bit, I was disintegrating into fragments.

"Can you eat?" Dimitris asked.

I shook my head no, too exhausted to answer. I looked around. Everybody appeared tired and heavy-eyed, even the volunteers. The whole atmosphere was drowsy, and I wanted to lie down, to disappear into a quiet slumber, but I knew that would be the kiss of death. I shook the cobwebs from my head and readied myself to depart.

"You're going to leave?" Nikos asked.

I shook my head in affirmation, again too tired to offer up any words.

"It will be light soon," Dimitris offered. "Though it's still pretty wet and cold; I think you ought to keep the shell."

"When will I see you again?" I asked.

"In Tegea."

"Okay," I said, and headed out. I had no idea where Tegea was. I wasn't sure if it was even in the same hemisphere, or cosmos. My world was slowly deconstructing, until there was nothing left except the primitive act of putting one foot in front of the other and repeating that action over and over again. Remain on course, I told myself, and just keep putting one foot in front of the other, one foot in front of the other. There are two ways to cope with pain. One is to put your head down and grunt through it. I didn't know the other way. With my head lowered, I trudged forward. I didn't have to go fast, I just had to go.

27

GO GREEK OR GO HOME

Dawn is the bewitching hour during an all-night run.
Alertness slips to a low, and a sleep-inducing lethargy
overtakes the system. As I ran through the misty predawn
dreamscape of the Arcadian foothills, it remained a fight
just to stay awake, as if tranquilizers had been infused into
my bloodstream and small weights quietly attached to my
eyelids. Lower and lower the shades drew across my field
of vision.

Thump . . . thump . . . thump, the monotonous, rhythmic
pulse of footsteps droned on metrically, like a vinyl record
skipping a groove. Slowly, ever so gradually, my eyelids
drooped downward, gradually darkening out what little light
was left coming in. Still, I pressed on.

When I reopened my eyes, I found myself in the middle
of the road. "What the heck?" I thought. I knew better than
to place myself in that kind of danger. So I meandered back
over to the shoulder and continued onward.

Then it happened again. I awoke, running down the middle of the road. That's when I realized that I was sleep running. I was literally falling asleep on the run. I was so

determined to keep going that I didn't fall over or stop. I just continued running, willing my body onward, while asleep. How long I had been asleep and how much distance I had covered while in this state of nocturnal locomotion was difficult to ascertain (after all, I'd been asleep), but it was more than just a few short steps, and when I looked back to trace the spot of my last conscious recollection, it appeared to be quite some distance behind me, perhaps several hundred feet. Shocking!

Even more startling was the realization that after this second bout of comatose running I reemerged feeling somewhat refreshed and rejuvenated, as though my body needed rest so desperately it had forced itself into a temporary shutdown mode to allow the cerebral network to reboot. After these two brief catnaps, I now felt a bit more coherent.

I've since talked with other ultramarathoners who have experienced similar episodes of cataleptic nocturnal locomotion (i.e., sleep running). I've also read accounts of people in war-torn regions falling asleep in motion while trying to escape an enemy pursuer. And there are reports of combat soldiers having fallen asleep on the battlefield with one eye open, in watchful observation of potential threats during intense military conflicts.

Unihemispheric slow-wave sleep (USWS), or asymmetric slow-wave sleep, refers to the ability to put half of one's brain to sleep while the other half remains awake. In contrast to normal sleep, in which both eyes are shut and both halves of the brain show reduced neural activity, during USWS only half of the brain is in deep sleep—a form of non–rapid eye movement sleep—and the eye corresponding to that particular half remains closed while the opposing eye remains slightly ajar. This phenomenon has not only been observed in chronically fatigued humans but also in a number of other terrestrial, aquatic, and airborne species, such as the swallows of

California and Baja California, during extensive, transconti-
nental migrations in which they might go weeks or even
months in motion without completing a single sleep cycle.

As the light of the looming sunrise progressively brightened the sky, my drowsiness subtly abated. The damp chill in
the air lingered thick in the lowlands, and the morning stillness idly held this mist in an aerosol-like spray that coated
my skin and hair in a fine layer of moisture. I shook my head
back and forth several times, sending a shower of condensa-
tion from my hair, the crystalline dewdrops temporarily suspended in the fiery flare of the rosy-fingered dawn.

The road began to rise onto the high, flat plateau above
Arcadia. The course proceeded through several sleepy villages and fertile groves of orchards, the fruit of which had
been in existence since the time of Pheidippides's own travels.
Given Herodotus's record, Pheidippides would have likely
passed through this very same section of Arcadia in these
same early morning hours, just as we were doing then.
Would he have eaten from these same trees? To think that an
ancient hemerodromos was running here 2,500 years ago fascinated me, and knowing that this was the land of my ancestral origins made the experience all the more visceral. I was
connected to this place in ways I could not know. My forebears
had walked these fields, tending to these very trees. The
ancient Greeks believed they were of this land, soil-sprung.
They hadn't come here from somewhere else; they were
autochthonous (earth-born), and this was the place of their origins, forever and always since the dawn of humanity. Formed
from white rock and blue sea, my ancestors raised their families in this land, fostered their hopes and dreams here, generation upon generation coming into and passing through life
in these same hills and plains that I now ran through. This
was their land, and in a timeless way, this was also my land.

Just as I was fully realizing the depth of my connection to

this place, a large diesel truck came barreling down the highway straight for me, interrupting my reflections and thrusting me back into the present-day reality of the modern Spartathlon. It was a stark reminder that while some things hadn't changed since ancient times, other things had. I veered off to the side of the road to avoid being hit by this 18-wheeled monstrosity as it roared past in an ear-splitting thunder.

Perhaps the only redeeming factor of having to run down these heavily trafficked roadways was that the loud roar of an approaching vehicle's engine could always be heard well in advance, thus providing sufficient notice that danger was fast approaching. There were no stealthy electric vehicles that snuck up on you without audible forewarning. Few Teslas traversed these byways (or one, even).

As the truck chugged past, it kicked up a small hailstorm of throat-choking particulates into the surrounding atmosphere, and I got a hardy taste of fresh morning air (yes, I'm being facetious). However, such was an unpleasant necessity for enduring the Spartathlon. Given that the race took place mostly on tarmac, there was no way to avoid these disagreeable encounters; they were all part of the challenge. I wasn't made for such accosting, but then again, what human was? We had created a world reliant on commerce for our very survival, and these modern machines were the muscles that powered such trade. In some ways we runners of the Spartathlon didn't seem right for this world. We were the ancient messengers that would have carried critical information, the force that would have driven trade between distant populations over mountains and valleys. We belonged to a place and time 2,500 years in the past.

Upward crept the sun, first cracking the eastern horizon and then moving higher into the sky. Temperatures warmed quickly, the cool predawn mist replaced by a muggy humidity that hung stagnant in the motionless air. Like most runners', my body glinted with a salty residue that abraded the flesh wherever fabric contacted skin. Much of enduring an ultramarathon is about how one manages and deals with minor miseries, and chafing is one unavoidable unpleasantness most athletes simply learn to bear. While it isn't severe enough to end a run, it is another contributing factor added to the expanding list of distresses. Over time, these minor maladies begin to exact a toll.

Warmer the day evolved. Brighter the sky shone, and more intense the piercing rays of the Southern Mediterranean sun became. At several checkpoints along the way I grabbed a cupful of water, managing to take small sips as I moved along, sometimes dumping the entire thing over my head. More runners appeared. Some sat slumped and motionless in chairs or were lying in cots at the aid stations, while others hobbled along, their limbs looking anesthetized as if half dead. A few of them tried to talk to me in labored, broken English. The gist of their message was a familiar one; they had read one of my books and were attempting to express their gratitude. Many of the themes in my writing are identifiable to any runner, regardless of the language one speaks, the color of one's skin, or the god one worships. This sacred brother- and sisterhood between runners is a bond we share. Although I had never met any of these fellow runners, they knew me, knew my family, knew of my struggles and joys. They intimately related to my story because it was also *their* story. Regardless of what place it was we occupied in this world, we shared the same emotions and experiences, and this commonality united us in a way that words could never adequately convey. Not even in my books.

The day wore on and the miles piled up, the bright glare of the sun distorting the landscape in a rippling mirage. The course seemed to go on and on endlessly, slowly pounding me into submission and demanding that I go to some deeper place to find the resolve needed to continue forging onward.

To finish the Spartathlon, you must give yourself up to it entirely. The pain had become so intense that I thought I would collapse, and then it went away . . .

The ancient Greek theologian Plotinus observed that when bodily pain seems beyond endurance, it can lead to a spiritual cleansing that obliterates the face of time until whole eons fall away like dead leaves from a tree. Those who have moved beyond the physical confines of pain have left the flesh and entered the illimitable realm of the spirit. I'd been running for more than 26 hours by this point, and my body was slowly moving beyond fatigue and exhaustion into a meditative transcendence. Step by step, I was departing from my corporeal body, losing my sense of identity, and slipping further into the province of spirit. It was a most glorious dismantling of self. My feet still clipped along, my arms still swung back and forth, and my chest still heaved, but my mind had largely relinquished jurisdiction. I was at once both vulnerable and powerful, a physical presence moving through this earth, though largely defenseless and exposed. An ultramarathon is a way to engage intimately with the world and at the same time escape from it.

The blasting of a car horn jolted me back to reality.

"*Focus, Karnazes! Focus!*" I told myself, a shot of adrenaline coursing through my veins. Wandering into oncoming traffic is never a good idea, especially when your mind is someplace else.

The Spartathlon was at once magnificent and repulsive. For every breathtaking Hellenic panorama and ebullient checkpoint volunteer came a contrasting dose of vile hideousness, each momentous high eventually eviscerated by a seemingly bottomless low. Why do men sail such seas, I wondered? Why not stay safely moored inside the harbor, sheltered from the storm? No one was forcing us at gunpoint to be out there, so why put ourselves through such intense suffering? The answer is that we Spartathletes seek to unlock a gateway that carries us deeper into the mysterious underworld of the human psyche, a place where great adventures await, yet shadowy dangers lurk. The battle is always within, and the Spartathlon provides a rare portal into oneself, a revealing glimpse at our true nature. Suffering provides a road to truth. This is where life is lived to its fullest, bare and susceptible yet completely engaged and whole, navigating the course when one is able and being carried by the tides when one is not. As the great explorer Marco Polo noted, the bold may not live forever, but the timid do not live at all. It is terrifying to let yourself go so completely, pushing your mind and body so far that virtually all control is lost. Yet it is also purifying. Confronting your fears helps makes you holy. That is why we ran the Spartathlon.

Tegea was once an important city in the Peloponnese, home to many writers, historians, and lyric poets, with an impressive stadium and a spectacular theater constructed entirely of brilliant white marble. My crew was there, waiting for me, though there was little they could offer. I sat with them for a moment, massaging my throbbing temples once again. More books appeared before me and I signed them. People crouched next to me to snap selfies. I smiled, though rather emptily, incapable of responding to the muffled noise and the flashes of light exploding in my face, staring blankly ahead like a deer caught in headlights.

Tegea sat 121 miles from the start. Word came to me that the American ultrarunning champion Jon Olsen had succumbed to heel problems and stomach issues and had dropped out. Jon was clearly no stranger to overcoming obstacles and dealing with adversity; it was thus a sobering reminder that even an athlete of extraordinary caliber could be stopped by this race. Learning his fate only reinforced the fact that absolutely no certainty exists with the Spartathlon, no givens or foregone conclusions can be drawn, regardless of one's skill. Failure is a very real possibility. I wondered how Dave was faring. Had he found his Coke and ice?

A tap on the shoulder disrupted my introspection. "Would you like some gum?" An older gentleman stood above me, and I nodded my head in affirmation. He handed me a piece. I popped it in my mouth and started to chew.

"Mastic?" I looked at him, "This is mastic, isn't it?"

"Indeed it is."

Harvested from a resin secreted by the ancient mastic tree, it tastes bitter at first, but after some chewing releases a refreshing, pine-cedar flavor. Mastic is said to have medicinal properties and grows on the southern side of the remote Greek island of Chios. I hadn't had a piece since I was an altar boy at Saint Sophia Greek Orthodox Church, where the priests used to chew mastic to moisturize their mouths prior to delivering a sermon. We all knew where they kept their private stash, in a small bowl behind the *epitafio*, and we would occasionally sneak a piece ourselves. Having a piece of mastic now tasted good, rejuvenating both for the mouth and for the soul.

"How do you feel?" the man asked.

"Not so good. It's been rough going, and it's sure to get rougher."

"Will you make it?"

"I'm not sure, but if I don't, they'll be carrying me off on a stretcher."

"Attaboy! You make us proud, Kostas. Remember the words of Winston Churchill?"

"Won't ever forget 'em."

Upon learning of Greek battle victories over the Germans despite insuperable odds, Churchill once quipped, "Hence, we will not say that Greeks fight like heroes, but that heroes fight like Greeks."

This had not been my best race. Far from it. I wouldn't be setting any records or achieving any of my personal goals, either. But what mattered most now was finishing what I'd started. I had to make it to Sparta.

Sure, there were other competitors in the race and the clock was ticking, but inevitably an ultramarathon is not a race against others or against a stopwatch; it is a match against oneself, a contest of you versus you. I knew my body well, knew how hard I could push it without going over the edge, because I'd pushed myself over the edge before. For it is only in knowing our limits that we can move beyond them, and I was adept at toeing that fine line between consciousness and collapse. At least I thought I was, just as every drunk believes he can drive a car.

At this juncture the paradigm had shifted from worrying about race results to merely getting the job done. I hadn't come here to start the race, but to finish it. As Aristotle once said, "Well begun is half done." Downshifting into a death march would be necessary if I were to harbor any hope of reaching the finish line. "Do what you can," Coach Wooden had counseled me. Shuffle to the best of your ability, I told myself, but do not stop. This is what it would take to reach Sparta, and I would do that which was necessary. When the music changes, so must the dance.

"I won't give up without a fight," I told the giver of mastic. "And now that battle must be fought."

I stood up, shook myself off, and prepared to give it everything I had, just as Pheidippides surely did. Go Greek or go home, even if that means in a body bag.

He looked at me amusingly. "From your lips to God's ears," he said.

Aid station sponge bath

28

THE TIDES THROUGH WHICH WE MOVE

I f you want to run, run a mile. If you want to experience a different life, run a marathon. If you want to talk to God, run an ultra. Five miles out from Tegea where that conversation was initiated the world began taking on a nebulous, pixilated quality. The surrounding landscape and fields of *horta* undulated to and fro like seaweed gently swaying in an ocean current. There was a shrill ringing in my ears like the high-pitched sound of an electrical wire, and it eventually drowned out all background noise and cast me inward, as if concealed within my own cocoon. Sensations and thoughts disappeared, bodily proprioception abated into thin air until little, if any, remained. I felt oddly removed—not present—as though held in an episodic déjà vu that wouldn't take place until sometime in the future.

Events unfolded before me, though I was strangely unaffected by them. I simply flowed down the road perceiving the occurrences as they happened, and that was all. Gone was the filter of ego, that internal voice which is perpetually evaluating situations as to how they might impact the self. For this is how we live, is it not? Are we not constantly processing and

analyzing incoming observations and episodes for the effect
they have upon us? Is what's happening positive for me, or
negative? we question. Is what I'm seeing, hearing, or feeling
potentially helpful, or harmful? Whether we are consciously
aware of it or not, the ego is incessantly scrutinizing events to
evaluate the consequences they have upon us. Perhaps this is
an evolutionary adaptation, but we are instinctually pro-
grammed for self-preservation.

But at this moment of time all of that fell away; there was
no such appraisal taking place any longer. And, in a mysterious sort of way, it was freeing. I was liberated from the self,
released from the burden of thought and worry, at one with
the universe and in synchronicity with the world, simply
floating along through space and time, detached from the
unbearable heaviness of being.

Slipping deeper into this fuzzy state of corporeal discon-
nection, a warm, flush feeling rushed over me. And then I
noticed something unexplainable on the earth below. Initially
the vision was hazy and formless, but as I peered more
intently at the image below me, it began to materialize and
take shape. There was a runner down there. I could see the
top of his head, and I could watch as his hair blew backward
in the wind. I observed his arms pumping like pistons and
could see the front of his left foot and then the front of his
right foot jutting outward with each forward stride.

The harder I peered, the more this form galvanized, yet
my vantage point was steadily drifting upward and away
from this animated emoji jogging below me. Higher and
higher I rose into the sky, as if I were being lifted in a hot air
balloon, the strutting stick man below becoming increasingly
diminutive the farther my viewpoint elevated skyward. The
higher I rose, the broader the perspective of the landscape
expanded until I could eventually see the entire region of
countryside all around. Then it occurred to me that this
place looked vaguely familiar, as if I'd been there before. I

must have been seated in a helicopter, or riding in an airship.

Yet something seemed strangely amiss with the picture, too. Something just wasn't right. I contemplated the scene, mentally deliberating what was going on, mulling over the illogicality of it all. But my mind seemed that of a child and could not form a rational understanding of the situation. There was this gnawing feeling in my gut that I was somehow more involved in the scenario than it appeared, but I could not comprehend how.

Then it struck me. That runner down below me was me.

I'd never had an out-of-body experience (OBE) before. Truthfully, I thought this to be the domain of mystics and clairvoyants, those who practiced intense meditation or who experimented with hallucinogenic drugs. I've since read reports of athletes engaged in extreme physical exertion—high-altitude climbing, deep-sea diving, endurance cycling—experiencing sensations of levitation. However, slight feelings of floating are one thing. Actually perceiving your body's location from a remote vantage point is a far greater magnitude of departure.

Autoscopy, as it is known, comes from the ancient Greek αὐτός (self) and σκοπός (watcher), and the term refers to the phenomenon in which an individual, while believing himself to be awake, sees his body's position from outside of his body. The impression of seeing the world from an elevated visuo-spatial viewpoint or extracorporeal perspective is most frequently observed in near-death experiences, in hospitalized victims suffering from traumatic medical emergencies or in those individuals with life-threatening illnesses.

While I remember most of the Spartathlon vividly, I have no recollection of certain segments along this stretch of the course, as though entire chunks of data were wiped from my mind or were never recorded in the first place. Sports psychologists talk about the importance of positive self-talk, but what happens when the voice inside your head goes silent?

The noise and chatter had gone quiet within, and I'd slipped into some bizarre deeper state of being. I don't think I was dead during that episode, though I wasn't fully alive, either. I was somewhere in between. It wasn't a markedly unpleasant experience, nor was it a resoundingly pleasant one. It just was. I can only articulate these things after the fact, when I possess the cognitive reasoning to reflect on the occurrence. At the moment in time, my mind seems to be unplugged and there is only a state of quiet nothingness.

Back on the Spartathlon route, the course had steadily climbed to an elevation nearly that of Bey's Ladder—some 3,200 feet—high above Tegea, though I don't remember any of it. It's all gone, removed. We passed through the small townships of Kamari and Manthirea, where the paved road twisted and turned through an evergreen landscape, though I scarcely remember any of that, either. But now, under a blazing sun, as I began the long descent into the Eurotas Valley, flickers of comprehension came bursting through periodically, like bright glimmers of luminosity popping off a crackling sparkler. Dimitris reminded me I hadn't put anything in my mouth in a long time (I heard his voice, at least, but don't remember seeing him). Cars honked as they drove past, people waving and hollering out the windows, checkpoints appeared and then disappeared. Sometimes I was keenly aware of my surroundings; other times I was not. I'd run 150 miles and was wholly consumed by the desire to will myself across that finish line.

There came a point where I found it almost impossible to put one foot in front of the other, and that's when everything that mattered most in my life became clear. I was there because I had to be. It was my destiny, my calling. In so many ways these were the most glorious footsteps of my life, yet in other ways they were the most unrelenting grunt work I'd ever undertaken, and a damn tough way to make a living. Like Greece itself, the Spartathlon had been a dichotomous experience.

From a competitive standpoint my performance was well below par. I knew this, and I was disappointed in that regard. But I also knew I must still conduct myself as a disheartened champion would. My personal ethos demanded that I always demonstrate *arête* and uphold my bestness, no matter how weakened my state. As the legendary ancient Greek athlete Archilochus once expounded, "O heart, my heart, no public leaping when you win; no solitude nor weeping when you fail to prove. Rejoice at simple things and . . . know the tides through which we move."

Paraphrasing Thomas Cahill in *Sailing the Wine Dark Sea,* "the tides through which we move . . . " is a chilling reminder that nothing lasts forever, that life ebbs and flows but eventually all is swept away by the currents of eternity. Let our temperament be humble in both glory and in defeat, let us maintain modesty in times of high achievement and honor in times of heartbreaking failure, and let us never forget that the illusion of permanence can deceive and that all things have their place and time but must inevitably come to an end. If we may conduct our life in accordance with this eternal truism, there is nothing more; we have lived life as best we can.

A procession of fans was waiting to escort me from the edge of town. Some drove scooters, some road bicycles, and others ran next to me. All were talking at once, asking me questions and hooting at spectators along the sidelines. Kids darted back and forth, nearly tripping me, screaming and laughing all the while. People cheered and clapped, "Bravo! Bravo Kostas!"

As we rounded the last corner and came running up the final stretch of roadway toward the finish, that cacophony and chaos of banter transformed into a melodious rapture. The pageantry of those last few steps is impossible to describe. I just glided inward as if surfing on clouds. To finish the Spartathlon race, you do something unique within the sporting world. There is no finish line to cross, no mat to step over or tape to break; instead, you conclude the journey by touching the feet of the towering bronze statue of King Leonidas in the center of town. The mayor of Sparta places an olive branch coronet upon the head of each finisher, and you are handed a golden goblet of water from the Holy River of Eurotas, just as Pheidippides had been given. There is no race finish as spectacular as that of the Spartathlon, and there will never be. This is it, the genuine article, the place it all began. Nothing will ever top it. Ever.

Pheidippides would have met with the equivalent of the mayor in his day, only that man would have been the king. Exhausted as he must have been from his long journey, his job was not yet complete. After arriving in Sparta, Pheidippides would then have to present a compelling case for why the Spartans should join the Athenians in battle. He'd have to pull himself together and appear poised and articulate, communicating with clarity and coherence. Herodotus recorded the moment thus:

Men of Sparta, the Athenians beseech you to hasten to their aid, and not allow that state, which is the most ancient in all of Greece, to be enslaved by the barbarians.

Apparently his plea was convincing, for it worked. The Spartan leaders agreed to bring their army to Athens to join forces against the Persians.

I was ushered into the medical tent for a mandatory racer's assessment. It was stifling inside and reeked like a public urinal. I've been through many postrace medical checks before, but never had I witnessed anything quite like this place. The scene was shocking, total carnage. Some runners were slumped over with their heads buried deep between their knees while others lay lifelessly on cots with IVs protruding from their arms. Many had splints or temporary casts on their legs, blood and sputum were splattered everywhere, drip bags hung like grapes on a vine, soft cries and moans echoed throughout, and people coughed and wheezed uncontrollably. Medics wearing surgical gloves darted about frantically trying to attend to all the wounded. One of them stopped and looked at me. "Were you in the race?" he asked. I nodded my head. "My God, you don't even look tired."

"Then may I go?" I felt like I was just getting in the way of things.

He excused me, and I stepped out onto the streets of Sparta. There was an assemblage of people waiting for me. They had more books and posters and another batch of things for me to sign. Many had driven for hours to meet me here. Some had come from islands on boats, and they wanted pictures and had special notes for me. Some even brought gifts and homemade platters of food to eat. I'd been running for nearly 35 hours straight, and a long line had formed to get my signature. My journey to Greece and the uncovering of my roots had been a transformative revelation, and the Spartathlon experience was the crowning jewel. Yet the race hadn't been easy. Although I was grateful for having finished, I was disappointed with my performance. But such were the tides through which I moved. There would be "no solitude nor weeping." Not now, not ever. *Sto kalo*, to the good. I would stand here until sunset signing things, smiling for photos, talking with others while holding my head high. These people had traveled far to see me. And now I realized, with great clarity, that I had traveled my entire lifetime to see them.

Finish of Spartathon with statue of King Leonidas in background.

29

THE TROPHY

Ivan Cudin of Italy won the race in 26 hours and 18 minutes, and Sugawara Hideo of Japan concluded the race in
35:57:03, fewer than 3 minutes before the cutoff. Somewhere
along the road, the hopes and dreams of 146 racers lay
dashed. They never reached Sparta; the sand in the hourglass
had run dry.

The drive back to Athens from Sparta was long, but I
was with my crew, and it was the first time I was able to formally thank them for their support during the race. Dimitris
said he'd never witnessed anything like it before. Like what, I
wondered? After all, he'd been at hundreds of races and was
the publisher of an ultrarunning magazine. He'd crewed for
the women's race winner, Lizzy Hawker, just the year before.
What could be so unique about the experience this time?

"All you had for the last 75 miles was water. You never
ate anything."

I explained to him that I couldn't. The nausea, you know.

"I know, I saw. But how you were able to get to that finish without eating anything was amazing. I've never seen
anything like it."

"Guess I just ran on stored reserves?"

"Oh no, I think it was more than that."

Perhaps it was. Perhaps I was simply acting out my destiny. Perhaps I needed to be at that finish line as much as I needed air itself. Something beyond my body carried me to Sparta, and I think we all sensed that.

My flight left early the next morning. I was due back in the United States to give a talk. As much as I would have preferred to stay in Greece a while longer, it was not meant to be. Life moved faster than I desired it to. Strangely, though, as we sat there preparing for takeoff, my mind was quieted. I was content. Somewhere along humanity's cultural progression we seem to have confused comfort with contentment, but I now realized that contentment doesn't come from comfort; contentment comes from living through great discomfort. As the plane's landing gear tucked up neatly into its compartment, I looked out the window one last time to see a shimmering sunrise over the mountaintops beyond Agios, rays of golden light beaming skyward into the heavens above. Once again, I sat awestruck by the majesty of this timeless land. Greece is a place for lovers, and Greece is a place for dreamers. Greece is a place for those who seek, and Greece is a place for those who seek escape. Greece is a place you go to lose yourself, and Greece is a place you go to find yourself. I had set out to find Pheidippides, and in the process I had found myself.

"Men search out God and searching find him," Aeschylus once said. This had been my search.

The long flight back to reality wasn't bad; my muscles weren't too sore and recovery came quickly. Part of the reason for this, I knew, was because I'd scaled back on my pace so drastically during the Spartathlon, downshifting into a lower gear and sacrificing performance for the certainty of finishing. I did what needed to be done to reach Sparta. My body could better tolerate this reduced output, and the amount of muscle and tissue destruction was thus minimized.

I learned that Dave had also gotten the job done. He said he'd probably drunk an entire case of Coke during the race, but he finished. It's amazing what a little sugar and caffeine can get a guy through (okay, a lot of sugar and caffeine). I did what I needed to do, and he did the same. *Philotimo* (respect and honor).

Here is the juncture where this book should end. It's the perfect Hollywood conclusion, is it not? The story contained a bit of drama, a little conflict, some ups and downs, but in the end all ended happily ever after. But there's a hitch, a meddlesome fly in the olive oil, if you will. You see, for one of the main characters involved in the plot there is still much unfinished business to contend with, for not everything in Sparta was as it seemed.

The issue, you see, is that the moon wasn't full.

You might be wondering why that matters. So what if the moon was half full, three-quarters full, or entirely full? Who cares? Well, the ancient Spartans cared. And they cared a lot, for established Spartan religious law forbade them from leaving for battle until the Karneian moon was at its fullest. These were men of great tradition, and not even the threat of pending annihilation would alter their principles.

This fact posed an interesting predicament for Pheidippides. Yes, the Spartans agreed to his request to come to Athens and battle the Persians, just not as quickly as the Athenians had hoped. The moon wouldn't be full for another 6 days' time. The Spartans were a people given to unflinching religious devotion, and Pheidippides would extend them all due respect in this regard. But at the same time, the situation was dire and their delay was horribly problematic, for in 6 days' time the Athenians might already be slaughtered by the Persians. Pheidippides had to let his people know about the delay, for such information could prove critical to the outcome of the war. So he did the unthinkable. After a brief cat-nap and some food, he awoke before sunrise and set out on the return trip of some 140 miles back to Athens. He had to let his countrymen know of the Spartan delay. After all, he was a messenger, and carrying news was his job. And never had there been more important news than this to carry.

The Spartans bid him farewell and assured him that in 6 days' time—when the moon was at its fullest—they would march for battle.

It may seem unimaginable that after running from Athens to Sparta, a man could pick back up and embark upon a return journey, but that is precisely what Pheidippides did. He was a man of duty, and whether or not he was in any physical condition to carry out this added task was irrelevant. He would do what needed to be done. And so off he ran.

One can imagine that his constitution would have been fairly compromised; I'd experienced this myself. Running from Athens to Sparta in the earth-scorching heat would render any man weakened, even the fittest of the fit. Now, operating on little sleep, Pheidippides found himself trudging back over a mountain pass in the Parthenion range high above Tegea. He'd already put a significant distance between himself and Sparta and was likely in a state of suspended delirium, when suddenly he had a vision of the god Pan standing before him. With the face of a human, but the body, feet, and horns of a goat, Pan was an unsettling figure to behold. What did this mountaintop god want?

Pan explained that while he still maintained loyalty to the Athenians, they must worship him properly in order to preserve the alliance. Pan had great powers that could distress and unravel an enemy; he would bestow the Athenians with these abilities, but only if they were to revere him as they should, as the god he was. Just as unexpectedly as this vision had occurred, the great god disappeared. But the sentiments Pan conveyed were not lost on Pheidippides.

Herodotus described this scene some 2,500 years ago; I wondered if that eerie presence I had encountered that night while high on the mountain ridge during the Spartathlon could have been this same ghostly god-creature. Was it a hallucination, or was it something more?

With unfathomable strength of body, mind, and spirit, Phei-

dippides arrived back in Athens in 2 days' time. However, the
Athenian citizens were gravely concerned when he showed up
unaccompanied. Where were the Spartans? Their hopes for
survival seemed dependent on Spartan reinforcements, but
these legendary warriors were nowhere to be seen. This was not
welcome news. Fear spread amongst the citizenry; what would
be their fate? An ominous cloud of anxiety and unrest pervaded
the city. The Spartans wouldn't be departing for 4 more days.

Pheidippides was informed that after he'd been dispatched to run to Sparta, the Athenian forces decided to
deploy to Marathon. Knowing this, he realized that despite
just having run to and from Sparta, he must immediately run
another 25 miles to the plains of Marathon to inform General
Miltiades and the Athenian forces of the Spartan delay. Talk
about no rest for the weary! Endurance never sleeps.

When he arrived in Marathon, the sight before him was
horrific. The entire plain was filled with Persian troops and
cavalry. Their encampment stretched for nearly as far as the
eye could see. To say the Greeks were the underdogs would be
putting it mildly. Most of the roughly 10,000 adult male Athenian citizens had mobilized to fend off the Persians, but it has
been estimated that there were as many as 50,000 Persians.
The Greeks were badly outnumbered, perhaps five to one.

Pheidippides found General Miltiades and the other
Greeks holed up in the foothills of the Pentele mountain
range overlooking the enemy encampment. They had sat in
this position for days, awaiting Pheidippides's and the Spartans's arrival. During that time, General Miltiades had kept
close observation over the Persian operations. He knew when
they arose in the morning and how long their deployment
lasted. Since the Persians tethered and hobbled their horses at
night, in the morning a groomsman had to untie them, feed
them, and prepare their saddlecloths and bridles. Doing these
things took time. Additionally, Miltiades noted, there existed
only one narrow pathway down to where the horses were
kept at night, so to deploy the cavalry into battle, they would

need to funnel them through this small gap. He thus surmised that in an urgent rush to fight, this slender exit would
create a massive bottleneck that would considerably slow the
release of both men and horses. General Miltiades was
already getting into the heads of the Persians.

Pheidippides delivered the message about the Spartan
delay. He also told about his encounter with Pan on the
mountaintop high above Tegea. This was taken as good news
and provided hope to the Athenians, for Pan would bring
them strength.

In their current position nestled along the Pentele mountain ridgetops, the Athenians held an advantageous battle
position over the Persians, one that blockaded the main
access point that led from Marathon to Athens. Even though
his forces were badly outnumbered, General Miltiades knew
the Persian leaders wouldn't attempt to launch an uphill
attack against a superior Greek position. He just needed to
wait for the Spartans to arrive. The military intelligence Pheidippides provided about the timing of the Spartan deployment had proved pivotal.

For a suspended moment of time, let us briefly digress to
dissect the genesis of the historical record. Herodotus mentions that after convening with the Spartans, Pheidippides
returned to Athens and then carried on to Marathon. The
narrative on this topic is delivered in concise, unelaborated
passages. In Herodotus's day, running great distances without rest was the work of a hemerodromos, that's all. His non-
chalance in describing Pheidippides's task likely resulted from
him stereotyping the role of all heralds as performing a similar duty, which necessitated no further examination of what it
meant, specifically, for a man to run 300 or more miles nearly
continuously. Further, because he was a scholar living some
50 years after Pheidippides, I doubt Herodotus would have
been a runner himself, and thus he would have lacked any
firsthand knowledge of what it meant for a human to undertake such a grueling endeavor. Instead, his cursory summation

was that a herald did what a herald did, and that was that.

Following Herodotus's lead, modern academics and historians have similarly adopted what could rightfully be considered a discounted appreciation of Pheidippides's feat. They have assigned great importance to the Battle of Marathon, but simply make perfunctory mention that some guy named Pheidippides, or Philippides, or Feidippideios or whomever, ran from Athens to Sparta, and then from Sparta to Marathon, via Athens. They cite this extraordinary accomplishment as if it were a casual stroll to the neighbors' house to borrow a cup of flour.

My point is that the annals of history have grossly under-recognized the significance of Pheidippides's superhuman act. It's no fault of anyone's, really; ultramarathoning is somewhat of an obscure activity, and it requires a fair amount of specialized knowledge and experience in the subject to provide any meaningful commentary or probing analysis on what it took to do what Pheidippides did. After having chased Pheidippides through the mountains and valleys of this ancient landscape, I can confidently assert that what he did was absolutely miraculous.

But back to the plains of Marathon. Having received the intelligence from Pheidippides about the Spartan delay, the Greeks hunkered down to await their arrival. The next evening, however, something completely unexpected happened. Under the cloak of darkness, two men on foot appeared at the Greek enclave. These men, it turns out, were fellow Greeks from the island of Eretria, which had been overthrown and captured by the Persians. They'd been taken hostage during the Persian siege of their island and were enslaved into forced labor by the enemy. Risking their lives, the pair had escaped from their captor that evening because there was urgent news they desperately needed to convey to their Greek countrymen.

The Persians, the Eretrians said, were up to something sneaky. They planned to divide into two groups, half their ranks setting sail in the morning around Attica to launch a surprise attack on Athens from the opposite coastline at the Bay of Phaleron, while the other half of the Persian forces were to remain at Marathon to keep the Greek army pinned down in their current position in the hills.

Now the Greeks were in trouble. The most prudent strategy in the face of this new Persian ploy would have been for General Miltiades and his army to immediately retreat to Athens to defend the city from this vantage point, as the Spartans were soon to arrive and could join the fight. Only, the Spartans weren't soon to arrive. Knowing this crucial piece of information changed everything.

Had Pheidippides not arrived in Marathon and delivered his news about the delayed Spartan departure, the Greeks would have retreated back to Athens only to wait in vain for the no-show Spartans, and without Spartan reinforcements the Athenians would have been hung out to dry, for alone they posed no match against this new, doubled-pronged Persian attack. Pheidippides saved the day. His message about the Spartan delay proved essential in averting what would have been certain catastrophe.

If returning to Athens in the absence of Spartan reinforcements was not a viable option, then what was the right thing to do? After great thought, General Miltiades decided that the Athenians would wake early the next morning and attack the current Persian position before they awoke and had time to set sail. It was the best thing to do given all of the dynamics at play. He gathered his troops around for a late-night briefing and explained to them that they were going to slightly alter their normal battle approach given the uniqueness of the situation and the distinctive configuration of the battlefield. The Greeks fought with shields and long, thrusting spears. They usually lined up in a tight phalanx formation, each man locking shields with his neighbor to form a seamless yet malleable continuous sheet of armor not unlike the interconnected protective shell of an armadillo. Plutarch described the phalanx as looking like "some ferocious cornered creature, stiffening its bristles as it turns to face its foe."

The Athenian phalanx was typically eight lines deep, but in this instance General Miltiades decided to thin the middle to four lines deep and reinforce the flanks with these additional layers. He also explained that instead of marching, they would need to move much quicker in this formation. In fact, they would need to run at the enemy. This innovative battle approach was unprecedented; no one had ever dared to charge the Persians head-on before. Miltiades reminded his men that they were fighting not just for their own lives, but also for the lives of all Greeks. This was their land, and it was the toil of their hands and those of their ancestors that had built everything they were defending. The Persian military, on the other hand, were slaves to a tyrant. These were not free men, but prisoners to a ruler who controlled everything. There was no democracy in Persia, only institutionalized slavery. The Greeks had built something worth fighting for, something worth defending and dying for. To these brave Athenians readying for battle, the fight was personal.

They rose early the next morning, before sunrise. A hearty stew of vegetables and barley was prepared for the morning meal. The Greeks readied themselves for battle, knowing that they would have to strike quickly and decisively, and that even then their odds of survival were small. I believe Pheidippides took up arms with the others.[1]

In the predawn darkness they snuck quietly down from their position along the hilltops like a colony of army ants. When they approached the valley, they noted that the Persians had yet to wake. Once at the bottom of the downslope,

---

1 This is my own conjecture; there is no historical record stating whether Pheidippides fought in this battle or not.

they came onto a flat exposed plain about a mile long that stood between them and the Persian position. As soon as they stepped out onto this open field, they would be spotted, and so they held up and silently fell into formation while remaining concealed within the rocks and crevasses of the foothills.

Slowly they began inching forward, shoulder upon shoulder. Farther along they crept, hoping to avoid detection for as long as possible. With about 1,000 meters separating the two forces, the Persian warning trumpets began blaring. The Greeks had been spotted. Seeing this, General Miltiades pointed at the Persians and roared, Κατά πάνω τους! (Charge at them!) The Greeks broke into a furious sprint, wildly screaming, *"Eleleu! Eleleu!"* to summon all their courage and strength for the ensuing confrontation.

Soon a barrage of arrows was launched by the Persian archers with their Scythian bows. The Greeks held up their shields to deflect the incoming projectiles. Some of the men were hit and fell, but others moved up in the phalanx to fill the void. They continued charging full-sprint, unabated by the archers' arrows.

The shields and spears the Greeks carried have been estimated to weigh somewhere between 45 and 75 pounds. Referred to as an Argive shield, these bronzed convex disks were so sturdy they could withstand the blow of an ax, but they were also too heavy to be wielded using only a central clasp. Instead, the back of the shield employed a dual bracing system consisting of a *porpax* (metal armband) through which the left arm was placed up to the elbow, and an *antilabe* (hand grip) to hold onto. The Greeks developed massive forearms to efficiently control these nearly impenetrable blockades and to effectively utilize their long thrusting spears, which were 7 to 8 feet in length and which they held with their right hand. These spears had foot-long metal tips and were counterbalanced by a chunky bronze butt-spike that could double as a bludgeoning weapon should the spear be broken. As a final piece of weaponry, the Greek hoplites carried a stout slashing sword that was tethered to their waistband. This smaller sword could be used in tight quarters or in close-proximity fighting when their thrusting spears were too long.

On top of all of this, these fighters wore heavy bronze Corinthian helmets, bulky armor breastplates, and greaves over their shins, covering from the ankle to the knees. Needless to say, charging for that distance with such weight on one's arms and encumbrances strapped to one's body is no easy task, but these men had trained assiduously to improve their endurance, strength, and stamina so that they could master such equipment. These were hoplites, and this is precisely the type of warfare they had prepared themselves for.

The Greeks needed to continue this aggressive pace without slowing, for the closer they got to the Persian front line, the more ineffective the Persian archers became and the more difficult it became for them to deploy their cavalry into battle. The Persians thought the Greeks were insane to be charging without cavalry or archers, but they steadied to meet the offensive with confidence, knowing that they possessed vastly superior numbers. The Persian military had conquered empires in the past, and they relished their reputation of invincibility.

The Greeks continued sprinting onward like stampeding wildebeests. They were scantily clad in loose-fitting tunics that allowed their legs full freedom of movement, and their muscles and armor gleamed in the morning sun. The Persians had never encountered such an untamed onslaught; this was not how traditional warfare was waged. Miltiades's approach was entirely disruptive, and it threw the enemy off-kilter. The Persians were lightly equipped, wearing only long white pantsuits with interlocking leather quills and feathered caps meant more to intimidate the enemy than to

provide legitimate protection of the head. The Persians stood
there dumbstruck, looking like some strange avian species.
All they carried for protection were insubstantial wicker
shields and swords. But what they did possess was a superior
quantity of fighters, and that was their advantage.

Not pausing to contemplate this numeric imbalance, the
Greeks continued charging relentlessly forward, the gleaming
bronze shield of each man overlapping and protecting his
neighbor, their phalanx line forming a continuous, interlocking wall of advancing armor. A hoplite warrior could be
stripped of everything, but he would never give up his shield.
The thrusting spear and slashing sword were offensive weapons, but the shield protected his neighbor, to which there was
no greater honor. Until death, a hoplite would always defend
his fellow fighter, and the shield was that sacred instrument by
which this was done. It would never be dropped or lowered, so
long as the heart continued to pump. Death before dishonor.

Onward they charged, bracing for impact.

When the Greeks crashed into the Persian front line, an
explosion reverberated into the air that, it has been said, could
be heard from miles away. Immediately the Persians were
pushed back as the Greeks fought like wild animals attacking
their prey. The two armies employed very different battle tactics. The Persians relied heavily on their skilled archers to
inflict heavy casualties from afar, and then the cavalry was
released to finish the job. They had never before encountered
such disorderly battle conduct. The Greeks moved like savage
beasts, knowing that they must strike quickly and decisively if
they were to stand any chance at all for survival. Their battle
strategy relied on the discipline and resoluteness of each hoplite warrior remaining in formation so that the phalanx stayed
intact and uniform; every man understood the importance of
his place in preserving this uniformity during the charge, protecting his neighbor, and presenting an impenetrable wall to
the enemy as they raced forward.

For the first time the Persians found themselves overwhelmed. Now that the Greeks were so swiftly upon them,
their archers were no longer effective. Despite their smaller
numbers, the Greeks were powerful in battle, thrusting their
spears and slashing with their swords, as they cut down the
Persian front line. Men screamed and moaned, limbs were
severed, and skin was pierced. Suddenly, the hunters had
become the hunted. The Persians' lightweight wicker shields
provided little protection against the mighty thrusts of a
Greek spear. It was a gruesome encounter, and the sights and
smells were hellish. Warfare in those days was a visceral
experience, the enemy lanced and dismembered at close
quarters. Homer masterfully captures the raw savagery of
ancient combat in this passage from *The Iliad*:

> At last the armies clashed at one strategic point, they
> slammed their shields together, pike scraped pike
> with the grappling strength of fighters armed in
> bronze and their round shields pounded, boss on
> wielded boss, and the sounds of struggle roared and
> rocked the earth. Screams of men and cries of tri-
> umph breaking in one breath, fighters killing, fight-
> ers killed, and the ground streamed blood.

The Greeks viewed war as glorious hell. There was no
higher honor, no greater deed than that of displaying courage
in combat, yet there was also no denying the tragedy of death
and the somber remorse for the fallen. The terror and gore
were at once joyous and grotesque. Homer continues:

> With that he hurled and Athena drove the shaft and
> it split the archer's nose between the eyes—it cracked
> his glistening teeth, the tough bronze cut off his
> tongue at the roots, smashed his jaw and the point
> came ripping out beneath his chin.

The battle raged on. The Persians kept coming and getting cut down, their thick, black blood spilling onto the earth and darkening the soil. Still, more and more of their ranks poured forth hoping to eviscerate the Greeks. There were so many Persian infantrymen that no matter how many were stopped, others quickly appeared as replacements. The Greeks continued battling as fiercely as they could. Their advancement had choked off the exit-way for the Persian cavalry and prevented these mighty horsemen from entering the battlefield. Holding this position and keeping these skilled cavalrymen at bay was imperative to Greek success.

They fought bravely against the never-ending procession of emerging combatants, but inevitably the Greek phalanx began to weaken at its center. As the Persians drove forward in the middle, the more heavily fortified hoplite flanks continued relentlessly driving the Persians backward on both the left and right sides. Sensing this weakness in the midpoint of the Greek line, the Persians poured more and more men into this enveloping gulf.

The whole thing was a trap. As soon as sufficient numbers of Persian men had entered this balloon in the middle of the line, General Miltiades gave a command, and the outer wings of the Greek phalanx swung inward to outflank the Persians and attack from behind. The invaders were now completely encircled by the Greeks and being assailed from every direction. Complete panic and pandemonium broke out amongst the invaders; the god Pan was clearly living up to his promise and casting his wrath upon these intruders.

General Miltiades had proven to be *polymechanos* (endlessly resourceful) and a brilliant tactician. The inventive battle plan he'd devised and choreographed was executed perfectly, and the surviving Persians turned and fled back to their vessels. The Greeks had emerged victorious.

Well, sort of. There were still a number of niggling issues that needed to be dealt with. Chiefly, many of the Persian

warships had already departed during the land battle and
had made their way southward from Marathon, rounding
Cape Sounion at the tip of Attica, and were speedily heading
toward the Bay of Phaleron to launch their counterattack on
Athens from the opposite coastline. The Greeks needed to
expeditiously make their way over to this location to head
them off. They were exhausted from the morning's fight, but
there was little time to spare. First, however, they needed to
honor tradition.

The process began by gathering discarded Persian war
artifacts and piling them at the point on the battlefield where
the enemy had been turned back. The word *trophy* comes
from the Greek *tropaion*, which derives from *trope* (a turning).
At the turning point in the battlefield this trophy of abandoned
Persian weapons was assembled. A large pyramid-shaped
mound of deserted Persian battle gear and armament was
erected at this spot. The trophy was now complete.

Next came the duty of tending to the fallen. Early Greeks
placed great importance on proper care and honor for the
deceased. By count, the Greeks had lost 192 men, compared
to 6,400 fallen Persians. A large communal grave was constructed and the bodies of the deceased placed into this hallowed burial mound, called the Soros. It would be a lasting
tribute to those Greeks who had sacrificed their lives at Marathon. The Soros remains visible to this very day.

With all the necessary postwar duties fulfilled, it was
now time to go for a run.

30

ONE MORE RACE

The sundial's shadow was rotating farther with each passing moment. It was time for the Greeks to mobilize. The Bay of Phaleron, where the departed Persian fleet intended to come ashore, was some 25 miles away along a rolling coastal road. Despite unthinkable fatigue, the battle-weary Greeks needed to reach this location as swiftly as possible. Additionally, another critical task had to be carried out. Someone had to inform the citizens of Athens about the battle's outcome.

What I'm about to propose is controversial, and no small amount of debate has swirled about the subject over the past few millennia, but this is my story and I'm sticking to it. Truth is, the real story of Pheidippides's final run will never be known. So permit me if you will, dear reader, a romantic departure from historical record to tell a concluding fictionalized version of what happened next to this venerated hemerodromos. We all have our fantasies, and this is mine.

The Greeks had to dispatch a messenger to Athens to deliver news from the battle. The ideal candidate for this role would have been, you guessed it, none other than the greatest herald the world has ever known, Pheidippides. This isn't just some fanciful delusion of mine, either. From an ultramarathoner's perspective, it makes perfect sense. Think about it. The

Athenians needed every able-bodied man they had to deploy
with them up the coastline to meet the incoming Persian fleet.
Of all the war-weary men, one might logically conjecture that
Pheidippides was most exhausted of them all. Clearly, he was
in deep pain. The others likely assumed that he would finally
seek rest right there at Marathon, his mission at last complete.
While they hustled up the coastline to head off the Persians,
Pheidippides would stay behind and recover.

But the valiant hemerodromos would have insisted otherwise. Pheidippides was not done yet. He knew there was one
last duty that needed completion, and he would have avowed
that he was both capable of carrying out this task and also
the best person to do so. Being personal friends with General
Miltiades, a level of trust existed between the two men. Pheidippides had most likely already removed his helmet, breastplate, and greaves to lighten the load in preparation for the
undertaking. And besides, he argued, the fact that he felt
great pain meant that he was still alive. And if he was still
alive, he could run to Athens. General Miltiades granted his
wish, and run he did.

His journey had been a long one, there was no denying
that, but it was not yet complete. Rest could wait another
day; there was still one more race to be run. And with that he
departed on a final marathon, knowing that soon it would all
be over and he could have his rest.

The other Athenians started their trek toward the Bay of
Phaleron in a forced march (literally a stride to the best of
one's ability). Some men would shuffle, some would run or
jog, slowing to catch their breath when necessary and picking
up the tempo when they were able. Each man moved as
quickly as he could, some running in pairs or in groups, others running solo, each focused on maintaining his fastest pace.

Over the miles, the group thinned and separated into a
long parade of hoplites scooting along the dirt pathway. As

the frontrunners passed through local villages, they called to
alert the residents. Soon, old men, boys, and women were collecting jars of water from the fountain houses and bringing
them to the passing warriors. The villagers set up makeshift
aid stations, not unlike those in a modern marathon, as they
were willing and eager to do all they could to help their fellow Greeks overcome the invading Persians. More and more
hoplites poured along the dusty roadway toward the Bay of
Phaleron, grabbing mouthfuls of water and food from these
aid stations as they passed.

In the meantime, Pheidippides ran. Over the hills and
through the valleys, along desolate stretches of rock and
earthen pathways, past orchards and fields of grapes, through
plenteous groves of olive trees he ran. Despite having covered
countless miles in the previous days, he was determined to
carry out this final mission and deliver news to his anxiously
waiting Athenian kinsmen. He drew upon any remaining
aristeia he could summon, his best self now shining more
brightly than ever. Once he fulfilled this duty, once he made
it to Athens and delivered his message, *then* could he rest, he
told himself. But not until then. With chin tucked low and
eyes fixed on the distant horizon, he continued relentlessly
placing one foot in front of the other, one foot in front of the
other.

And so did his fellow countrymen. Onward they rushed
toward the Bay of Phaleron.

As the Greeks ran to head them off, the Persian oarsmen
pulled at their paddle handles, whips lashing those who
showed fatigue. The Persian leaders drove each man to complete exhaustion, and when they crumpled on the boat's
wooden planks, they were dragged away and replaced with
another. The only concern of these leaders was launching a
counterattack on the city of Athens; the welfare of their men
meant nothing. There was plenty of this resource to go around.

Dusk was falling as the Persian fleet rounded the final

headland. The rowers pulled steadily, under orders to come ashore along the northern beaches of the cove. As they approached the landing site within the bay, they noticed something coming over the ridge on the cliffs above. It was a Greek hoplite. First there was one, then another. And still others appeared. More and more Greeks began arriving until the entire clifftop was lined with men three deep.

The Persian leaders cursed! As terribly as they wanted to squash these blasted Hellenes, they weren't willing to make landing at a disadvantaged battle position in the face of a large, determined, and victorious force of hoplite warriors. They had no choice but to order their ships about and paddle away in retreat. It was another crushing defeat for the Persians, another mortal wound to a previously invincible power. They would have a long slog back to Persia to mull over this implausible upset victory by the Greeks.

The Greeks cheered and clasped arms as they watched the Persian warships slowly receding off into the distance. General Miltiades's sentiments remained a bit more subdued, however, for he realized that news of the failed Persian conquest would enrage King Darius. Watching the Persian warships fading off into the distance was not the end of things, Miltiades feared; it was just the beginning. Despite the Greek triumph that day, he thought about the ramifications their success would bring. The Persians would be back, and future wars were sure to ensue. Miltiades was saddened by this knowledge. As Herodotus wrote: "No one is so foolish as to prefer war to peace. In peace children bury their fathers, while in war fathers bury their children." Miltiades knew that many fathers would be burying their children when the Persians eventually came back.

Meanwhile in Athens, the citizenry debated the most appropriate course of action to take in the midst of swirling uncertainty. Had the Persians slaughtered the Greeks at Marathon? Were they now en route to the city to rape, pillage, and

enslave the remaining Athenian citizens? If the Persians had
been successful in their conquest at Marathon, remaining in
Athens posed grave danger, for they would stand no chance
against these barbaric foreign invaders. Should they flee the
city? There had been many sleepless nights in Athens, especially by those mothers who gazed worriedly at their children, wondering if the Persian butchers had savagely cut
down their fathers. There could be no rest until they knew
with certainty what had happened at Marathon.

Just then a sentry on lookout spotted something moving
over the horizon. It was a ghostly figure, a man swaying and
staggering, tripping and stumbling along, though picking
himself back up and continuing onward. Who was this person? The sentry looked closer for telltale signs of identity but
couldn't make out much detail. One thing was for certain: It
was not the enemy. And even if it were, this individual was in
no shape to put up a fight.

Pheidippides's perceptions flitted between light and dark.
Interludes of hazy lucidity revealed a landscape veneered in
silvery metallic hues, as if a river of liquid mercury had
poured down from the sky embossing the earth. Waves of
translucent ripples percolated upward from the ground, the
surface rising and falling fluidly underfoot. A cathartic trill
echoed within his ears like that of a thousand angels crying,
his body drifting reflexively onward. Before him, on a hill
high above, stood a heavenly formation of cottony alabaster,
a sanctity of peace towering in the clouds majestically, as if
home to the gods. That was where he must go, he understood. Up these streets in which he'd played as a child, to this
place above the world. One more ascent to that sacred mountaintop temple and then, at long last, he could have his rest.

Others were awaiting his arrival at the Acropolis, a solitary
figure gliding phantom-like through the hallowed entranceway
and onto the main grounds. They watched transfixed, unsure
of what to do, unsure of what would happen next, as this angel-

like form made its way toward the gathered group. The air was eerily still, motionless, as he came before them, pulling up directly in front of the assemblage and bringing himself to a halt. They stared, amazed by his presence, inspecting his body and his mental constitution, assessing his state of being. There was a dreamlike moment of pause, when time seemed suspended. What would transpire in the next moments?

Pheidippides tried to mount a response, but nothing came. He tried again, to no avail. His body was nearly lifeless, seemingly incapable of anything more. Others moved to his aid but were held back by their fellow Athenians.

In a final consecrated act of determination, Pheidippides drew in his breath, seized all his might, and burst forth: *"Nike! Nike!"* (Victory! Victory!) *"Nenikekamen!"* (Rejoice, we conquer!) he cried out, proudly thrusting both arms into the air in a show of defiance and pride.

A palpable sense of ease rushed over the crowd, the tension of days of anguished waiting released and washed away in an instant. However, there was no outward celebration, no open expressions of joy or delight. All present felt an uplifting sensation that Greece had been saved, but no one could take their eyes off this travel-weary hemerodromos standing before them. His once powerful and ever-enduring frame was now terribly withered and depleted, yet there was nothing they could do. It was past that point. They watched as he gradually lowered to one knee, and then to the other. His body gracefully folded onto the ground, toppling earthward and twisting softly sideways to come to a rest upon its back, his eyes and heart facing skyward. He peered longingly into the distant universe as the twilight of his life passed before him, those last magnificent glimmering rays of sunlight slowly fading to black. He drew in a final precious breath of warm, sweet air, a gentle smile spread across his face, and then his eyes slid silently shut. Finally, at long last, Pheidippides would have his rest. Eternal and forever rest, rest in peace.

CONCLUSION

The Spartans eventually arrived in Athens and learned of the battle's outcome. They were impressed by the Athenian victory, yet General Miltiades warned that the triumph at Marathon would not spell the end of Persia's thirst for Greek blood. He was right: A decade after the Battle of Marathon, in 480 BCE, Persian King Darius's son Xerxes invaded Greece. At the famous Battle of Thermopylae, the Spartans lived up to their fearless reputation. Under the leadership of Spartan King Leonidas, a group of a mere 300 elite mountain warriors went to battle against a huge contingency of Persians numbering in the hundreds of thousands. Xerxes demanded that the Spartans lay down their arms, to which King Leonidas replied with but two words, *Molon labe* (come and take them).

Xerxes's messenger threatened that if the Greeks did not surrender, the Persians would attack with the full brunt of their military might. He said the sheer mass of their archers' incoming arrows would blot out the sun, to which the Spartan warrior Dienekes appreciatively replied, "So much the better; then we shall fight our battle in the shade."

The Persian messenger went on, "We will destroy you, and we will capture your women."

"Hah!" the Spartan laughed. "You do not know our women."

On the morning of the battle, Leonidas advised his men to eat a hearty breakfast, "for tonight we dine in the underworld," he told them. Three hundred Spartans held strong at Thermopylae. "*AROO! AROO! AROO!*" was their battle cry as they fearsomely stood their ground, watching the endless throng of Persians advancing upon them. Many armies have made the claim that they would fight to the death, but usually death comes with no other alternative. If given an opportunity to flee, others have, but not the Spartans. Even when the option of retreat existed, they chose instead to stay and fight. They fought with their shields and their thrusting spears. And when those were stripped from them, they fought with their knives. And when those were stripped from them, they fought with their bare hands. And when they were cut to the ground and lay dying, they fought with their teeth. These men lived large, and although they lost the battle of Thermopylae to the Persians that day, all 300 Spartans died with valor, making the ultimate sacrifice in the hope of preserving the freedom of others. Flesh will eventually return to earth; the end is the same for all humankind. To a Spartan, a noble life cut short was preferable to a withering existence of quiet desperation. Either way, the final destination was identical. At the battlefield of Thermopylae an everlasting epitaph to those Spartans who lost their lives on that day poignantly reads:

GO TELL THE SPARTANS,
STRANGER PASSING BY, THAT HERE,
OBEDIENT TO THEIR LAWS, WE LIE.

And thus we are once again reminded that dying is part of living, that without death there would be no life, without darkness there would be no light. From a thorn a rose emerges and from a rose a thorn. The ancient Greeks lived close to these dualisms, honest and in celebration of the insuperable realities of existence, both the glorious and the tragic. "Not life, but good life, is to be chiefly valued," Socrates said shortly before drinking the poisonous hemlock. Only when the unbearable sorrow of our doomed fate is recognized and embraced can we see the true beauty in things and live a life beyond the ordinary. We worship the gods because they are immortal, but the gods envy us because we are not. Theirs is a race with no finish line, an endless string of days and nights stretching on for eternity. The gods observed that human mortality is what gives life magic, that the tragedy of inevitable death is preferable to the sameness of forever life. An existence that stretches on indefinitely is not a blessing, they realized, but a curse.

Here, at this juncture, let us take a moment to examine the historical significance of Pheidippides's feat and the Battle of Marathon. What would have happened if Pheidippides had failed to reach Sparta or had been incapable of running back from Sparta to Marathon? Here's what plausibly may have happened. Upon receiving midnight news that the Persians were planning on deploying half their troops up to the Bay of Phaleron to launch a bifurcated offensive, the Athenians who were hunkered down in the hillsides above Marathon would have prudently retreated back to Athens. Doing so offered a better defense strategy against a two-sided Persian attack, and because they believed Pheidippides and the Spartans would be arriving shortly, it made all the more sense to abandon their current position and retreat to Athens. Hence, there would have been no battle at Marathon.

This is no trivial matter. For if Pheidippides had failed in his ultramarathon conquest, what has been called the most critical battle in world history might never have occurred. Without word from Pheidippides that the Spartans were delayed, the Athenians would have returned back to the city only to wait in vain for the Spartans. Pheidippides provided a key piece of military intelligence that prevented such a chain of events from occurring, and thus the battle was ultimately waged at Marathon. This profound revelation has been hiding in plain sight for the past 2,500 years, perhaps only waiting for someone to tear into the history books and examine the record through the lens of an ultramarathoner. Pheidippides's historic run, quite literally, saved the world.

Now, historians are always reluctant to speculate on what would have happened had the outcome of a particular event been different, but I am not a historian. What would have happened had there been no Battle of Marathon and the Persians successfully overthrew the Greeks in Athens? The world as we know it would be a very different place, that is for sure. The liberal enlightenment of Western society and the gradual ascendancy of the great principles that cultivated European civilization would have been lost. The nascent ideology of democracy would have vanished, possibly forever, and the burgeoning ideal of self-governance by the people would have been thrust back into the dark ages of Persian totalitarianism. The great ancient works of Greek art and architecture would not exist. There would be no Parthenon, no Myron, and no Iktinus. Pythagoras and his theorem would disappear, and the development of modern mathematics and engineering would have suffered as a consequence. Plato would be gone, as would Aristotle. Drama, tragic comedy, and story development would have evolved very differently, if at all. So much of the way we live our lives today has its roots in that prolific period of human development following the Battle of Marathon. And, most important for us runners, had Pheidippides failed in his conquest, we would have no marathon.

Those men who fought on the plains of Marathon and then ran along the coastline to the Bay of Phaleron to head off the Persian counterattack became legends. Known as the *marathonomachoi*, they were revered throughout the land. The victory at Marathon became a defining event in Greek history. Dramatic depictions of the battle were displayed in friezes on the Temple of Nike at the Acropolis. Even as the years passed, the *marathonomachoi* were distinguished from others. "Veterans of Marathon, tough as oak or maple," Aristophanes described them.

In a modern incarnation of the *marathonomachoi*, the so-called Grizzled Vets are a small group of marathoners who have completed each of the 30 successive Big Sur International Marathons, completing one of the toughest 26.2-mile courses along the California coastline from Big Sur to Carmel in procession over 3 decades. Which brings us to the question: Why 26.2? Why has that particular distance become the modern-day standard for the marathon? Why are we not running something like 300 miles, the distance Pheidippides ran from Athens to Sparta and back?

The answer probably has to do with the outcome of that final run from the battlefield of Marathon to Athens. You see, Pheidippides was a hemerodromos, and running great distances is what hemerodromoi did. It might seem remarkable to us today that a man could cover such a vast distance on foot, but that was the role of an ancient Greek herald. In essence, when Pheidippides ran to Sparta and back, he was just doing his job. As I mentioned earlier, Herodotus never emphasized this extraordinary feat of endurance and stamina as being anything out of the ordinary, and modern scholars have largely adopted that same position without much analysis, which some might say is a glaring oversight, especially anyone who has ever attempted to run such a distance.

At any rate, 600 years after the fact, the historians Plutarch and Lucian didn't focus on Pheidippides's run to

Sparta and back but instead drew attention to that final run from the battlefield of Marathon to Athens.[1] Why highlight this shorter run when a much greater feat of athleticism occurred in Pheidippides's round-trip run from Athens to Sparta? Here's the answer: Because in that final jaunt from the battlefield of Marathon to Athens, the messenger died at the conclusion. To the ancient Greeks, nothing could be nobler than tragically dying after performing a heroic deed for one's country. It was the highest possible calling.

The 18th-century British poet Robert Browning captured this quintessence in dramatic, lyrical style:

So, when Persia was dust, all cried, "To Acropolis!

Run, Pheidippides, one more race! The meed is thy due! Athens is saved, thank Pan, go shout!"

He flung down his shield and ran like fire once more: and the space 'twixt the fennel-field

And Athens was stubble again, a field with fire runs through,

Till in he broke: "Rejoice, we conquer!" Like wine through the clay,

Joy in his blood bursting his heart, he died—the bliss!

The legend of a man dying after a gallant act of valor is what perpetuated through the ages, and this is the story that we're left with today. Along the way, facts have been distorted, names have been altered, and circumstances rearranged to hold the narrative, as is the case with many great historic tales. This is how the enduring lore of Marathon as we now know it came to evolve.

---

1   It must be noted that neither Plutarch nor Lucian refers to Pheidippides by name as being the individual who ran from Marathon to Athens after the battle. In fact, they assign this to a runner named Eucles or Thersippus. Herodotus never mentions this final marathon at all.

Still, why 26.2? The true distance from Marathon to Athens on the pathway an ancient foot messenger would have traveled was closer to 25 miles. So how did we eventually settle on 26.2? The evolution of this story has its twists and turns as well.

It begins with the end of the ancient Olympics in 394 CE. The original Greek Olympic movement was conceived as an event in which all citizens participated, regardless of one's status or profession. Athletic competition was part of being Greek, something cherished and prized, and everyone joined in the Games and took part. Yes, the winners were recognized, but participation by all was chiefly valued, and everyone who competed received the same laurel or olive-branch wreath.

Over time, however, this founding spirit began to falter, and professionalism and elitism crept into the Games. Originally all athletes were amateurs and trained only in their spare time, but suddenly professionally paid athletes were entering the games, sometimes sponsored by the wealthy citizen class. As the years progressed, the Olympics lost their way entirely and became more about cutthroat competition and winning at all costs. Intense rivalries, even hatreds, developed among athletes of different sporting disciplines who were all vying for the limelight in an effort to gain notoriety over one another. Ironically, it was a Roman emperor, Theodosius I, not a Greek, who abolished the Games. His reason for doing so was that the Games had deteriorated into a ritualistic spectacle rather than a sporting event.

Equally ironic, it was a French nobleman, Baron Pierre de Coubertin, not a Greek, who revived the Games in 1896 when the first modern Olympics were held in Athens. De Coubertin sought to bring back the spirit of the original games. Sounding like an ancient Greek scholar, the Frenchman wrote, "The important thing in the Olympic Games is not to win, but to take part; the important thing in life is not triumph, but the struggle; the essential thing is not to have conquered but to have fought well." In an even stranger twist of plot, a marathon run was introduced in these modern Games and became the premier attraction, even though no footrace of such duration had existed during the original ancient Greek Olympics. The marathon race was the final anchor event of these modern Games, and the distance was set at 24.85 miles following the ancient route from the plains of Marathon to Athens. Perhaps providentially, a Greek athlete, Spiridon Louis, won this first marathon.

The inaugural modern Olympics were a success, and this new marathon race became a highlight of the Games. The Olympics took place in different countries around the globe and grew into a popular spectator event. A problem arose during the 1908 Games in London, however. The royal family wanted the marathon to finish in front of their viewing box at the newly constructed White City Stadium, so the King of England altered the distance of the race to 26 miles plus 385 yards to accomplish this end. The rest, as they say, is history.

Running 24.85 miles wasn't easy in the first place, and running 26.2 miles made it even harder. Adding incremental distances to a race of that duration increases the difficulty exponentially. Perhaps no one captures this better than legendary marathoner Frank Shorter, who, when struggling to keep up with his rival Kenny Moore during the 1971 Pan American Games, breathlessly muttered at the 21-mile mark, "Why couldn't Pheidippides have died here?"

Shorter went on to capture the gold medal in the marathon at the 1972 Summer Olympics and become one of the all-time marathoning greats. The competitive aspect of the sport really developed during his era, and the quantum leaps in performance were profound. Marathoning was largely a male-dominated sport, and anyone intent on running a marathon dedicated a good portion of his life to the endeavor. Elite athletes running extraordinarily fast times dominated the sport. In 1970 there were an estimated 25,000 marathon finishers in the United States, and the average finish time was under 3 hours and 30 minutes.

In recent years marathoning has gone through a dramatic democratization. In 2014 an estimated 542,000 individuals completed a marathon in the United States, and participation was divided equally between women and men. Marathoning has now become a more mainstream pursuit and something achievable by nonelite athletes, those who train in their spare time. Average finish times have become slower, 4:17 for males and 4:42 for females, but far more citizens participate in these events, and the spirit surrounding a marathon race is more supportive and all-inclusive than in bygone years. This modern Olympic sport that was never an original Olympic sport has grown to epitomize the ancient Olympic principles, even though those initial Olympic ideals disappeared thousands of years ago. How convoluted, and very Greek, is all of that?!

Despite its growing popularity, there is nothing easy about finishing a marathon. No matter if you are an elite front-runner or an anxious first-timer, the undertaking is fearsome. And that is because the marathon is not about running; it is about salvation. You see, we spend so much of our lives doubting ourselves, thinking that we're not good enough, not strong enough, not made of the right stuff. The marathon offers an opportunity for redemption. Opportunity, I say, because the outcome is uncertain. Opportunity, I say, because it is up to you, and only you, to make it happen.

There is no luck involved in finishing a marathon. The ingredients required to tackle this formidable challenge are straightforward: commitment, sacrifice, grit, and raw determination. Plain and simple.

So you set about your training to prepare your body for the rigors of running 26.2 miles. You refuse to compromise, dedicating yourself wholeheartedly to the contest at hand, pouring everything you've got into it. But you know that the marathon will ask for more. In the dark recesses of your mind, a gloomy voice is saying, *"You can't."* You do your best to ignore it, but that nagging voice of self-doubt won't go away.

The marathon shakes you to the core. It deconstructs your very essence, stripping away all of your protective barriers and exposing your inner soul. At a time when you are most vulnerable, the marathon shows no pity. The marathon tells you that it will hurt you, that it will leave you demoralized and defeated, crushed and lifeless in a heap alongside the road. The marathon tells you that it can't be done, not by you. *"HA!"* it taunts you, *"In your dreams . . . "*

You fight back, however, and stand courageously at that starting line, nervously awaiting the gun to go off. When it does, you put your head down and charge into the abyss, knowing honestly in your heart's heart that you either paid your dues or that you skimped along the way. There is no lying to oneself here. The marathon sees right through excuses, shortcuts, and self-transgressions. You can't fake your way through a marathon.

All goes well for the first half. But slowly, step by step, the pain mounts as the intensity of the endeavor amplifies. You remain steadfast, knowing that you did not skimp in your training, that you did not take shortcuts, and that every footstep was earned through months and years of rigorous preparation and hard work. Still, with each draining thrust forward, that little nagging inclination of self-doubt in the back of your mind grows progressively louder.

Then, at mile 20, the looming voice of uncertainty is all you can hear. It hurts so badly that you want to stop. It hurts so badly that you must stop. But you don't stop. This time, you ignore that voice, you tune out the naysayers who've told you that you're not good enough, not strong enough, not made of the right stuff, and you listen only to the passion within your heart. That burning desire tells you to keep moving forward, to continue putting one foot in front of the other no matter what. Courage comes in many forms, and running a marathon demands the courage to keep trying and to not give up regardless of how dire things become. And dire things do become. At the 26-mile mark you can barely define the course any longer, your vision faltering as you teeter perilously on the edge of consciousness.

And then suddenly before you, front and center, looms the finish line. Tears stream down your face as you realize you may finish. Finally, after years of torment and toil, you can answer back to that nagging voice of uncertainty in your head with a resounding, "Oh yes I can!"

You burst across that finish line and are forever liberated from the prison of self-doubt and limitations that has held you captive. You have learned more about yourself in the past 26.2 miles than you have known in your entire life. You have freed yourself everlastingly from those chains that bind. Even if you can't walk for a week, even if you are confined to your bed, never have you been so free.

As they carry you away from the finish line, wrapped in a flimsy Mylar blanket, barely able to keep your head upright, you are at peace. That daunting adversary that has haunted you an entire lifetime is now your liberator, your fondest ally. You have done what few will ever do—you have done what you thought you could never do—and it is the most glorious, unforgettable awakening ever.

You are, above all, a marathoner, and you will wear this distinction not only with the medal they place around your neck, but also deep within your heart, for the rest of your God-given years. Nothing can ever take that away from you. As with Pheidippides, you are part of a sacred fraternal order of the few and the proud. You have kindred spirits across borders and across time. Others may admire you, congratulate you, and tell you they are proud of you, but only those who cross that finish line know the true feeling. A marathoner is not just something you are, but someone you've become.

EPILOGUE

I n the course of writing this book, life moved forward (imagine that). Professor Cartledge retired from Cambridge, though I don't think a man of such deep intellectual curiosity ever truly retires. Emeritus just means he won't be teaching classes any longer, which will give him more time to devote to his studies. I get the feeling he will only pick up the pace in his "retirement."

P-J's family has grown since we first started working on the project together, and her grandmotherly duties have multiplied. She and her husband, Stephen, now preside over a clan of rambunctious grandkids. Yet, as grounded as she is in the countryside of England, I still get the sense P-J is restless, that for her there are journeys still to be undertaken, new worlds still waiting to be uncovered. As much information as she provided me, and as fascinating as her research on the ancient Greek hemerodromoi was to me, the one question I never got around to asking her was *Why?* Why did this stately woman from the British countryside find such interest in the plight and travels of an ancient Greek hemerodromos, Pheidippides? It seemed like a rather obscure topic of interest for an Englishwoman living in Yorkshire.

Finally, after the manuscript was completed and we'd

spent several years working together, I sent her an e-mail to inquire where this passion had arisen. Why of all possible topics did this one hold such interest to her? It was a typically curt digital communication, all of a single brisk sentence, asking the question, "Why?" Below is the unedited response I received from her:

The question of "Why?" is not that easy to answer. I could give a blow-by-blow account of the origin and growth of the whole thing, but that would really be an answer to the question of "How?" Your "Why?" requires something different, and I think it is this:

Pheidippides's journey became inextricably entwined with a personal journey, for me, for Stephen, and for the pair of us, both of mind and of body—a journey which, in its turn, has shone some light, albeit imperfectly, on what he endured.

One aspect of it has been, and is still, a journey into the experience of Greece, of the physical country herself AND the often fragmentary written records about her (far more numerous and diverse than I had ever imagined), from Herodotus to the 20th century.

But, in a manner more difficult to describe, trying to follow Pheidippides led us on a trek through our own capabilities and limitations, as well as into the reality of Greece, her bones and sinews as well as her heart, and our response to, and relationship with, her. I say "Greece" but of course I really mean the Peloponnese. And of all the Peloponnese, a sort of wry love affair with Arcadia, with its mountains and little hanging plains, its oaks and stones, its wayward watercourses and *katavothres*.

When, occasionally, I re-read my first journal, recording our first trek—15 miles, with 35-40 lbs each of kit on our backs—from Argos over Mt. Ktenias in

the snow & down to Achladokampos, one February
day in 1992, I laugh out loud to think how naive I
was (and how mad the kind people in the village
clearly thought us!). But I'm also thrilled, every time,
to re-live our first meetings with people who were so
good to us that day, and who became such friends to
us thereafter; and to remember how our first view
from the top of the higher pass over Ktenias across to
the great cone of Parthenius was so exactly as I had
imagined it from the maps and the accounts of Paus-
anias and Leake! I realise afresh that I never anticipated, then, what a journey this would be, and it's
not over even now (there are still questions we want
to settle, and I daresay that settling them will throw
up yet more, and more, unto the ages of ages!).

Nor did I anticipate how much we would dis-
cover of the achievements and sufferings, generosity
and fears, customs, hardihood & precious knowledge
of those we encountered, both in the past (the runners, writers, warriors, scholars, ancient figures, freedom fighters, Gentlemen Travelers, even the *kalderimi*
road-builders!), and as we went along, through that
beautiful and terrible terrain. Nor that we'd acquire,
painfully, some inkling of what might have been
meant by "Pan," through our own occasional suffering of that terrifying feeling of being utterly overwhelmed by the prospect of what was required of us.

For that matter, we learnt a lot about our own
married relationship, discovered some marvelous
complementarities, developed a special language,
refined a method of eating, and mercifully never
both suffered "Pan" simultaneously; that's not to say
that we didn't also lose our tempers with each other
from time to time! Actually, trekking together, with
the added strength that companionship supplies,

gives some indication of how much harder it is to struggle alone. I did do some of the walking alone, and the comparison is pretty convincing.

If you take all of this and wind it around Pheidippides's own journey, I think it led, finally and most importantly, to a realisation of the splendour of what he accomplished. Does this answer, in some way, your question of "Why?" I hope so.

I would say this indeed answers my question, and in a more beautiful way than I could ever imagine. And these are the types of responses I routinely received from my oft-rushed and unintelligible questions. Every answer P-J provided left me more enthralled, more energized to continue seeking.

But alas, this journey has come to a resting point. As this book draws to a conclusion, I want to thank you, dear reader, for joining with me on this voyage of discovery and self-discovery. In getting to know Pheidippides, I have gotten to know myself. I have become more aware of who I am and have learned to appreciate the forces that have shaped my life. I hope that you have enjoyed our excursion, and I hope that you have learned and have perhaps even been inspired to find yourself. As I type these final words, my curiosity about Pheidippides and the ancient Greek hoplite athletes is as strong as it was the day I typed the opening sentence. Perhaps stronger. The Greek-born biographer Plutarch noted that the tales of the excellent can lift the ambitions of the living. There are still treasures to be uncovered, and there are still untraveled roads to be explored. But now is not the time for that; now is the time for me to honor Pheidippides in the highest way possible. With the final words in this manuscript typed, now is the time for me to close this computer and go for a run . . .

ACKNOWLEDGMENTS

There are many people I'd like to thank for helping to bring this book to life. Mom and Dad, thank you for keeping our Greek spirit alive and for instilling Hellenic values in me from the day I was born. To my wife, Julie, and our daughter and son, Alexandria and Nicholas, thank you for venturing to Greece with me and discovering the magic of this enchanting land firsthand.

Carole Bidnick, my literary agent, it started with *Ultramarathon Man* and four books later, we still like each other! I'm sure our friendship will endure for many years to come.

To my editor at Rodale, Mark Weinstein, thank you for continuing to believe in me even when I lost belief in myself. You challenged me to be better and pushed me to strive higher, and I rose to the occasion because of this. Thanks for that not so subtle nudge.

Also at Rodale, I wish to express my gratefulness to Gail Gonzalez, Aly Mostel, and Joanna Williams, as well as to David Willey and the entire crew at *Runner's World* for supporting me and for supporting the sport, activity, and lifestyle of running. Who would ever think such a simple act could have such profound meaning in our lives?

I want to thank Peter Polous for his ongoing friendship

Runs end, running lasts forever. Thank you Pheidippides. Pylos, Greece.

and brotherhood, and for making some of the best damn olive oil in the world! To Akis Tsolis and the team at Focus on Sports, you guys have been terrific to work with, world class. We've built the Navarino Challenge into something special, something we can all take pride in. Of course, I owe a debt of gratitude to Achilleas Constantakopoulos and the staff of Costa Navarino for making the Navarino Challenge possible in the first place. And thank you to the other athletes at the Navarino Challenge, Spyros Gianniotis, Alexandros Nikolaidis, and Mandy Persaki for representing Greece so proudly.

To the organizers and tireless volunteers of the Spartathlon, thank you for creating an event that is unparalleled in the world of sports. My heartfelt appreciation goes out to Dimitris Troupis and Nikos Kalofyris for sharing in the adventure with me, and to Babis Giritziotis for doing such an outstanding job of capturing it. Finally, thank you to Mike Arnstein for relentlessly insisting that I do the Spartathlon. *Just go, drop everything, nothing else matters,* you persisted, *this is who you are.* I'm not sure how you knew these things, but you were right. Thank you for never giving up on me.

To Ellie Flenga and the fine folks at Holmes Place gym, thanks for extending membership reciprocity whenever I'm visiting Athens. Nothing better than having a nice place to clean up after a run and workout. And to my poor Greek instructor, Dafni Dedopoulou, you have the patience and good humor of a saint despite my continued butchery of the Greek language. Thank you. No, Ευχαριστώ. Hey, I got that one right!

And, lastly, thank you to the Greek people for embracing me so warmly. It would be easy for me to tell you to be strong and to weather the storm bravely, but that would be unfair since I face no such struggle or hardship in my life. What I can say is that nothing seems to bring people together like shared suffering. This is something we runners know. You have suffered together as a country, and I see the bonds tightening ever more strongly on each subsequent visit to Greece. The battered economy may have taken its toll on the nation's finances, but the Greek spirit perseveres. Long live Greece!

Generations of Spartathletes

ABOUT THE AUTHOR

Dean Karnazes was named by *Time* magazine as one of the 100 Most Influential People in the World and by *Men's Health* magazine as one of the 100 Fittest Men of All Time. He has raced and competed across the globe and once ran 50 marathons, in all 50 US states, in 50 consecutive days. The recipient of an *ESPN* ESPY award and three-time winner of *Competitor* magazine's Endurance Athlete of the Year, Dean lives with his wife and family in the San Francisco Bay Area.

For more, visit www.Ultramarathon.com.

*Carrying the Olympic Torch through
San Francisco.*

INDEX

Boldface references indicate photographs.